ELECTRICAL AND INSTRUMENTATION ENGINEERING

DR. P. ELAMURUGAN

Dedication to God Almighty,Family Members and beloved Student friends

Contents

Foreword

Electrical engineering (sometimes referred to as **electrical and electronic engineering**) is a professional engineering discipline that deals with the study and application of electricity, electronics and electromagnetism. The field first became an identifiable occupation in the late nineteenth century with the commercialization of the electric telegraph and electrical power supply. The field now covers a range of sub-disciplines including those that deal with power, optoelectronics, digital electronics, analog electronics, computer science, artificial intelligence, control systems, electronics, signal processing and telecommunications.

Instrumentation engineering deals with the design of devices to measure physical quantities such as pressure, flow and temperature. The design of such instrumentation requires a good understanding of physics that often extends beyond electromagnetic theory. For example, radar guns use the Doppler effect to measure the speed of oncoming vehicles. Similarly, thermocouples use the Peltier-Seebeck effect to measure the temperature difference between two points.

Electrical and Instrumentation engineers are responsible for **designing, developing, installing, managing and maintaining equipment which is used to monitor and control engineering systems, machinery and processes**

Preface

ELECTRICAL AND INSTRUMENTATION ENGINEERING

UNIT I TRANSFORMER

Introduction - Ideal and Practical Transformer – Phasor diagram-– Per Unit System – Equivalent circuit- Testing- Efficiency and Voltage Regulation– Three Phase Transformers –Applications-Auto Transformers, Advantages- Harmonics.

UNIT II DC MACHINES

Introduction – Constructional Features– Motor and Generator mode - EMF and Torque equation –Circuit Model – Methods of Excitation- Characteristics – Starting and Speed Control – Universal Motor- Stepper Motors – Brushless DC Motors- Applications

UNIT III AC ROTATING MACHINES

Principle of operation of three-phase induction motors – Construction –Types – Equivalent circuit, Speed Control - Single phase Induction motors -Construction– Types–starting methods. Alternator: Working principle–Equation of induced EMF – Voltage regulation, Synchronous motors- working principle-starting methods – Torque equation.

UNIT IV MEASUREMENTS AND INSTRUMENTATION

Functional elements of an instrument, Standards and calibration, Operating Principle , types -Moving Coil and Moving Iron meters, Measurement of three phase power, Energy Meter,Instrument Transformers-CT and PT,DSO- Block diagram- Data acquisition.

UNIT V BASICS OF POWER SYSTEMS

Power system structure -Generation , Transmission and distribution , Various voltage levels,Earthing – methods of earthing, protective devices- switch fuse unit- Miniature circuit breaker moulded case circuit breaker- earth leakage circuit breaker, safety precautions and First Aid.

Acknowledgements

I thank the Management,Faculty Members ,Staffs of N.S.N. College of Engineering and Technology and Student friends who helped me and made it a worthwhile experience in my career.

CHAPTER ONE

TRANSFORMER

INTRODUCTION

A transformer is an electrical device, having no moving parts, which by mutual induction, it transfers electrical energy from one circuit to another at the same frequency, usually with changed values of voltage and current.

- There are two or more stationary electric circuits that are coupled magnetically.
- It involves interchange of electric energy between two or more electric systems.
- Transformers provide much needed capability of changing the voltage and current levels easily.
- They are used to step-up generator voltage to an appropriate voltage level for power transfer.
- Stepping down the transmission voltage at various levels for distribution and power utilization.

CONSTRUCTION OF TRANSFORMER

The main components of transformer are ,

1. Magnetic core

2. Windings

3. Insulation

4. Insulating oil

5. Expansion tank

6. *Temperature gauge*
7. *Oil gauge*
8. *Buchholz relay*
9. *Breather*
10. *Bushings*
11. *Cooling arrangements*

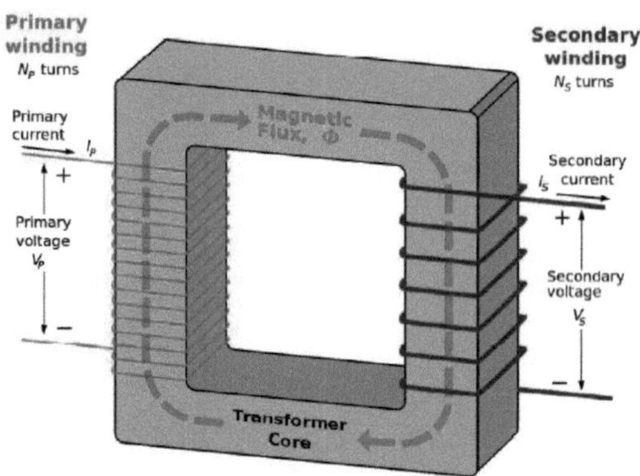

Figure 1.Construction of Transformer

Magnetic core

Magnetic circuit consists of an iron core. The transformer core is generally laminated

and is made out of a good magnetic material like silicon steel. The laminations are insulated from each other by coating then with a thin coat of varnish.

The two types of transformer cores are,

1. **Core type**
2. **Shell type**

Core type transformer

- It has only one magnetic path
- It has two limbs for the two windings
- It is made up of two L-type stampings

The coils are usually are of cylindrical type. For transformers of higher rating stepped core with circular cylindrical coils are used. For transformers of smaller rating, rectangular coils with core of square or rectangular cross section is used.

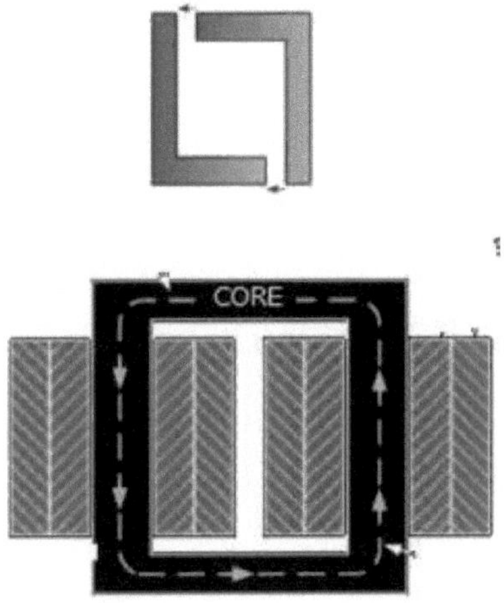

Figure 2.Core Type

Shell type transformer

- It has two parallel paths for magnetic flux
- It has three limbs. The two windings are carried by the central limb.
- It is made up of E and I type stampings
- The coils used are of multilayer disc type.

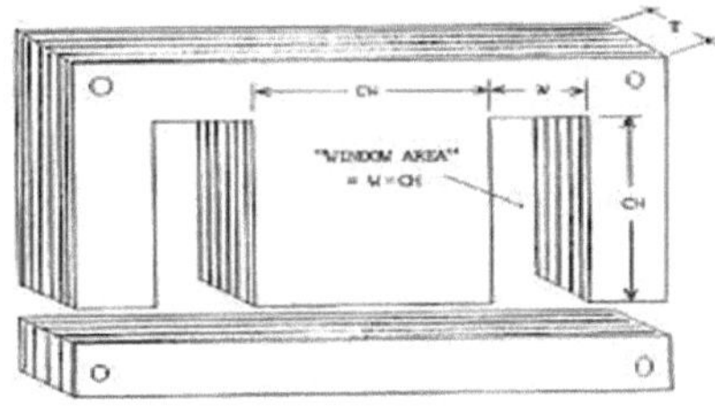

Figure 3.Shell Type

Windings

Windings are made up of copper. There are two types of windings in a transformer. They are,

1. Primary windings
2. Secondary windings

Insulation

Paper is still used as the basic conductor insulation. Enamel insulation is used as the inter-turn insulation of low voltage transformers. For power transformers enamelled copper with paper insulation is used.

Insulating oil

The oil used in a transformer protects the paper from dirt and moisture and removes the heat produced in the core and coils. It also acts as a insulating medium.

Expansion tank or conservator

A small auxiliary oil tank may be mounted above the transformer and connected to main tank by a pipe. Its function is to keep the transformer tank full of oil.

Temperature gauge

Every transformer is provided with a temperature gauge to indicate hot oil. It is self contained weather proof unit made of alarm contacts.

Oil gauge

Every transformer is fitted with an oil gauge to indicate the oil level present inside the tank. The oil gauge may be provided with an alarm contact which gives an alarm when the oil level has dropped beyond permissible height due to oil leak or due to any other reason.

Buchholz relay

The first warning that a fault is presented may be given by the presence of bubbles in the oil. The gas operated relay gives an alarm in case of minor fault and to disconnect the transformer from the supply mains in case of severe faults.

Breather

The simplest method to prevent the entry of the moisture inside the transformer tank is to provide chambers known as breather. The breather is filled with some drying agents, such as calcium chloride or silica gel. This drying agents absorbs moisture and allow dry air to enter the transformer tank. The drying agent is replaced periodically as routine maintenance.

Bushings

Connections from the transformer windings are brought out by means of bushings.Bushings are fixed on the transformer tank.

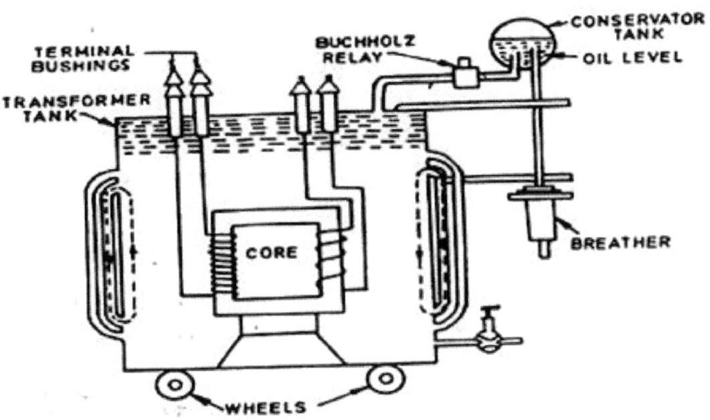

Figure 4.Schematic Arrangement of Transformer

Cooling arrangements

The various methods of cooling employed in a transformer are,

1. Oil immersed natural cooled transformers
2. Oil immersed forced air cooled transformers
3. Oil immersed water cooled transformers
4. Oil immersed forced oil cooled transformers
5. Air blast transformers

Oil immersed natural cooled transformers

In this type, the core and coils are immersed in insulating oil contained in an iron tank. The heat produced in the core and windings is conduct by the circulation of oil to the surface which dissipates heat to surroundings. In transformers of larger output, the dissipation surface is increased by providing large number of tubes on its sides. The oil not only keeps the windings cool but also provides additional insulation.

Oil immersed forced air cooled transformers

In this type, the core and windings are immersed in oil and cooling is increased by forced air over the cooling surfaces. The air is forced over external surfaces such as tank, tubes and radiators by means of fan mounted external to the transformer.

Oil immersed water cooled transformers

In this type, the core and windings are immersed in oil and cooling is increased by circulation of cold water through the tubes immersed in oil.

Oil immersed forced oil cooled transformers

In this type, the core and windings are immersed in oil and cooling is achieved by forced oil circulation. In this method of cooling forced oil circulation is obtained by a centrifugal pump which is located at either the oil inlet or outlet. The pump motor used for cooling is designed to operate totally immersed in the cooling oil being circulated.

Air blast transformers

Here the transformer is cooled by a forced circulation of air through core and windings. It is used in substations located in thickly populated places where oil is considered a fire hazard. The air supplied is filtered to avoid dust entering the ventilating ducts.

OPERATION OF TRANSFORMER

The transformer works on the principle of electromagnetic induction.

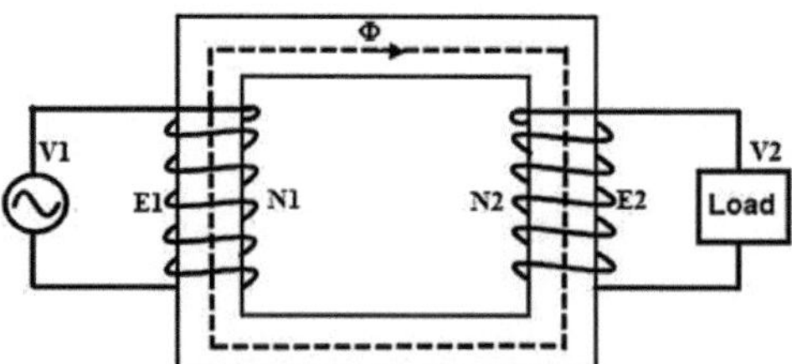

Figure 5.Operation of Transformer

When the primary winding is connected to an AC source, an exciting current flows through the winding. As the current is alternating, it will produce an alternating flux in the core which will be linked by both the primary and secondary windings. The induced emf in the primary winding (E_1) is almost equal to the applied voltage V1 and will oppose the applied voltage. The induced emf in the secondary winding (E_2) can be utilized to deliver power to any load connected across the secondary. Thus power is transferred from the primary to the secondary circuit by electromagnetic induction.

The flux in the core will alternate at the same frequency as the same frequency of the supply voltage. The frequency of induced emf in secondary is the same as that of the supply voltage. The magnitude of the emf induced in the secondary winding will depend upon its number of turns.

In a transformer, if the number of turns in the secondary winding is less than those in the primary winding, it is called a step down transformer, when the number of turns in the secondary winding is higher than the primary winding, it is called a step up transformer.

As per faraday's laws of electromagnetic induction, an emf is induced in the secondary coil. If the secondary coil circuit is closed, a current flow in it and thus electrical energy is transferred from the first coil to the second coil.

EMF EQUATION OF TRANSFORMER

Let,

N1-Number of primary turns

N_2- Number of secondary turns

ϕ_m-Maximum value of the flux in the core in wb

B_m - Maximum value of the flux density in the core in wb/m^2

A-Area of the core in m^2

F -Frequency of the AC supply in Hz

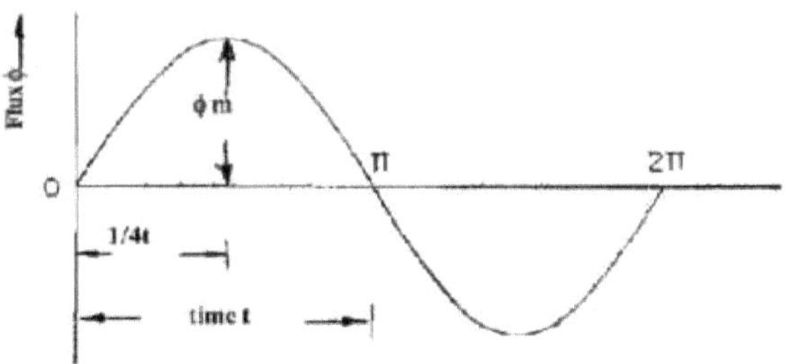

Figure 6:Flux in the Core

The flux in the core increases from zero to Φm in one quarter cycle (1/4 second) Therefore, average rate of change of flux = Φm/(1/4f) = 4f Φm

Average emf induced per turn = Average rate change of flux x 1 =4f Φm Volts

Rms value = Form factor × Average value

Form factor =Rms value/Average value = 1.11

RMS value of induced emf per turn = 1.11 x 4f Φm = 4.44f Φm Volts

RMS value of induced emf in primary, E1 = 4.44f Φm N1 Volts

RMS value of induced emf in secondary, E2 = 4.44f Φm N2 Volts

In an ideal transformer on no load, V1 = E1, V2 = E2

TRANSFORMATION RATIO

For an ideal transformer,

$V_1 = E_1;\ V_2 = E_2$ and $V_1 I_1 = V_2 I_2$

$$\frac{V_2}{V_1} = \frac{I_1}{I_2};\ \frac{E_2}{E_1} = \frac{I_1}{I_2}$$

$$\frac{E_2}{E_1} = \frac{N_2}{N_1}$$

$$\frac{E_2}{E_1} = \frac{N_2}{N_1} = \frac{V_2}{V_1} = \frac{I_1}{I_2} = K$$

$$\text{Voltage ratio} = \frac{E_2}{E_1} = K$$

$$\text{Current ratio} = \frac{I_2}{I_1} = \frac{1}{K}$$

Note:If N2 >N1, i.e., K>1, then transformer is a step up trans former. If N2<N1, i.e., K<1, then transformer is a step down transformer.

IDEAL TRANSFORMER

100% efficient or no loss transformer is called ideal transformer. It consists of purely inductive coil and loss free core. Windings are wound on a core.

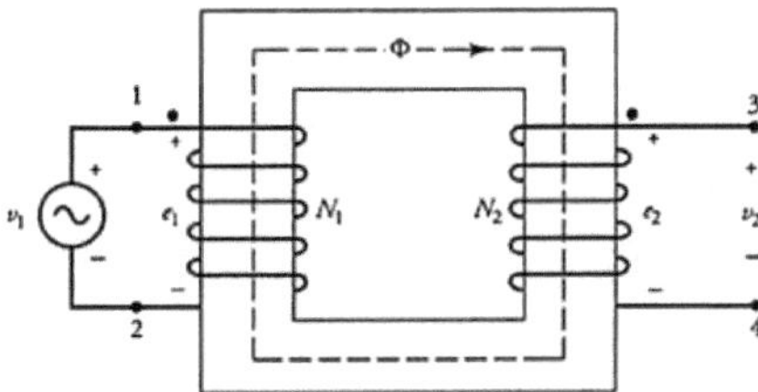

Figure 7.Ideal Transformer

Here the ideal transformer secondary is open. The AC supply is connected to the primary winding. A current flows through the primary winding. Th is current is called magnetizing current. It is denoted as Iμ. This current is mainly used to magnetise the core. The value of magnetizing current is small. It is lagging V1 by 90° the current Iμ produces an alternating flux Φ.Iμ and Φ are inphase. This changing flux is linking with primary andsecondary windings. Due to the alternating flux, a self induced emf is produced in the primary winding. It is denoted as E1 and equal to and in opposition to V1. It is known as counter emf or back emf of the primary winding. Similarly, an induced emf E2 is produced in the secondary winding, because the alternating flux is linking with secondary winding. This emf is known as mutually induced emf. This emf E2 is in opposition to V1 and its magnitude is proportional to the rate of change of flux and number of secondary turns.

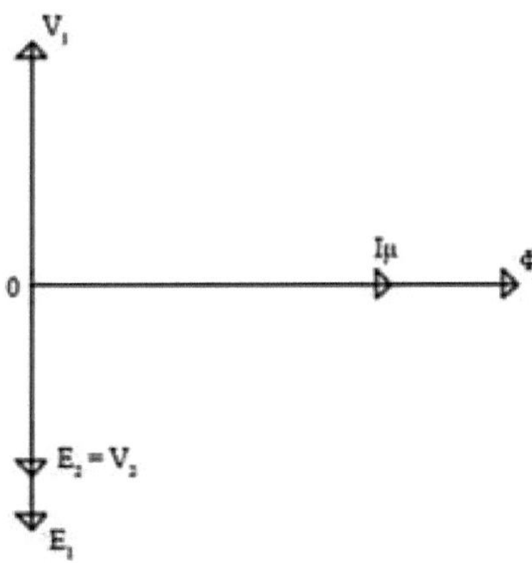

PRACTICAL TRANSFORMER ON NO -LOAD

If the primary wind ing is connected to an alternating voltage and secondary winding is left open, then the transformer is said to be on no load.

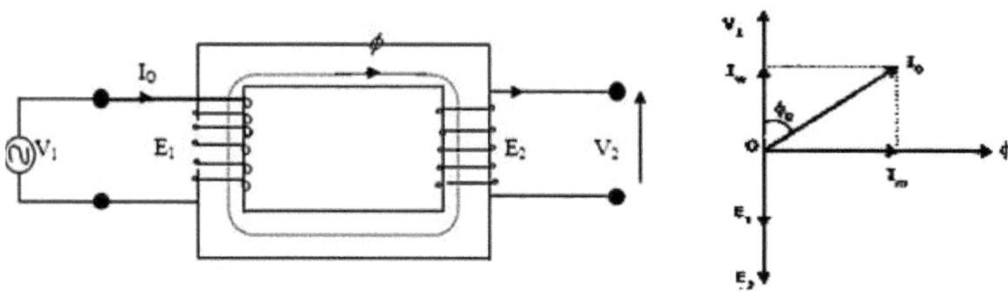

Figure 8.Pratical Transformer on No Load

When the secondary winding is connected to a load, then the transformer is said to beon load. Due to this load condition, the secondary current I2 is flowing through the load.

Let the supply be V_1 volts. This causes an alternating current to flow through the primary. Since secondary is open, this current is called no load primary current (I_o). This I_o establishes a flux Φ weber in the core.Thus $I_o$is not at 90° behind V_1, but lags it by an $_0<90^o$. No load input power, $P_o = V_1 I_o \cos\Phi_{0.}I_o$ has two components.

1. Active or working or iron loss or wattfull component (I_w), which is inphase with V_1.

$I_w = I_0 \cos\Phi_0$

2.Reactive or magnetizing or wattles component (I_μ), which is in quadrature with V_1.

$\mathbf{I\mu} = I_0 \sin\Phi$

$$I_o = \sqrt{I_w^2 + I_\mu^2}$$

Where, $\cos\Phi_o$ - no load power factor

From the above discussion, the following points are noted.

1. The no load primary current Io is very small as compared to the full load primary current.
2. As I is very small, the no load primary copper loss is negligible this no load input power is practically equal to the iron or core loss of the transformer.

TRANSFORMER ON LOAD

When the secondary winding is connected to a load, then the transformer is said to be on load. Due to this load condition, the secondary current I_2 is flowing through the load.

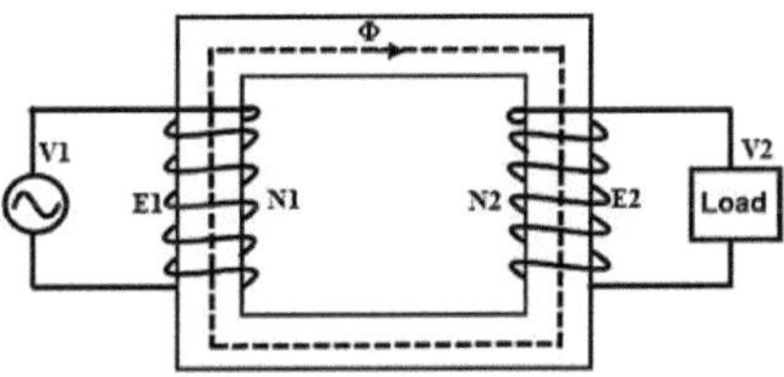

Figure 9: Transformer on Load

The phase angle between V_2 and I_2 depends on the type of load. When the load is resistive I_2 will be inphase with V_2. When the load is inductive I_2 will be lagging V_2 and when the load is capacitive I_2 will be leading V_2. Here the primary winding draws no-load current I_o.This I_o set up flux Φ.

The secondary current I_2 produces flux Φ_2. This flux Φ_2 opposes no load flux Φ and decreases the no load flux. Due to this, induced emf E_1 is reduced and V_1 dominates over E_1 and thus causes additional current I_2 to flow through the primary. I_2' is also known as load component of primary current. This current is in antiphase with I_2. I_2'establishes flux Φ_2'. This flux Φ_2' is equal in magnitde but opposite in direction to the flux Φ_2.Hence Φ_2' and Φ_2 cancel each other.

Thus when the transformer is loaded,

1.The flux passing through the core is same as that at no load i.e., flux is constant at no load as well as loaded condition. That is why transformer is also called a constant flux apparatus.

2. The total primary current, I_1 will be vector sum of I_0 and I_2'.

Transformer winding resistance

In the practical transformer, the windings have some resistances. The primary winding has primary resistance. It is denoted as R_1. Similarly the secondary winding has secondary resistance. It is denoted as R_2.

Transformer winding leakage reactance

In practice, all the flux generated by the primary winding does not link with the secondary winding. Some part of the flux passes through air rather than around the core. This flux is called the primary leakage flux. It is denoted as Φ_{L1}. The primary leakage reactance is denoted as X_1. Similarly, a leakage flux is set up in the secondary winding.This flux is called the secondary leakage flux.It is denoted as Φ_{L2}.The secondary leakage reactance is denoted as X_2.

Vector diagram of transformer on Load

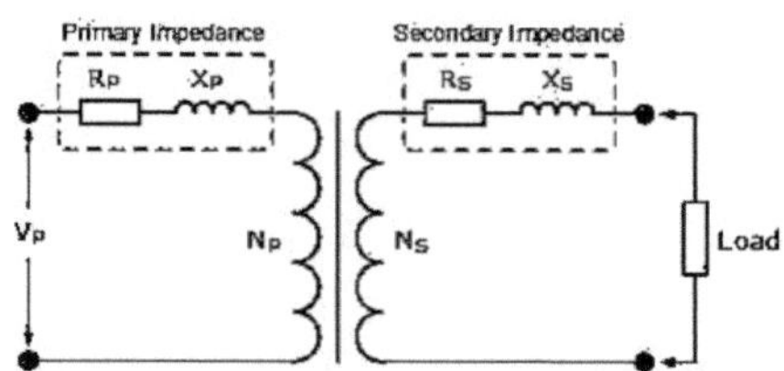

Figure 10.Vector Diagram of Transformer On Load

Consider two cases.

1. When such a transformer is assumed to have no winding resistances and leakage reactances.
2. When the transformer has winding resistances and leakage reactances.

Case (i) No winding resistances and leakage reactances (R1, R2, X1, X2 neglected)

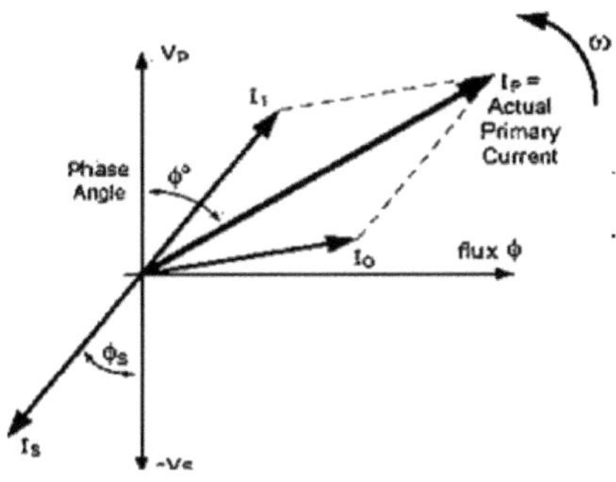

Figure 11. Lagging Power Factor

Case (ii) Transformer with resistances and leakage reactances

Consider R_1, R_2, X_1 and X_2. Practical transformer having winding resistances and leakage reactances. Input voltage is applied to the primary winding. Current I_1 is flowing through the primary winding.

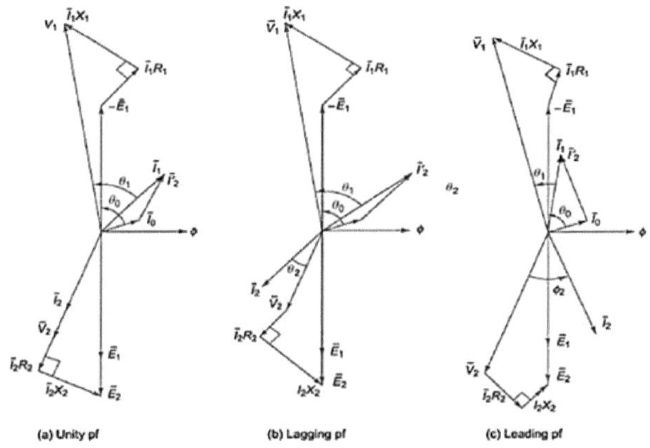

Figure 12.Vector Diagram

SHIFTING IMPEDANCES IN A TRANSFORMER

The resistance and reactance of the winding can be transferred to the other side by appropriately using the factor K^2.

Referred to primary

When secondary resistance or reactance is transferred to the primary, it is divided by K^2. It is then called equivalent secondary resistance and reactance referred to primary and is denoted by R_2 and X_2.

Equivalent resistance of transformer referred to primary

$R_{01} = R_1 + R_2' = R_1 + (R_2/K^2)$

Equivalent reactance of transformer referred to primary

$X_{01} = X_1 + X_2' = X_1 + (X_2/K^2)$

Equivalent impedance of transformer referred to primary

$$Z_{01} = \sqrt{R_{01}^2 + X_{01}^2}$$

It shows the resistance and reactance of the secondary referred to the primary. Note that secondary now has no resistance and reactance.

Referred to secondary

When primary resistance and reactance is transferred, it is multiplied by K^2. It is then called equivalent primary resistance and reactance referred to the secondary and is denoted by R_1 and X_1.

Equivalent resistance of transformer referred to secondary

$R_{02} = R_2 + R_1' = R_2 + K^2R_1$

Equivalent reactance of transformer referred to secondary

$X_{02} = X_2 + X_1' = X_2 + K^2X_1$

Equivalent impedance of transformer referred to secondary

$$Z_{02} = \sqrt{R_{02}^2 + X_{02}^2}$$

It shows the resistance and reactance of the primary referred to the secondary.Note that primary now has no resistance and reactance.Per-Unit System

Another approach to solve circuits containing transformers is the per-unit system. Impedance and voltage-level conversions are avoided. Also, machine and transformer impedances fall within fairly narrow ranges for each type and construction of device while the per-unit system is employed.The voltages, currents, powers, impedances, and other electrical quantities are measured as fractions of some base level instead of conventional units.

Quantity per unit=Actual Value/ Base value of quantity

Usually, two base quantities are selected to define a given per-unit system. Often, such quantities are voltage and power (or apparentpower).In a 1-phase system:Ones the base values of P (or S) and V are selected, all other base values can be computed from the equations.In a power system, a base apparent power and voltage are selected at the specific point in the system. Note that a transformer has no effect on the apparent power of the system, since the apparent power into a transformer equals the apparent power out of a transformer.

$$P_{base}, Q_{base}, \text{ or } S_{base} = V_{base} I_{base}$$

$$Z_{base} = \frac{V_{base}}{I_{base}} = \frac{(V_{base})^2}{S_{base}}$$

$$Y_{base} = \frac{I_{base}}{V_{base}}$$

As a result, the base apparent power remains constant everywhere in the power system. On the other hand, voltage (and, therefore, a base voltage) changes when it goes through a transformer according to its turn ratio. Therefore, the process of referring quantities to a common voltage level is done automatically in the perunit system.

Ex 1: Sketch the appropriate per-unit equivalent circuit for the 8000/240 V, 60 Hz, 20 kVA transformer with $r_c = 159$ kΩ, $x_m = 38.4$ kΩ, $r_{eq} = 38.3$ Ω, $x_{eq} = 192$ Ω.

Sol: To convert the transformer to per-unit system, the primary circuit base impedance needs to be found.

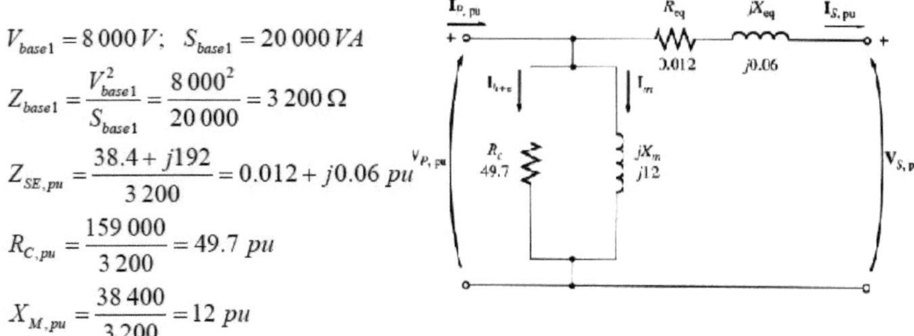

$$V_{base1} = 8\,000\,V;\quad S_{base1} = 20\,000\,VA$$

$$Z_{base1} = \frac{V_{base1}^2}{S_{base1}} = \frac{8\,000^2}{20\,000} = 3\,200\,\Omega$$

$$Z_{SE,pu} = \frac{38.4 + j192}{3\,200} = 0.012 + j0.06\ pu$$

$$R_{C,pu} = \frac{159\,000}{3\,200} = 49.7\ pu$$

$$X_{M,pu} = \frac{38\,400}{3\,200} = 12\ pu$$

EQUIVALENT CIRCUIT OF A TRANSFORMER

An equivalent circuit is merely a circuit interpretation of the equations which describe the behavior of the system.

Under no load condition, the primary of a transformer draws no load current I_o. It is mainly used to supply the iron loss and to produce the flux in the core. The effect of iron loss is represented by a non-inductive resistance R_o and the magnetizing current is represented by X_o. Both of them are connected in parallel with primary winding. This circuit is known as exciting branch or no-load branch (R_o and X_o). In this equivalent circuit,

R_1, X_1 - Primary winding resistance and reactance in Ω

R_2, X_2- Secondary winding resistance and reactance in Ω

R_o -No-load resistance in Ω

X_o - No-load reactance in Ω

I_o - No load primary current in A.

I_1 - Full load primary current in A.

I_2 - Full load secondary current in A.

I_2 -Load component of primary current in A.

I_w - Working component

I_{μ}- Magnetising component.

E_1 - Induced emf in primary winding in V
E_2 - Induced emf in secondary winding in V
Z_L - Load impedance in Ω
K - Transformation ratio

Equivalent circuit of a transformer referred to primary

If all the secondary parameters are transferred to the primary side, we get the equivalent circuit of a transformer refe rred to primary. Note that when secondary parameters are referred to primary, resistances and reactances are divided by K^2, voltages are divided by K and currents are multiplied by K. this circuit is called the exact equivalent circuit of a transformer.

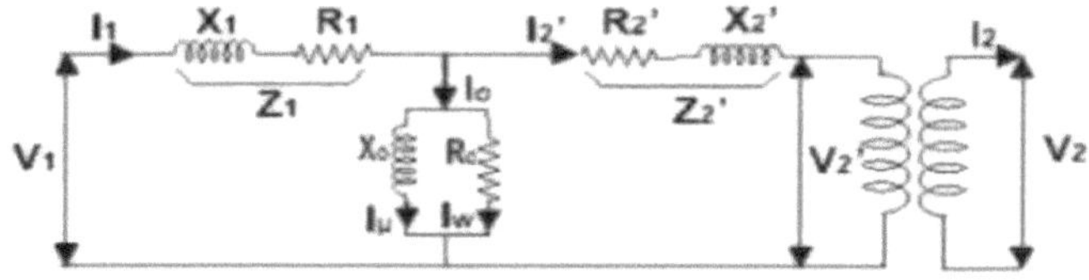

Figure 13.Equivalent Circuit of Transformer refered to Primary

$R_2' = R_2/K^2$
$X_2' = X_2/K^2$
$I_2' = KI_2$
$Z_L' = Z_L/K^2$
$V_2' = V_2/K$
$R_0 = V_1/I_W$
$X_0 = V_1/I_\mu$

Approximate equivalent circuit

The no load current Io is only 1-3% of rated primary current. So I_2 is practically equal to I_1. Due to this, the equivalent circuit can be simplified by transferring the excit ing branch (R_0 and X_0) to the left position of the circuit. This circuit is known as approximate equivalent circuit of the transformer.

$R_{01} = R_1 + R_2'$

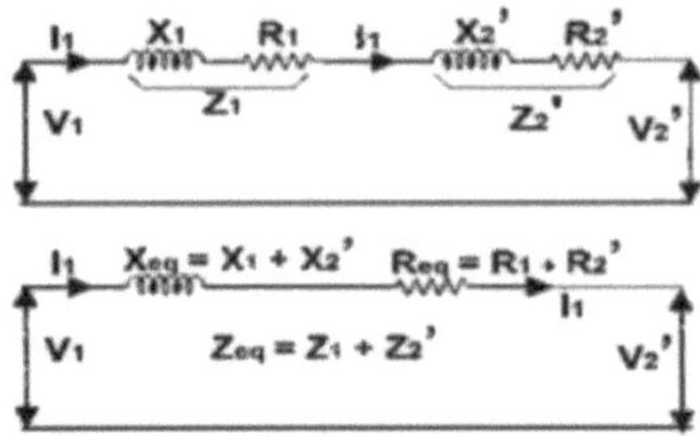

Figure 14: Approximate Eqivalent Circuit of transformer refered to primary

$X_{01} = X_1 + X_2'$
$R_{01} = R_1 + R_2$

$$Z_{01} = \sqrt{R_{01}^2 + X_{01}^2}$$

Similarly, the parameters referred to secondary are,

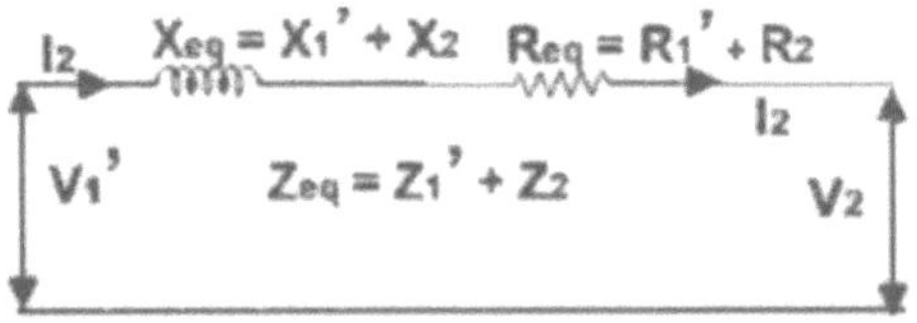

Figure 15.Approximate Eqivalent circuit of Transformer refered to secondary

$R_{02} = R_2 + R_1' = R_2 + K^2R_1$
$X_{02} = X_2 + X_1' = X_2 + K^2X_1$

$$Z_{02} = \sqrt{R_{02}^2 + X_{02}^2}$$

VOLTAGE REGULATION OF A TRANS FORMER

It is defined as the variation of no-load to full-load voltage of either the primary or secondary as percentage of no-load voltage.The purpose of voltage regulation is to determine the percentage of voltage drop between no load and full load.

Voltage Regulation={Voltage(at no load)-Voltage(at full load)}/Voltage(at no load)

For an ideal transformer, regulation is 0% since voltage drops, due to R1, X1, R2, X2 are negligible .

Lagging power factor

Voltage regulation is given by,

$$\% \text{ regulation} = \frac{I_1 R_{o1} \cos\phi + I_1 X_{o1} \sin\phi}{V_1} \times 100$$

Leading power factor

Voltage regulation is given by,

$$\% \text{ regulation} = \frac{I_1 R_{o1} \cos\phi - I_1 X_{o1} \sin\phi}{V_1} \times 100$$

Unity power factor

Voltage regulation is given by,

$$\% \text{ regulation} = \frac{I_1 R_{o1}}{V_1} \times 100$$

RATING OF A TRANS FORMER

The copper loss depends on current and iron loss depends upon voltage. Hence the total loss in a transformer depends upon volt-ampere (VA) only an not on the phase angle between voltage and current i.e., it is independent of load power factor. That is why the rating is given in KVA and not in KW.

APPLICATIONS OF TRANSFORMER

Transformers are used in,

- Transmission and distribution

- Radio and TV circuits, telephone circuits, control and instrumentation circuits.

LOSSES IN A TRANSFORMER

In any transformer, there are no friction or windage losses. The losses occuring are,

1. Core or iron loss
2. Copper loss

Core or iron loss

Iron loss is caused by the alternating flux in the core and consists of *hysteresis and eddy current loss.*

Hysteresis loss, $P_h = K_h B_{max}^{1.6} f$

Eddy current loss, $P_e = K_e B_{max}^{2} f^2$

Where, K_h - Proportionality constant which depends upon the volume and quality of the core material

K_e - Proportionality constant which depends upon the volume and resistivity of the core material

B_{max} -Maximum flux density in the core

f -Frequency of the alternating flux

Both losses depends upon maximum flux density and supply frequency.

Hysteresis loss can be minimized by using steel of high silicon content for the core loss and eddy current loss can be minimized by using very thin laminations of transformer core.

Copper loss

This loss is due to ohmic resistance of the transformer winding. If I_1 and I_2 are the primary and secondary currents respectively and R_1 and R_2 are the respective resistances of the primary and secondary windings, the copper losses occurring in primary and secondary windings will be $I_1^2R_1$ and $I_2^2R_2$ respectively. So total copper losses will be $(I_1^2R_1 + I_2^2R_2)$. These losses vary as the square of the load current.

EFFICIENCY OF A TRANS FORMER

$$\text{Transformer efficiency}, \eta = \frac{outputpower}{inputpower}$$

$$\eta = \frac{outputpower}{outputpower + losses} = \frac{outputpower}{outputpower + ironlosses + copperlosses}$$

Output power = $V_2 I_2 \cos\Phi$

V_2 – secondary terminal voltage on load

I_2 - secondary current at load

$\cos\Phi$ – power factor of the load

$$\eta = \frac{nV_2 I_2 \cos\phi}{nV_2 I_2 \cos\phi + P_i + n^2 P_{cu}} = \frac{nKVA\cos\phi}{nKVA\cos\phi + P_i + n^2 P_{cu}}$$

P_i – Iron loss

P_{cu} – Copper loss

Note:At full load, n = 1;
At half load, n = 1/2

CONDITION FOR MAXIMUM EFFICIENCY

Output power = $V_2 I_2 \cos\Phi_2$
If R_{o2} is the total resistance of the transformer referred to secondary, then,
Total copper los, $P_{cu} = I_2^2 R_{o2}$
Total losses = $P_i + P_c$

$$\eta = \frac{outputpower}{inputpower} = \frac{outputpower}{outputpower + losses} = \frac{V_2 I_2 \cos\phi_2}{V_2 I_2 \cos\phi_2 + P_i + P_{cu}}$$

$$\eta = \frac{V_2 I_2 \cos\phi_2}{V_2 I_2 \cos\phi_2 + P_i + I_2^2 R_{o2}}$$

Dividing both numerator and denominator by I_2,

$$\text{We get, } \eta = \frac{V_2 \cos\phi_2}{V_2 \cos\phi_2 + \frac{P_i}{I_2} + I_2 R_{o2}}$$

The condition for maximum efficiency is obtained by differentiating the denominator and equating it to zero.

$$\frac{d}{dI_2}(\text{denominator}) = 0$$

$$\frac{d}{dI_2}\left(V_2 I_2 \cos\phi_2 + \frac{P_i}{I_2} + I_2 R_{o2}\right) = 0$$

$$\left(0 - \frac{P_i}{I_2^2} + R_{o2}\right) = 0$$

Iron Loss = Copper Loss(or)Constant Loss=Variable Loss

$P_i = I_2^2 R_{02} = P_{cu}$

Hence the efficiency of a transformer will be maximum when copper losses are equal to iron losses.

Load current corresponding to maximum efficiency is given by,

$$I_2 = \sqrt{\frac{P_i}{R_{o2}}}$$

Load corresponding to maximum efficiency is given by,

$$= \text{Full load KVA} \times \sqrt{\frac{Ironloss}{Fullloadcopperloss}}$$

All Day Efficiency or Energy Efficiency

Large capacity transformers used in power systems are classified broadly into Power transformers and Distribution transformers. The former variety is seen in generating stations and large substations. Distribution transformers are seen at the distribution substations.

The basic difference between the two types arises from the fact that the power transformers are switched in or out of the circuit depending upon the load to be handled by them. Thus at 50% load on the station only 50% of the transformers need to be connected in the circuit. On the otherhand a distribution transformer is never switched off. It has to remain in the circuit irrespective of the load connected. In suchh cases the constant loss of the transformer continues to be dissipated. Hence the concept of energy based efficiency is defined for such t ransformers. It is called '**all day**' efficiency.

All day efficiency = Energy out put of the transformer over a day/ Corresponding energy input.

The ratio of the output in kwh to input in kwh of a transformer over a 24 hour period is known as all-day efficiency.

$$\eta_{all\text{-}day} = \frac{kwhoutputi\ n24hours}{kwhinputin\ 24hours}$$

AUTO TRANSFORMER (OR) VARIAC

A transformer in which part of the winding is common to both the primary and secondary is known as an autotransformer.The autotransformer differs from a conventional two winding transformer in the way in which the primary and secondary are irrealated. In the conventional transformer, the primary and secondary windings are completely insulated from each other but are magnetically linked by a common core. In the autotransformer, the primary and secondary windings are conn ected electrically as well as magnetically, infact a part of the single continuous winding is common to both primary and secondary.

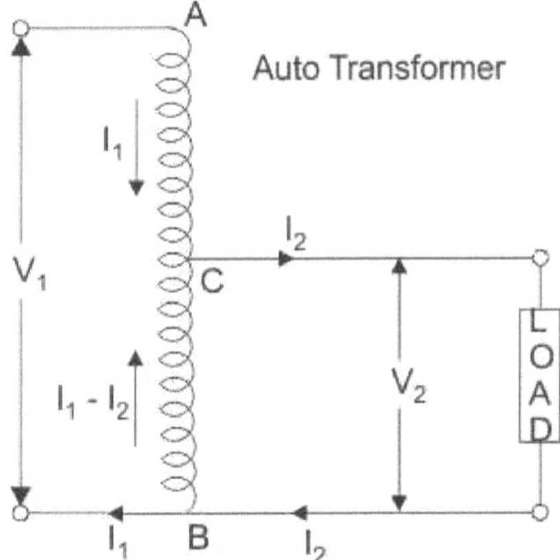

Figure 16.Auto Transformer

Advantages

1. Higher efficiency
2. Small size
3. Smaller exciting current
4. Lower cost

5. Better voltage regulation

6. Required less copper

Disadvantages

1. If the ratio of transformation K differs from unity, the economic advantages of auto transformer over two winding transformer decrease.
2. The main disadvantage of an autotransformer is due to the direct electrical connection between low tension and high tension sides. If primary is supplied at high voltage, then an open circuit in the common winding BC, would result in the appearance of dangerously high voltage on the low voltage side. This high voltage may be detrimental to the load and the persons working there. Thus a suitable protection must be provided against such an occurance.
3. The short circuit current in an autotransformer is higher than that in a two winding transformer.

Applications

1. Autotransformers are used for starting of induction motors and synchronous motors.
2. Continuously variable autotransformer finds application in electrical testing laboratories.
3. Autotransformers are used as boosters to increase the voltage in AC feeder.
4. As furnace transformers for getting a convenient supply to suit th furnace winding from 230V AC supply.

Harmonics

Harmonics: The distortion in a sinusoidal wave is generally defined in terms of various harmonics components. Harmonics are defined as the content of signal whose frequency is an integral multiple of the system frequency of the fundamental. Typical harmonics for a 50 Hz system (fundamental frequency) are the 5th (250 Hz), 7th (350 Hz), 9th (450 Hz)

Transformers: Harmonics in transformers cause an increase in the iron and copper losses. Voltage distortion increase losses due to hysteresis and eddy currents and causes overstressing of the insulation material used. The primary effect of power line harmonics in transformer is, thus the additional heat generated. Other problems include possible resonance between the transformer inductance and the system capacitance, thermal fatigue due to temperature cycling and possible core vibrations.

Source of harmonics: (1) Transformers under no load and light loads (2) Saturated Reactors (3) Thyrister controlled motor drives (4) Arc Furnaces (5) Arc Welders (6) Conduction Furnaces (7) Gas discharging lighting-low pressure/ high pressure Sodium vapour lamps (8) High-pressure Mercury vapor lamps (9) CFL/fluorescent tube lights (10) Energy conservation devices e.g. soft starters, electronics ballast and fan regulators (11) Rectifiers (12) UPS (13) Static VAR compensator (14) HVDC transmission system (15) Solar power conversion

Why to worry for harmonics: Voltage distortion is generally very harmful because it can increase the effective peak value and also the RMS current in some devices connected to the network. For a capacitor, impedance decreases drastically as it is inversely proportional to the frequency. Under normal circumstances the voltage distortion in primary electrical distribution network is minimal and can usually be ignored from a practical point of view. On the other hand distortion of current wave shape is common particularly when electronic equipment is connected to the network or when non-linear loads are connected. Current distortion, in general, causes overheating due to increase in the losses and affects all electrical machines, transformers etc. This causes derating of equipment. The amount of derating will depend upon which harmonics are present and the magnitude of the individual current and resistance.

Filters for harmonics

For healthy operation of power system, two things serve as guidelines:

1. The consumer is responsible for maintaining current distortion within permissible/acceptable levels.

2. The electricity board is responsible for maintaining voltage distortion within permissible/acceptable levels.

There are different types of filters:

– Single tuned filters.

– High Pass (first, 2nd or third order etc.)

A capacitor with a series reactance can be so designed as to tune to a given harmonic. It offers almost a zero impedance parallel path and absorbs a particular harmonic. At the fundamental frequency, it also helps in power factor correction. Thus, wherever filters are required, a portion of the P.F. capacitor bank is converted into a filter or filters. A filter bank increases the cost of capacitor installation because of extra circuit breakers and reactors.

Undesirable harmonic current is prevented from flowing into power system by use of high series impedance to block them or direct them by means of low impedance shunt path.

Series filters should be designed to carry full load current and should be insulated to full rated voltage of the system, while shunt filters are less expensive and provide reactive compensation in fundamental frequency. Therefore, it is generally preferred to use shunt filters.

- Defines the total harmonic content of current or voltage
- Ratio of the RMS of the harmonic content to the RMS of the Fundamental, as % of Fundamental

$$\text{THD} = \sqrt{\frac{\text{sum of squares of amplitudes of all harmonics}}{\text{square of amplitude of fundamental}}} \times 100$$

Mathematically,THD of a voltage wave form can be defined as,

$$\text{THD} = \sum_{h=2}^{h=\infty} \sqrt{\frac{V_h^2}{V_1^2}} \times 100$$

Three Phase Transformers

Electric power is generated in generating stations, using three phase alternators at 11 KV. This voltage is further stepped up to 66 KV, 110 KV, 230 KV or 400 KV using 3 phase power transformers and power is transmitted at this high voltage through transmission lines. At the receiving substations, these high voltages are stepped down by 3 phase transformers to 11 KV. This is further stepped down to 400 volts at load centers by means of distribution transformers. For generation, transmission and distribution, 3 phase system is economical. Therefore 3 phase transformers are very essential for the above purpose.

Construction of Three phase Transformer

Three phase transformers comprise of three primary and three secondary windings. They are wound over the laminated core as we have seen in single phase transformers. Three phase transformers are also of core type or shell type as in single phase transformers. The basic principle of a three phase transformer is illustrated in figure in which the primary windings and secondary windings of three phases are shown. The primary windings can be inter connected in star or delta and put across three phase supply.

The three cores are 120° apart and their unwound limbs are shown in contact with each other. The center core formed by these three limbs, carries the flux produced by the three phase currents I_R, I_Y and I_B. As at any instant $I_R + I_Y + I_B = 0$, the sum of three fluxes (flux in the center limb) is also zero.

Therefore it will make no difference if the common limb is removed. All the three limbs are placed in one plane in case of a practical transformer as shown in figure.

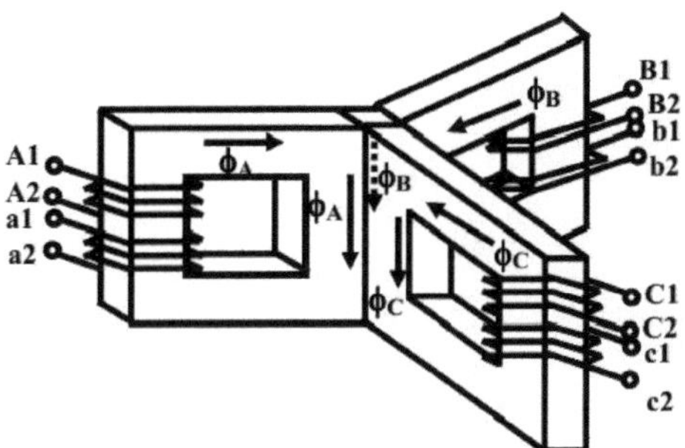

Figure 17. Three Phase Core type Transformer

The core type transformers are usually wound with circular cylindrical coils. The construction and assembly of laminations and yoke of a three phase core type transformer is shown in figure.

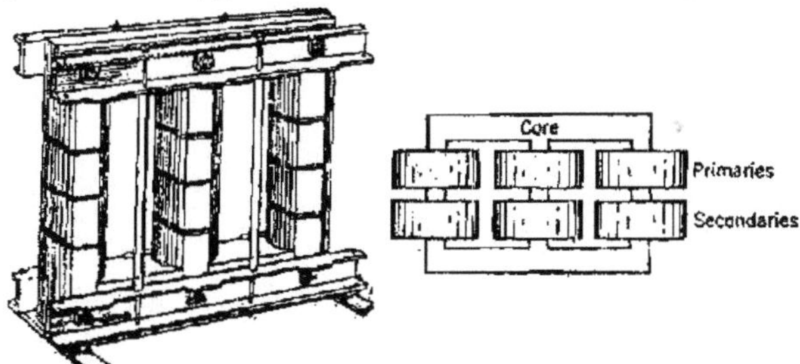

Figure 18.Threephase Core type Transformer Winding and Construction

In the other method the primary and secondary windings are wound one over the other in each limb. The low-tension windings are wound directly over the core but are, of course, insulated for it. The high tension windings are wound over the low— tension windings and adequate insulation is provided between the two windings.The primary and secondary windings of the three phase transformer can also be interconnected as star or delta.

Advantages of Three-phase transformers over Single-phase transformers

Inexpensive: Compared with single-phase transformers, 3-phase transformers are cheaper. It has a lower cost when compared to three units of a single-phase transformer.

Lightweight: Three-phase transformers are light in weight and smaller in size than single-phase transformers, which means they take up less space.

Assembly in the least time: Very easy to assemble. We can get a single-phase source from three-phase transformers, while the opposite is not valid.

Higher efficiency: The three-phase transformer performs its functions more efficiently and delivers more power than a single-phase transformer.

Easier to install: Pre-wired 3-phase transformer is ready to install, making the installation very easy and smooth.

Easy transportation: To provide the same output, the material used to fabricate the core of a 3-phase transformer is very little compared to that of 3 single-phase transformers. Therefore, they aren't only easy transportation but also lower shipping costs.

Disadvantages of 3-phase transformers

The more significant cost of standby units: The individual cost of redundant equipment is high and makes it difficult to repair or correct any problems. In a 3-phase transformer, a common core is shared across all three units. Therefore, if the unit is defective or is damaged, the entire three-phase transformer must be shut down.

Cost of repair: Repair costs for 3-phase transformers are higher because it is very costly to change each component. Hence, for service recovery, the spare unit cost is higher when compared with single-phase transformers.

Reduced capacity: Because the 3-phase transformer is self-cooled, the transformer's power is also reduced simultaneously.

Fault correction: In the event of a fault in any phase of a 3-phase transformer, the fault is transferred to the other two phases. Therefore, the entire unit needs to be replaced.

Three Phase Transformer connections

The identical single phase transformers can be suitably inter-connected and used instead of a single unit 3—phase transformer. The single unit 3 phase transformer is housed in a single tank. But the transformer bank is made up of three separate single phase transformers each with its own, tanks and bushings. This method is preferred in mines and high altitude power stations because transportation becomes easier. Bank method is adopted also when the voltage involved is high because it is easier to provide proper insulation in each single phase transformer.

As compared to a bank of single phase transformers, the main advantages of a single unit 3-phase transformer are that it occupies less floor space for equal rating, less weight costs about 20% less and further that only one unit is to be handled and connected.

There are various methods available for transforming 3 phase voltages to higher or lower 3 phase voltages. The most common connections are (i) star — star (ii) Delta—Delta (iii) Star —Delta (iv) Delta — Star.

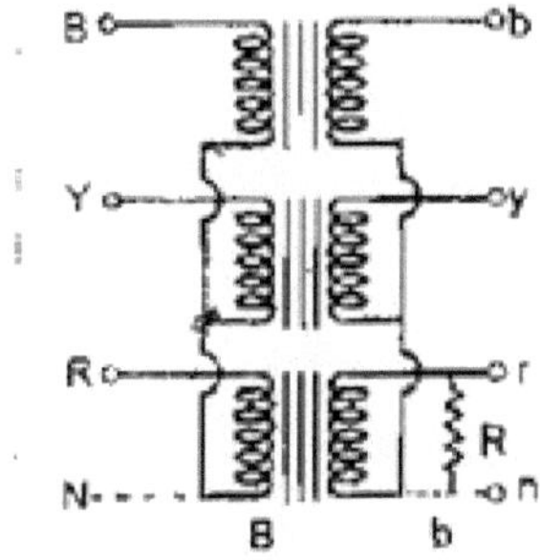

Figure 19.Star-Star Connection

The star-star connection is most economical for small, high voltage transformers because the number of turns per phase and the amount of insulation required is minimum (as phase voltage is only 1/3 of line voltage. In the figure a bank of three transformers connected in star on both the primary and the secondary sides is shown. The ratio of line voltages on the primary to the secondary sides is the same as a transformation ratio of single phase transformer.

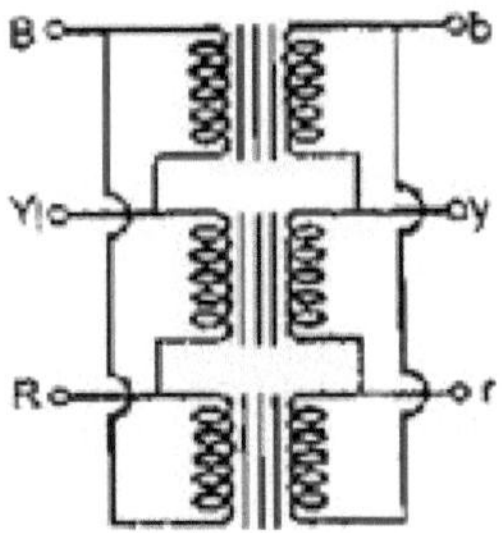

Figure 20. Delta- Delta Connection

The delta— delta connection is economical for large capacity, low voltage transformers in which insulation problem is not a serious one. The transformer connection are as shown in figure.

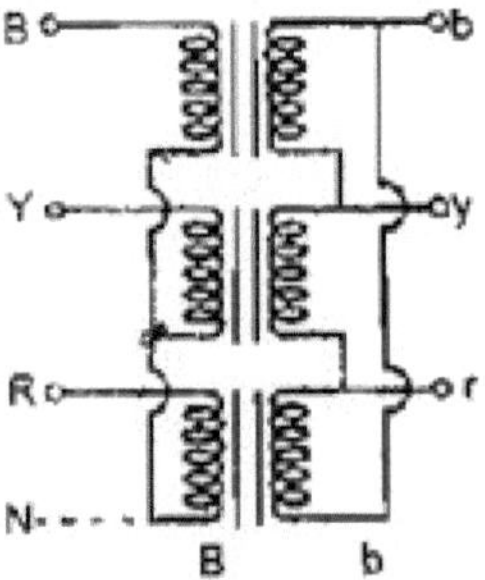

Figure 21. Star- Delta Connection

The main use of star-delta connection is at the substation end of the transmission line where the voltage is to be stepped down. The primary winding is star connected with grounded neutral as shown in Figure. The ratio between the secondary and primary line voltage is 1/3 times the transformation ratio of each single phase transformer. There is a 30° shift between the primary and secondary line voltages which means that a star-delta transformer bank cannot be paralleled with either a star-star or a delta-delta bank.

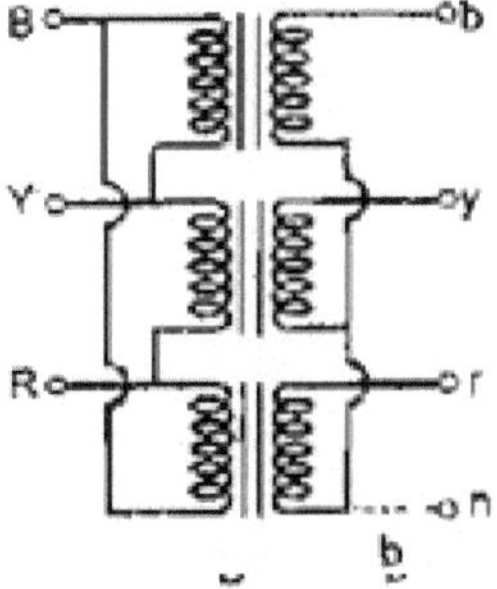

Figure 22.Delta-Star Connection

Delta-Star connection is generally employed where it is necessary to step up the voltage. The connection is shown in figure. The neutral of the secondary is grounded for providing 3-phase, 4-wire service. The connection is very popular because it can be used to serve both the 3-phase power equipment and single phase lighting circuits.

Parallel operation of three phase transformer

Advantages of using transformers in parallel

- To maximize electrical power system efficiency
- To maximize electrical power system availability
- To maximize power system reliability
- To maximize electrical power system flexibility

Conditions for parallel operation

Certain conditions have to be met before two or more transformers are connected in parallel and share a common load satisfactorily. They are,

1. The voltage ratio must be the same.
2. The per unit impedance of each machine on its own base must be the same.
3. The polarity must be the same, so that there is no circulating current between the transformers.
4. The phase sequence must be the same and no phase difference must exist between the voltages of the two transformers.

Problems:

1. A sinusoidal flux o.o2 wb links with 55 turns of a transformer secondary coil. Calculate the rms value of the induced emf in the secondary. The supply frequency is 50 Hz.

Given data :

Supply frequency f =50 Hz, No. of secondary turns N_2= 55,

Flux ϕ = 0.02mwb

Maximum flux ϕ_m $= \sqrt{2 \times \phi}$

$= \sqrt{2 \times 0.02}$ = 0.028 wb

To find:

RMS value of induced emf in the secondary (E_2)

Solution:

$$E_2 = 4.44 f \phi_m N_2 = 4.44 \times 50 \times 0.028 \times 55$$

E_2 = 341.8 V

2. The no load current of transformer is 15 A at a power factor of 0.2 when connected to a 460 V, 50 Hz supply. *F the primary winding has 550* turns, Calculate i) The magnetising component of no-load current, ii) The iron loss, iii) The maximum value of the flux on the core.

Given data :

The no-load current I_o = 15 A, Power factor = 0.2, V1 = 460 V

supply frequency f= 50 Hz Primary turns N_1= 550,

Solution:

i) Magnetising component of no-load current I_μ

$$I_\mu = I_o \sin\phi_o = 15 \times 0.98 = 14.7A$$

ii) Iron loss (W_o) = $V_1 I_o \cos\phi_o = 460 \times 15 \times 0.2 = 1380\ W$

iii) Maximum value of the flux (ϕ_m)

$$E_1 = 4.44 f \phi_m N_1$$

$$\phi_m = \frac{E_1}{4.44 f\ N_1} = \frac{460}{4.44 \times 50 \times 550} - 3.77 mwb$$

3. A 220/110 V, 10 kVA transformer has primary winding resistance of 0.25 Ω and a secondaryresistance of 0.06 Ω .Determine the primary and secondary current at rated load, the total winding resistance referred to the primary and total winding resistance referred to the secondary.

Given data:

$V1 = 220$ V, $V2 = 110$ V, $R1 = 0.25\ \Omega$, $R2 = 0.06\ \Omega$, rating = 10 kVA

To find:

I_1, I_2, R_{o1}, R_{o2}.

Transformation ratio $K = \frac{V_2}{V_1} = \frac{110}{220} = 0.5$

Total winding resistance referred to primary

$R_{01} = R_1 + R_2 = \frac{R_1 + R_2}{k^2} = 0.25 + \frac{0.06}{0.5^2}$

$R_{01} = 0.49\ \Omega$

Total winding resistance referred to secondary

$R_{02} = R_2 + R_1$

$= R_2 + R_1 k^2$

$= 0.06 + 0.25 \times 0.5^2$

$R_{02} = 0.1225\ \Omega$

4. The required no load voltage ratio in a 150 kVA, 50 Hz single phase transformer is 5000/250 V. Find the efficiency at half rated kVA, Unity power factor and also efficiency at full load 0.8 pf lagging if the full load copper losses are 1800 W; core losses are 1500 W.

Given data:

Transformer rating = 150 kVA   Supply Frequency = 50 Hz

Primary voltage = 5000 V,   Secondary voltage = 5000 V,

full load copper loss P_{cufl}= 1800 W core loss P_1 = 1500 W

Solution:

i)Efficiency at half rated kVA, UPF

$$n = {}^{1}/_{2} = 0.5,\ \cos\phi = 1$$

$$\%\eta = \frac{n\,kVA\cos\phi}{n\,kVA\cos\phi + P_1 + n^2 \times P_{cufL}}$$

$$= \frac{\frac{1}{2}\times 150\times 10^3\times 1}{\frac{1}{2}\times 150\times 10^3\times 1 + 1500 + \left(\frac{1}{2}\right)^2\times 1800}$$

$$\boxed{\%\eta = 97.46\%}$$

ii)Full load kVA at $0.8pf, \cos\phi = 0.8$

$$\%\eta = \frac{kVA\cos\phi}{kVA\cos\phi + P_1 + P_{cufL}}$$

$$= \frac{150\times 10^3\times 0.8}{150\times 10^3\times 0.8 + 1500 + 1800}\times 100$$

$$\boxed{\%\eta = 97.33\%}$$

5. A 500 kVA transformer has an iron loss of 500 W and full load copper loss 700 W. Calculate the efficiency at 3/4th full load 0.8 power factor.

Given data:

Transformer rating = 500 kVA, Iron loss $P_1 = 500$ W

Full load copper loss $P_{cufL} = 700$ W, power factor $\cos\phi = 0.8$

Load = 3/4th full load

To find:

Efficiency at 3/4th full load and 0.8 pf

Solution:

$n = ¾$; $\cos\phi = 0.8$

$$\%\eta = \frac{n\,kVA\cos\phi}{n\,kVA\cos\phi + P_1 + n^2 \times P_{cufL}} \times 100$$

$$= \frac{\frac{3}{4}\times 500\times 10^3 \times 0.8}{\frac{3}{4}\times 500\times 10^3\times 0.8 + 500 + \left(\frac{3}{4}\right)^2 700}\times 100 = \frac{300000}{300000+500+393.75}\times 100$$

$\%\eta = 99.7\%$

CHAPTER TWO

DC MACHINES

INTRODUCTION

Applications such as light bulbs and heaters require energy in electrical form. In other applications, such as fans and rolling mills, energy is required inmechanical form. One form of energy can be obtained from the other form with the help of converters. Converters that are used to continuously translate electrical input to mechanical output or vice versa are called electric machines. The process of translation is known as electromechanical energy conversion. An electric machine is therefore a link between an electrical system and a mechanical system. In these machines the conversion is reversible. If the conversion is from mechanical to electrical, the machine is said to act as a generator. If the conversion is from electrical to mechanical, the machine is said to act as a motor. Hence, the same electric machine can be made to operate as a generator as well as a motor. Machines are called ac machines (generators or motors) if the electrical system is ac and dc machines (generators or motors) if the electrical system is dc.

ELECTROMAGNETIC CONVERSION

Three electrical machines (dc, induction, and synchronous) are used extensively for electromechanical energy conversion. In these machines, conversion of energy from electrical to mechanical form or vice versa results from the following two electromagnetic phenomena:

1. When a conductor moves in a magnetic field, voltage is induced in the conductor.

2. When a current-carrying conductor is placed in a magnetic field, the conductor experiences a mechanical force.

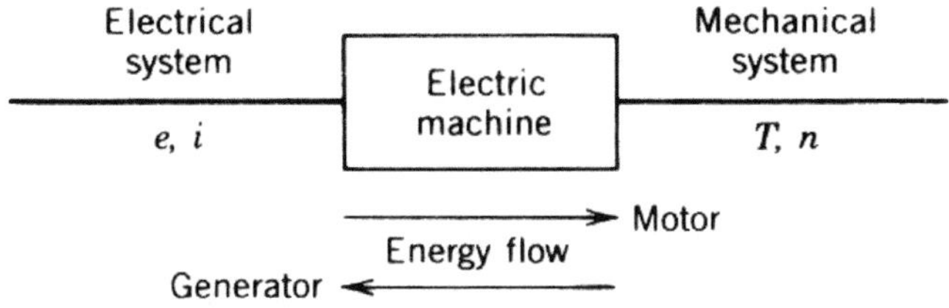

Figure 1: Electromechanical Energy Conversion

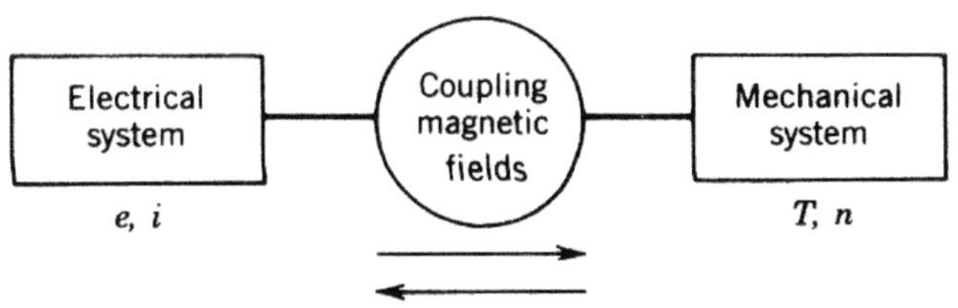

Figure 2:Coupling Field between Electrical and Mechanical System

Note that in both motoring and generating actions, the coupling magnetic field is involved in producing a torque and an induced voltage. The basic electric machines (dc, induction, and synchronous), which depend on electromagnetic energy conversion, are extensively used in various power ratings.

DC MACHINES

The dc machines are versatile and extensively used in industry. A wide variety of volt–ampere or torque–speed characteristics can be obtained from various connections of the field windings.

Although a dc machine can operate as either a generator or a motor, at present its use as a generator is limited because of the widespread use of ac power. The dc machine is extensively used as a motor in industry. Its speed can be controlled over a wide range with relative ease. Large dc motors (in tens or hundreds of horsepower) are used in machine tools, printing presses, conveyors, fans, pumps, hoists, cranes, paper mills, textile mills, rolling mills, and so forth. Additionally, dc motors still dominate as traction motors used in transit cars and locomotives. Small dc machines (in fractional horsepower rating) are used primarily as control devices—such as tachogenerators for speed sensing and servomotors for positioning and tracking. The dc machine definitely plays an important role in industry.

CONSTRUCTION

In a dc machine, the armature winding is placed on the rotor and the field windings are placed on the stator. The essential features of a two-pole dc machine are shown in Figure. The stator has salient poles that are excited by one or more field windings, called shunt field windings and series field windings. The field windings produce an air gap flux distribution that is symmetrical about the pole axis (also called the field axis, direct axis, or d-axis).

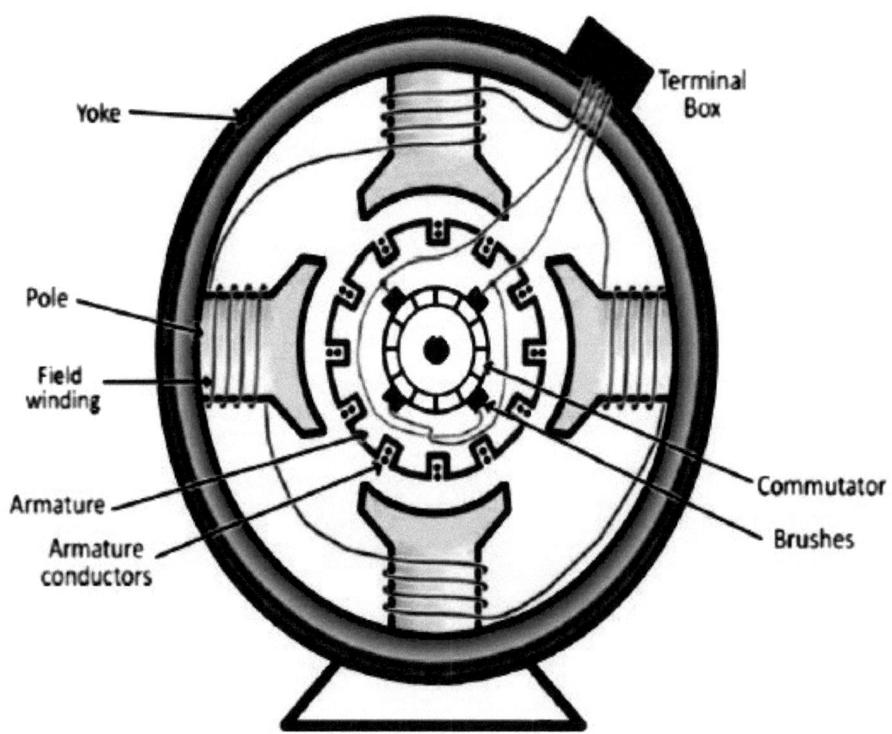

Figure 3. Cross sectional view of DC Machine

The construction of DC generator and DC motor are the same. Any DC generator can be run as a DC Motor and vice-versa. The main parts of dc machine includes,

1. Yoke or Magnetic frame
2. Pole core and pole shoes
3. Field winding
4. Armature-Armature core, Armature winding.
6. Commutator
7. Brushes

Yoke:

- The outer frame of a dc machine is called as yoke. It acts as a protecting cover for DC machine.
- It provides mechanical support for the poles.
- It carries the magnetic flux produced by the poles.
- Material used: Small machine: cast iron, Large machine: cast steel

Pole core, pole shoes:

- Pole core carries field winding which is necessary to produce the flux.
- Pole shoes spread out the flux in the air gap and also to reduce the reluctance.
- They support the exciting coils.
- Material used: Small machine: cast iron, Large machine: cast steel

Inter poles:

- Inter poles or the commutating poles are fixed to the frame in between main poles.
- They are used for improve commutation.

Field winding:

- The field winding is placed on the pole core.
- To carry the current and to produce the magnetic flux.
- Material used: It is made up of aluminum or copper.

Armature:

It is further divided into two parts namely:

(i)Armature core

(ii) Armature winding

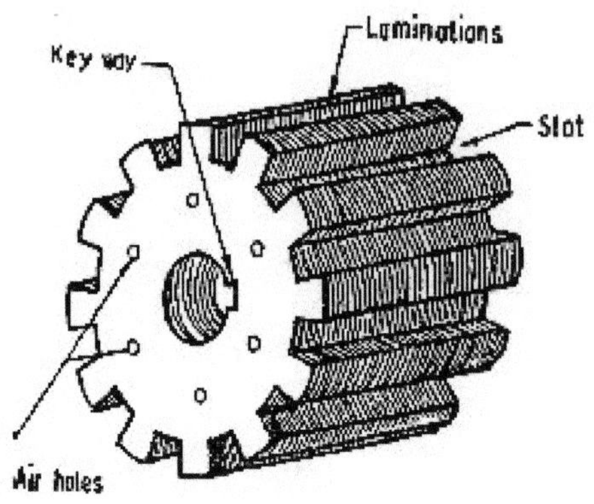

Figure 4: Armature

Armature core:

- It is cylindrical in shape with slots on its outer periphery.
- It is mounted on the shaft.
- It provides the house for armature conductors.
- Material used: Small machine: cast iron, Large machine: cast steel

Armature winding:

- The armature windings are placed into the slots on the armature surface.
- The ends of the coils are soldered with commutator segments.
- Functions: When the armature rotates an emf is induced in the armature conductors in case of generators.
- Material used: Copper.

Commutator:

- The basic nature of emf induced in the armature conductor is alternating.

- This needs rectification in case of DC generator, which is made possible by a device called commutator.
- Material used: Copper.

Brushes :

Brushes are usually made from carbon or graphite. They rest on commutator segments and slide on the segments when the commutator rotates keeping the physical contact to collect or supply the current.

Working of DC Generator:

A dc generator works on the principle of Faradays laws of electromagnetic induction. It produces dynamically induced emf. It states that whenever the magnetic lines of force i.e., flux linking with a conductor or a coil changes, an emf is induced in that conductor or coil. The change in flux associated with the conductor can exist only when there exists a relative motion between a conductor and the flux. It is achieved by rotating conductor with respect to flux.

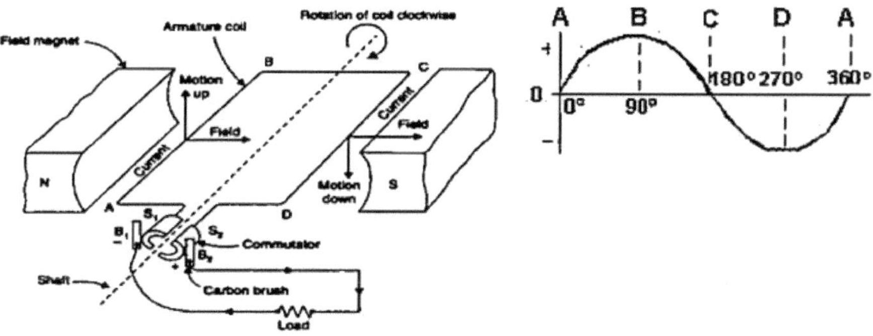

Figure 5: Working of DC generator

Let's us consider, the rectangular loop of conductor is ABCD rotates clockwise, magnetic field lines passing through it changes. When coil AB moves upwards and arm CD moves downwards. According to Fleming Right hand rule, the induced current in the armature coil flows in the direction ABCD.

When coil sides ABCD and magnetic flux are moving parallel to each other ($\theta = 0°$), then coil sides are not cut by the flux lines, hence no emf is induced.

When coil sides ABCD moves at an angle to the magnetic flux($\theta = 0°$ to $90°$), then there is a low emf induced in the conductor.

When coil sides ABCD and magnetic flux are perpendicular to each other($\theta = 90°$), then there is a maximum rate of flux is cut by the conductor. Therefore the emf induced is maximum. Again the emf induced decreases with coil sides moves at an angle to the magnetic flux ($\theta = 90°$ to $180°$) and reaches zero emf.

In second half of the rotation($\theta = 180°$ to $360°$), the coil sides move under a pole of opposite polarity and the direction of induced emf is reversed.

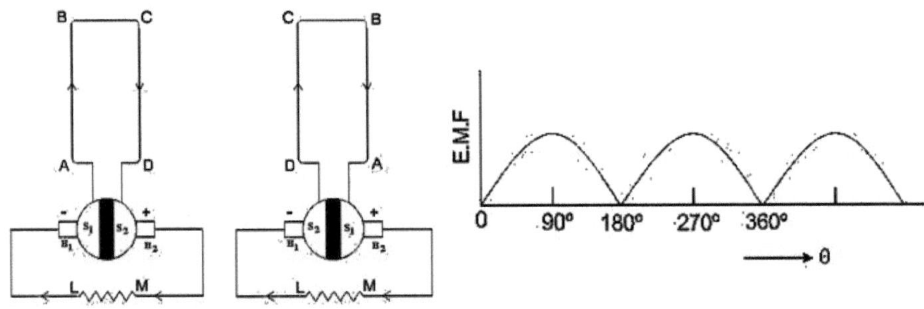

Figure 6.Waveform of Current through Load Circuit

It is seen that in the first half of the revolution current flows always along $ABCDS_2B_2MLB_1S_1$. In the next half revolution, in the figure the direction of the induced current in the coil is reversed. But at the same time the position of the segments S_1 and S_2 are also reversed which results that brush no B_1 comes in touch with the segment S_2. Hence, the current in the load resistance again flows from M to L. The waveform of the current through the load circuit is as shown in the figure. This current is unidirectional.

EMF equation of dc generator

φ= Flux/pole in weber.

N=Speed of armature in RPM

P=Number of poles

N/60=Speed of armature in RPS

Z= Total number of armature conductors.

E = EMF induced in any parallel path in the armature in volts

A=Number of parallel paths

According to Faraday's law, the induced emf is proportional to the rate of change of the magnetic flux.

i.e ., e =-dφ/dt

Let us consider a single conductor moving during one revolution.

*dφ=φ*P weber*

Number of revolutions per second=N/60 seconds.

Time taken to complete one revolution, dt=60/N seconds.

According to Faraday's laws of electromagnetic induction.

EMF generated/conductor = dφ/dt ....(1)

*Substituting, dφ=φ*p and dt=60/N in equation (1) gives =φ*p/(60/N)*

EMF generated/conductor =φNp/60 volts

Number of conductors in one path of armature =z/A

*EMF generated/path = (φpN/60) *(z/A) volts*

For wave winding, A=2

*EMF generated/path = (φpN/60) *(z/2) volts*

= φpNz/120 volts

For lap winding, A=P

*EMF generated/path = (φpN/60) *(z/P) volts*

= φNz/60 volts.

Types of DC generators

DC generators are classified according to their methods of field excitations,

1. Separately excited DC generator.
2. Self excited DC generator

-DC shunt generator

- DC series generator

-DC compound generator

Separately excited DC generator

A dc generator whose field winding is energised from an independent external dc source is called separately excited dc generator.

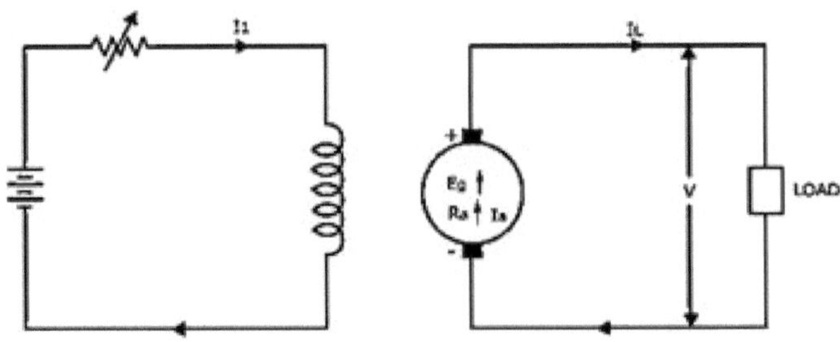

Figure 7: Seperately Excited DC Generator

Armature current $I_a=I_L$

Generated emf $E_g=V+ I_a R_a+ V_{Brush}$

Power developed in the armature = $E_g I_a$

Power delivered to load=V I_a

Self excited DC generator

Self-excited DC Generator is a device, in which the current to the field winding is supplied by the generator itself. In self-excited DC generator, the field coils may be connected in parallel with the armature in the series, or it may be connected partly in series and partly in parallel with the armature windings.

A shunt DC generator is shown figure, in which the field winding is wired parallel to armature winding so that the voltage across both are same. The field winding has high resistance and more number of turns so that only a part of armature current passes through field winding and the rest passes through load.

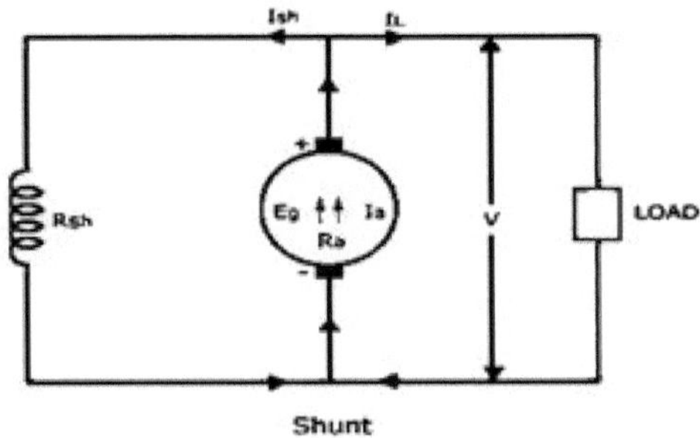

Figure 8. DC Shunt Generator

- Field winding is connected in parallel with armature.
- It is a "constant speed" machine.

Shunt field current $I_{sh}=V/R_{sh}$
Armature current $I_a = I_L + I_{sh}$
Generated emf $Eg=V+ I_a R_a + V_{Brush}$
$I_a R_a$=Voltage drop in the armature resistance
V_{Brush} = Voltage drop at connects of the brush

A series DC generator is shown below in which the armature winding is connected in series with the field winding so that the field current flows through the load as well as the field winding. Field winding is a low resistance,thick wire of few turns. Series generators are also rarely used.

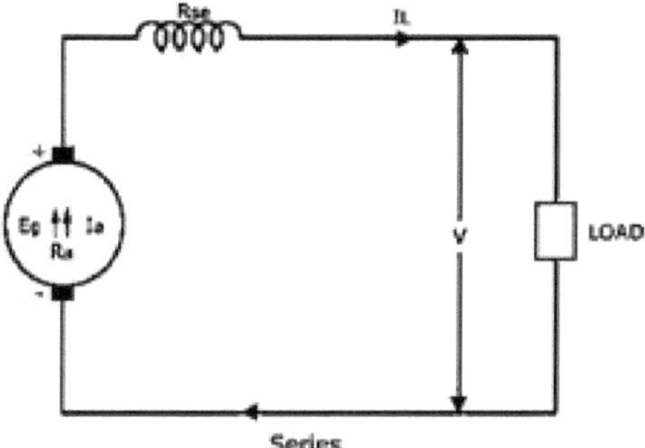

Figure 9:DC Series Generator

i. The field winding is connected in series with armature.
ii. Same current flows through field as armature.

$I_a=I_L=I_{se}$
Generated emf $E_g=V+ I_a R_a + I_a R_{se} + V_{Brush}$
$I_a R_{se}$= Voltage drop in the series field winding resistance

A compound generator is shown in figure below. It has two field findings namely Rsh and Rse. They are basically shunt winding (Rsh) and series winding (Rse). Compound generator is of two types – 1) Short shunt and 2) Long shunt

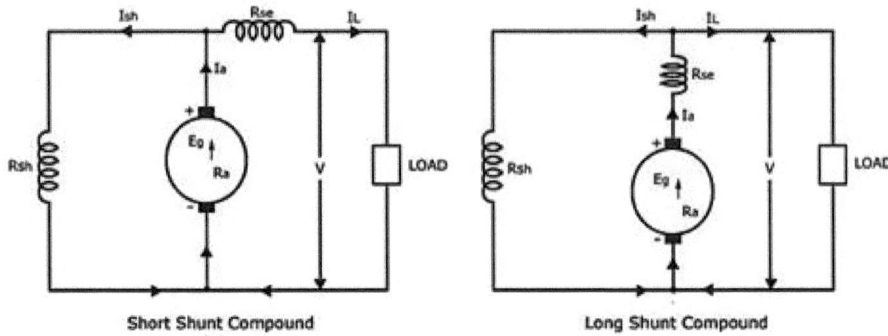

Figure 10:DC Compound Generator

Short shunt:- Here the shunt field winding is wired parallel to armature and series field winding is connected in series to the load.

Load current,$I_L=I_{se}$

Shunt field current,$I_{sh}=(V+I_{se}R_{se})/R_{sh}$

Generated emf,Eg=V+ Ia Ra+Ise Rse+ VBrush

Long shunt:- Here the shunt field winding is parallel to both armature and series field winding (Rse is wired in series to the armature).

Series field current $I_{sc}=I_a=I_L+I_{sh}$

Shunt field current $I_{sh}=V/R_{sh}$

Generated emf $E_g=V+I_a(R_a+R_{se})+V_{Brush}$

CHARACTERISTICS OF DC GENERATOR

There are three types of characteristics in DC generator.

a. Open circuit characteristics (OCC) (or) Magnetisation characteristics [E_g Versus I_f]
b. Internal characteristics (or) Total characteristics [E Versus I_L]
c. External characteristics (or) Voltage regulated characteristics [V Versus I_L]

SEPARATELY EXCITED DC GENERATOR:

From equation $E_g=(p\Phi zN)/60A$, it is clear that the induced emf is proportional to the flux. If the speed is kept constant, and the flux is varied, then the induced emf also varies.

Open circuit characteristics:

If N is constant, ϕ increases E_g increases. Fig. shows the separately excited circuit diagram for OCC. The variation of flux with the induced emf is called the no-load magnetisation curve (or) saturation curve of the generator. Measurement of flux is difficult, instead the curve is plotted between field current (I_f) and induced emf (E_g).

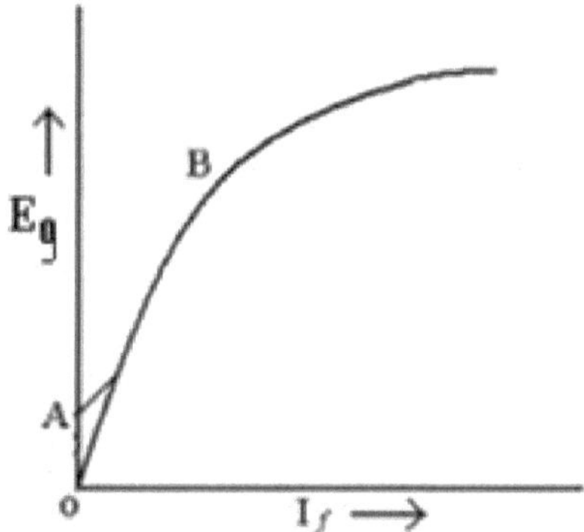

Figure 11:Open Circuit Characteristics

When the field current is zero, there is some flux due to residual magnetism and this causes a small induced emf (OA) is shown in the above figure.

From the characteristics of separately excited d.c generator, it is clear that, as the field current is increased, the induced emf increases linearly from A to B. As I_f further increased, emf also increases slowly. At point D saturation has set in and any further increase in field current does not produce any increase in induced emf.

Internal and External Characteristics:

- The internal and external characteristics are obtained due to armature reaction drop and armature resistance drop.
- Armature reaction means the effect of magnetic field set up by armature current the distribution of flux under main poles of a generator.

Fig. shows internal and external characteristics. The dotted line represents armature current versus no load induced emf .It is only for ideal

D.C generator. There is no voltage drop in ideal generator.

For practical generator, there are two cases.

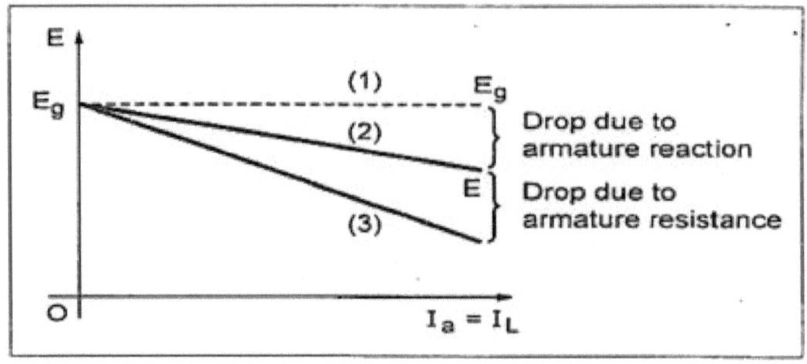

Figure 12: Internal and External characteristics

a.Internal Characteristics

This curve is drawn between the emf (E) and armature cument (I_a). By increasing the I_a induced emf, E will decrease due to armature reaction is shown in Fig. This is represented as curve (2).

b.External Characteristics:

This curve is drawn between the terminal voltage (V) and armature current (I_a).By increasing I_a, the induced emf again decreases due to armature resistance. This is represented as curve (3) in Fig.

DC MOTOR

A dc motor is a machine that converts electrical energy into mechanical energy.

Principle of operation:

The basic principle of operation of DC motor is a "Whenever current carrying conductor is placed in magnetic field, the conductor experiences a force tending to move it". The force whose direction is given by Fleming's Left-Hand Rule and whose magnitude is given by F=BIl Newton.

B=Magnetic field intensity in wb/m2

I=Current in Amperes

L=Length of the conductor in meter.

Operation:

i. When voltage is applied to the loop of wire a current flows, and a magnetic field is created that will interact with the field of the magnet.
ii. The repulsion and attraction of the fields will cause the loop to turn.
iii. The loop moves away from the strong field toward the weak field.
iv. The direction of the rotation can be determined by "right-hand rule".

In a dc motor, the stator poles are supplied by dc excitation current, which produces a dc magnetic field.

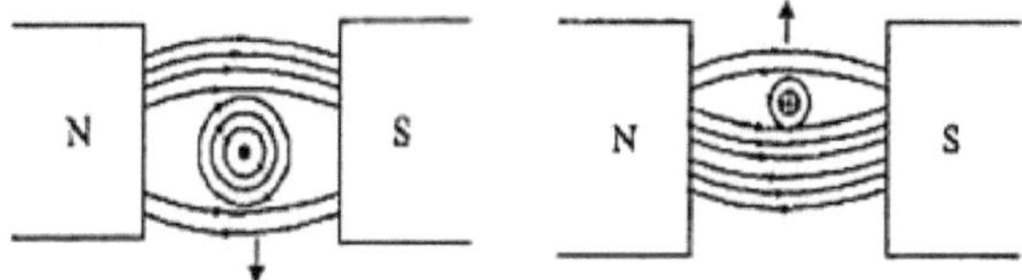

Figure 13.Interaction of two fluxes and force experienced by the conductor

- The rotor is supplied by dc current through the brushes, commutator and coils.
- The interaction of the magnetic field and rotor current generates a force that drives the motor .
- A current is supplied to the coil by a battery and the torque acting on the current-carrying coil causes it to rotate.

Figure 14.Direction of rotation of Conductor

Back emf of a Motor:

i. As the coil rotates in a magnetic field, an emf is induced in the coil.
ii. This induced emf always acts to reduce the current in the coil and is called **back emf**.
iii. The back emf increases in magnitude as the rotational speed of the coil increases.

$E_b=(\phi\ Z\ N/60)*(P/A)$

Types of DC motors

DC Shunt Motor

The field winding is connected in parallel with armature. It is a "constant speed" machine.

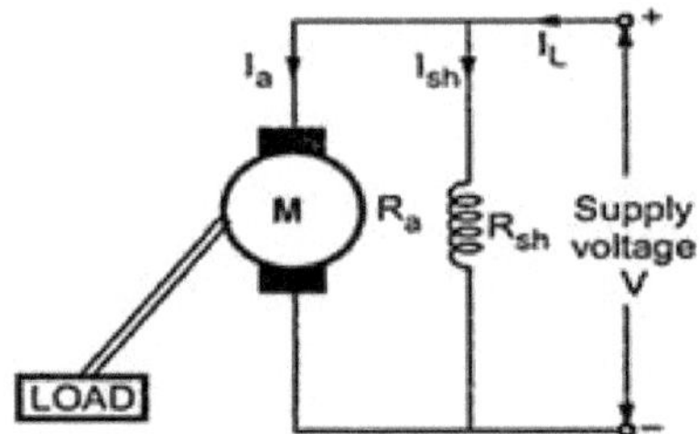

Figure 15.DC Shunt Motor

Shunt field current $I_{sh}=V/R_{sh}$
Armature current $I_a=I_L-I_{sh}$
Supply voltage $V= E_b + I_a R_a + V_{Brush}$
$I_a R_a$=Voltage drop in the armature resistance
V_{Brush} = Voltage drop at connects of the brush
Input current $I_L=P_L/V$

DC Series Motor

The field winding is connected in series with armature. The current flows through field as well as armature are same.

$I_a=I_L=I_{se}$

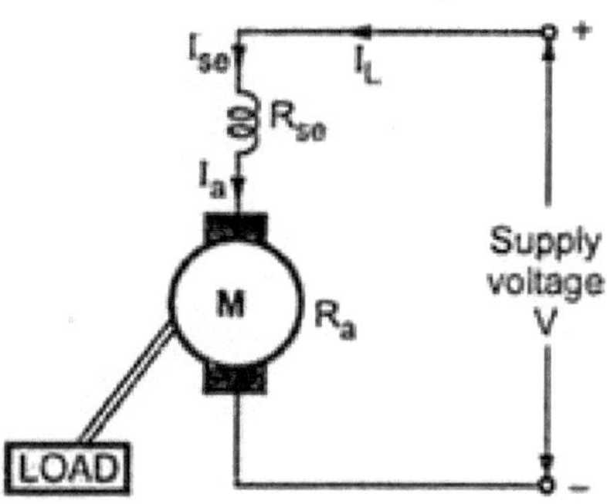

Figure 16: DC Series Motor

Supply voltage $V = E_b + I_a R_a + I_a R_{se} + V_{Brush}$

$I_a R_{se}$= Voltage drop in the series field winding resistance $I_L = P_L / V$

Compound Motor

- If the shunt and series field aid each other it is called a cumulatively excited machine.
- If the shunt and series field oppose each other it is called a differentially excited machine.

Depending upon these two winding connections, it is further classified into two types

1. Long shunt compound Motor
2. Short shunt compound Motor

Long Shunt

Shunt field winding is connected across both series field winding and armature winding.

Series field current $I_{se} = I_a = I_L - I_{sh}$ (or) $I_L = I_a + I_{sh}$

Shunt field current $I_{sh} = V/R_{sh}$

$V = E_b + I_a R_a + I_a R_{se} + V_{Brush}$

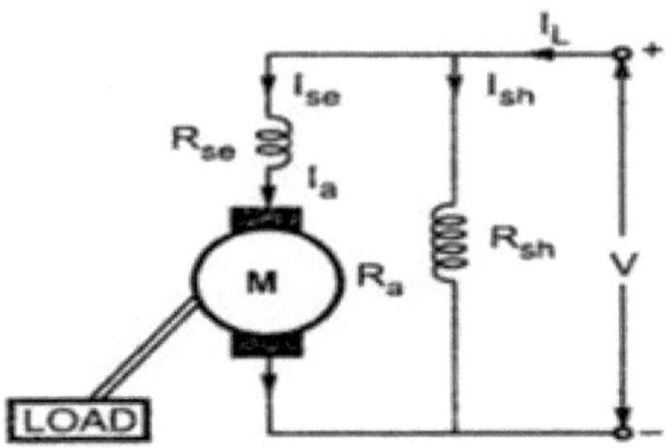

Figure 17: Long Shunt Compound Motor

Short Shunt

The Shunt field winding is connected in parallel with the armature and this combination is connected in series with series field winding.

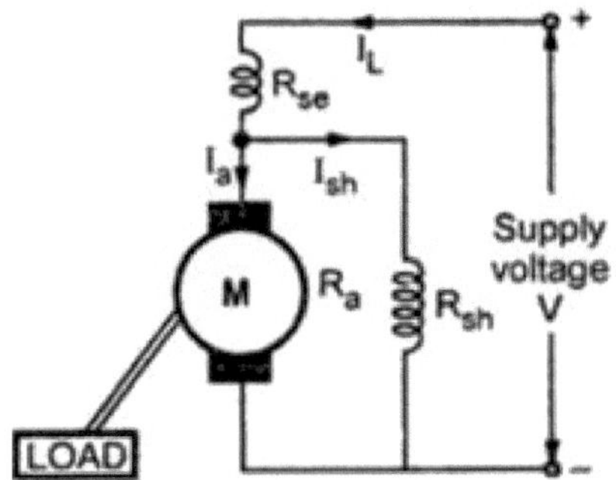

Figure 18:Short Shunt Compound Motor

Load current $I_L = I_{se}$

Shunt field current $I_{sh} = (V - I_{se}R_{se})/R_{sh}$

$V = E_b + I_aR_a + I_aR_{se} + V_{Brush}$

Characteristics of DC Motor

DC motors are shunt, series or compound motors. We are generally interested in the following three characteristics.

i. Speed - armature current characteristics
ii. Torque - armature current characteristics
iii. Speed - torque characteristics

DC Series Motor

The motor in which the field winding is connected in series with the armature is called series motor.

i) Speed-armature current characteristics

As the flux depends on the field current I_{se} which is same as the line current, the flux is not constant with loads. The speed equation

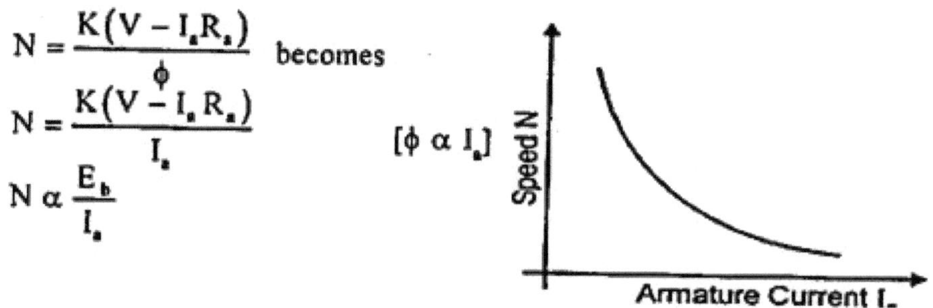

Speed -Armature Current Characteristics

From the above equation it is clear that by, increasing the armature current, speed will decrease. It is shown in figure.

DC Series motor should never be started without some load. Otherwise the motor speed will rise to a dangerous value and get damaged.

ii)Torque - armature current characteristics

We know that $T\alpha\phi\, I_a$. In DC series motor, flux is directly proportional to armature current. i.e.,

$\phi\, \alpha I_a$.

$T\alpha\phi I_a$ before saturation

$T\alpha\, I_a^2$ after saturation

At light load,armature current I_a and hence fluxϕ is small.But as I_a increases T_a increases as the square of thecurrent.Hence this characteristic is a parabola. It is shown in figure.

After saturation,the flux is constant.i.e ϕ is independent of I_a, hence $T\alpha$ I_a.So the curve becomes a straight line.

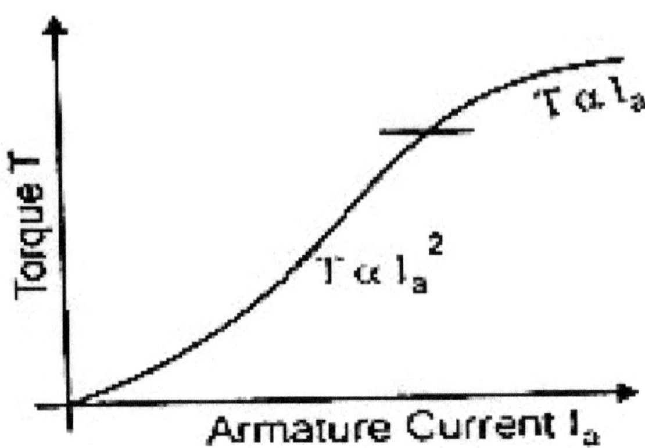

Torque -Armature Current Characteristics

iii) Speed-torque characteristics

This characteristics can be got from the above two characteristics. Here the DC series motor speed is high, the torque is low and vice- versa. It is shown in figure.

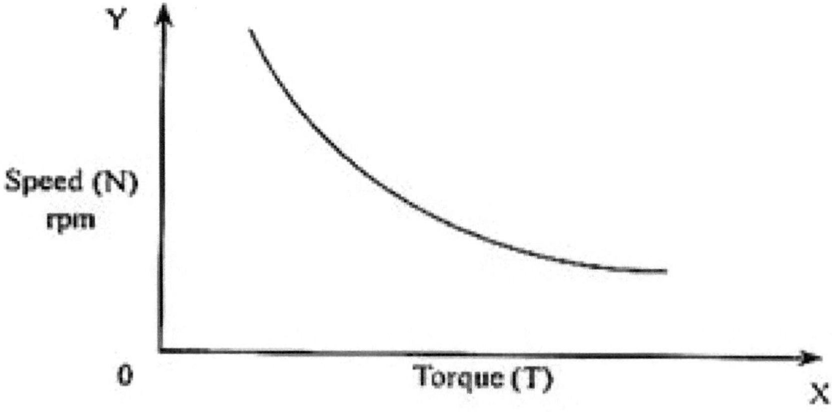

Speed Torque Characteristics

DC Shunt Motor

The shunt motor is constructed as follows Here the field winding is connected in parallel to the armature winding.

Shunt motor normally called as constant speed motor.

In DC Shunt motor

$I_L = I_a + I_f$

Since, the field winding is directly connected to supply voltage 'v' which is also constant, the field current If is also constant.

i) Speed - armature current characteristics

The speed equation of the DC motor is

$$N = K\left(\frac{V - I_a R_a}{\phi}\right)$$

Since I_{sh} and ϕ are nearly constant, $N = K (V - I_a R_a)$ where K is a constant. This implies that speed is nearly constant except for a small drop. This is shown in figure

Due to this characteristics, the DC shunt motor acts as a constant speed motor. The main applications are machine tools, lathes, driving shafting, wood-working machines and for all other purposes where constant speed is needed.

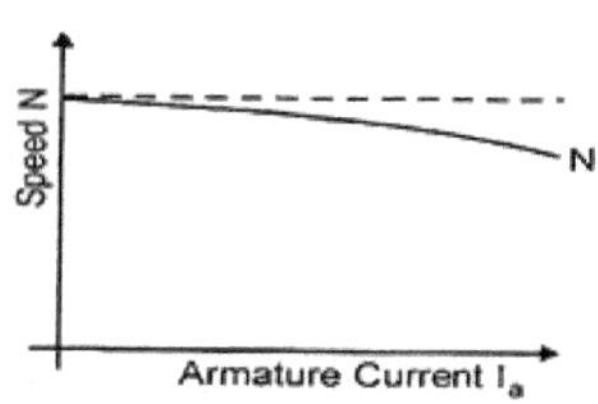

Speed Armature Current Characteristics

ii)Torque - armature current characteristics

It is also called electrical characteristics. The DC shunt motor torque is directly proportional to flux and armature current. i.e.

$$T \alpha \phi I_a$$

Here, ϕ is constant

$$\therefore \quad \boxed{T \alpha I_a}$$

So when the armature current increases, the torque also increases. It is shown in figure

The dotted line is indicated as a shaft torque.

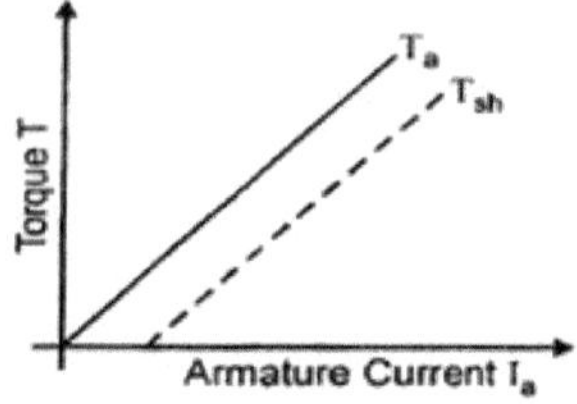

Torque Armature Current Characteristics

iii) Speed – Torque characteristics

It is also called mechanical characteristics. This characteristic can be got from the above two characteristics. It is shown in figure. Here, when the load torque increases, the speed slightly decreases.

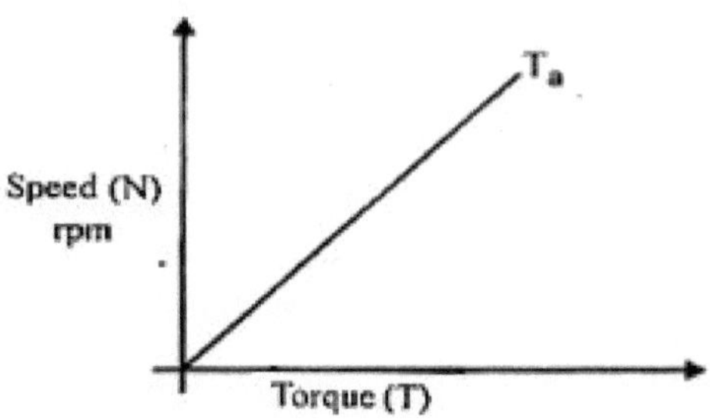

Speed Torque Characteristics

Starting methods of dc motors

Need for Starter in case of DC motor

At starting, when the motor is stationary, there is no back e.m.f. ($E_b = 0$) in the armature. Consequently, if the motor is directly switched on to the mains, the armature will draw a heavy current ($I_a = V/R_a$) because of small armature resistance. This current will damage the motor.

The voltage and current equation of dc motor is given by

$V = E_b + I_aR_a$

Where, E_b - Back emf, R_a - Armature resistance, V - Supply voltage

From the voltage equation, current drawn by dc motor is

$I_a=(V - E_b)/R_a$

$E_b = 0$ (Starting)

This high starting current may result in:

(i) Burning of armature due to excessive heating effect,

(ii) Damaging the commutator and brushes due to heavy sparking,

(iii) Excessive voltage drops in the line to which the motor is connected.

In order to avoid excessive current at starting, a variable resistance (known as starting resistance) is inserted in series with the armature circuit. This resistance is gradually reduced as the motor gains speed (and hence E_b increases) and eventually it is cut out completely when the motor has attained full speed.

As an example, 5H.P, 220V shunt motor has a full-load current of 20A and an armature resistance of about 0.5 Ω. If this motor is directly switched on to supply, it would take an armature current of 220/0.5 = 440 A which is 22 times the full-load current.

The starting operation of a d.c. motor consists in the insertion of external resistance into the armature circuit to limit the starting current taken by the motor and the removal of this resistance in steps as the motor accelerates. When the motor attains the normal speed, this resistance is totally cut out of the armature circuit. It is very important and desirable to provide the starter with protective devices to enable the starter arm to return to OFF position.

(i) When the supply fails, thus preventing the armature being directly across the mains when this voltage

is restored. For this purpose, we use no-volt release coil.

(ii) When the motor becomes overloaded or develops a fault causing the motor to take an excessive

current. For this purpose, we use overload release coil.

Types of dc motor starters

There are three types of starters namely:

1. Two point starter
2. Three point starter
3. Four point starter

Two point starter

The two point starter is used to start the dc Series motor

The two types of TWO point starter

1). 2- Point starter with No Load Protection 2). 2-Point starter with No Volt Protection

TWO Point Starter with No Load Protection

A two point starter is used for starting a DC series motor which has the problem of over-speeding due to the loss of load from its shaft. At this point, we have to keep in mind that, a DC series motor never be started without load. A two point starter is shown in figure.

Here for starting the motor, the control arm is moved clockwise from its OFF position to the ON position against the spring tension. The control arm is held in the ON position by an electromagnet. The Hold ON electromagnet is connected in series with the armature circuit. If the motor loses its load, current decreases and hence the strength of the electromagnet also decreases. The control arm returns to the OFF position due to spring tension, thus preventing the motor from over-speeding. The starter arm also returns to the OFF position when the supply voltage decreases appreciably. The L and A or F are the starter terminals which are connected with the supply and motor terminals.

L – Line (Supply) F – Field A – Armature

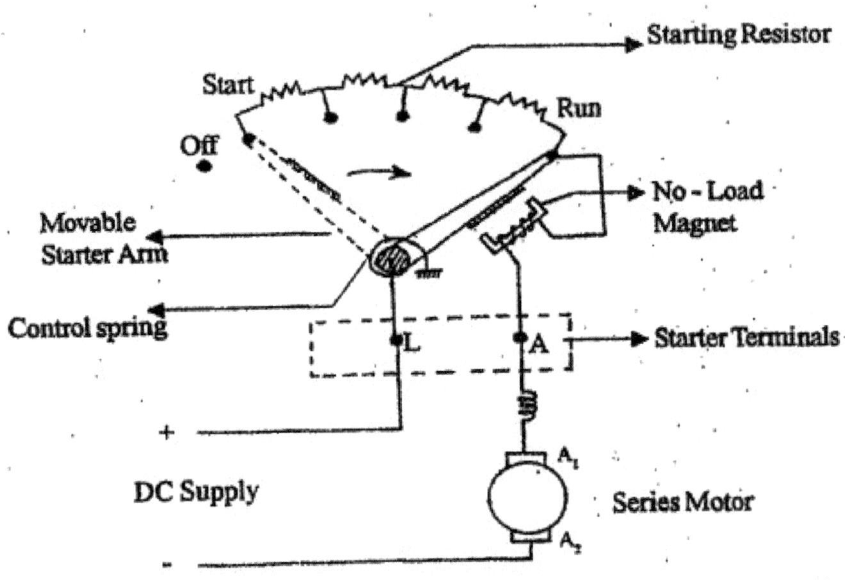

Typical Control Circuit for Starting DC Series Motor using TWO point starter with No Load Protection

No load protection:

When the DC series motor is started without any load, the starting current is very low due to the absence of load, the No-Load armature current is very low because of starting resistance. Since the magnet is not sufficiently energized to attract the starting handle. So, if the starter handle is placed at run position it returns back to the off position due to spring action. The DC series motor is now switched off and No Load protection is thus accomplished.

TWO Point Starter with No Volt Protection

This is a special starter with three terminals such as L_1, L_2 and A

L_1 - Terminal that is connected with supply main

L_2 - Terminal that is connected to a resistance R and No Volt magnet.

A - The terminal that is connected to armature and series field

The operation this starter is similar to the two point starter with no load protection. Now handle is gradually moved from off position, full starting resistance is connected to armature of the dc series motor and the high starting current is limited. Finally handle reach the RUN position. Where the entire starting resistance is removed from the series circuit. The handle is kept at run position due to the presence of No-Volt magnet, which is connected across the DC supply through the resistance R. If there is no resistance then No-Volt magnet circuit acts as a short circuit. The starting resistance is connected to terminal A. The terminal A is connected to series field winding and armature of DC series motor.

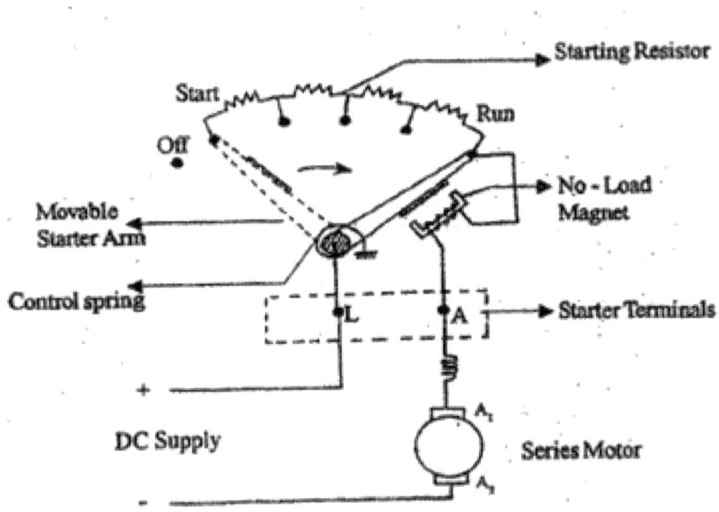

Typical Control Circuit for Starting DC Series Motor using TWO point starter with No Volt Protection

Three Point Starter

This type of starter is widely used for starting shunt and compound motors.

Schematic diagram

Fig. shows the schematic diagram of a three-point starter for a shunt motor with protective devices. It is so called because it has three terminals L, F and A. The starter consists of starting resistance divided into several sections and connected in series with the armature. The tapping points of the starting resistance are brought out to a number of studs. The three terminals L, F and A of the starter are connected respectively to the positive line terminal, shunt field terminal and armature terminal. The other terminals of the armature and shunt field windings are connected to the negative terminal of the supply.

The no-volt release coil is connected in the shunt field circuit. One end of the handle is connected to the terminal L through the over-load release coil. The other end of the handle moves against a spiral spring and makes contact with each stud during starting operation, cutting out more and more starting resistance as it passes over each stud in clockwise direction.

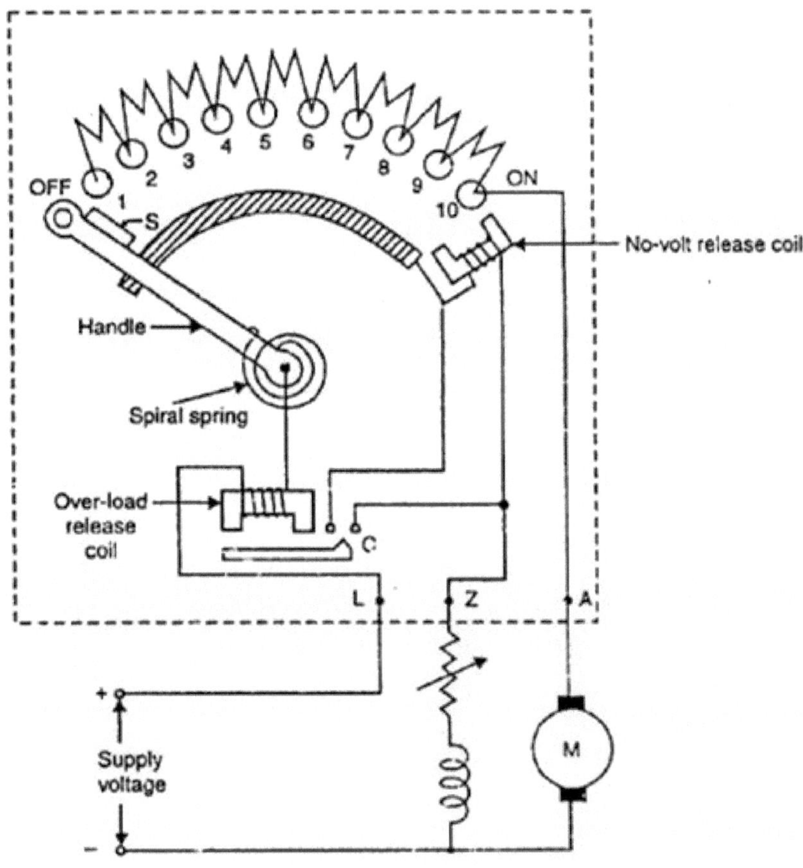

Three Point Starter

Operation

(i) To start with, the d.c. supply is switched on with handle in the OFF position.

(ii) The handle is now moved clockwise to the first stud. As soon as it comes in contact with the first stud, the shunt field winding is directly connected across the supply, while the whole starting resistance is inserted in series with the armature circuit.

(iii) As the handle is gradually moved over to the final stud, the starting resistance is cut out of the armature circuit in steps. The handle is now held magnetically by the no-volt release coil which is energized by shunt field current.

(iv) If the supply voltage is suddenly interrupted or if the field excitation is accidentally cut, the no-volt release coil is demagnetized and the handle goes back to the OFF position under the pull of the spring. If no-volt release coil were not used, then in case of failure of supply, the handle would remain on the final stud. If then supply is restored, the motor will be directly connected across the supply, resulting in an excessive armature current.

(v) If the motor is over-loaded (or a fault occurs), it will draw excessive current from the supply. This current will increase the ampere-turns of the over-load release coil and pull the armature C, thus short-circuiting the no volt release coil. The no-volt coil is demagnetized and the handle is pulled to the OFF position by the spring. Thus, the motor is automatically disconnected from the supply.

Drawback

In a three-point starter, the no-volt release coil is connected in series with the shunt field circuit so that it carries the shunt field current. During speed control, speed is varied through field regulator; the field current may be weakened to such an extent that the no-volt release coil may not be able to keep the starter arm in the ON position. This may disconnect the motor from the supply when it is not desired. This drawback is overcome in the four point starter.

Four Point Starter

The disadvantage of a three point starter is overcome in a four point starter by connecting the hold-on coil across the line instead of in series with the shunt field circuit. This makes a wide range of field adjustments possible.

The connection diagram for a four point starter is shown in Fig. Therefore, when the starting arm touches the starting resistance, current from the supply is divided into three paths. One through the starting resistance and armature, one through the field circuit and one through the NVR coil.

A protective resistance is connected in series with the NVR coil (or) Hold-on magnet coil. With this arrangement, any change of current in the shunt filed circuit not at all affect the current passing through the HOLD-ON coil because the two circuits are independent of each other. It means that the electromagnetic pull exerted by the Hold-on coil will always be sufficient and will prevent the spring from restoring the starting arm to OFF position no matter how the field rheostat or regulator is adjusted.

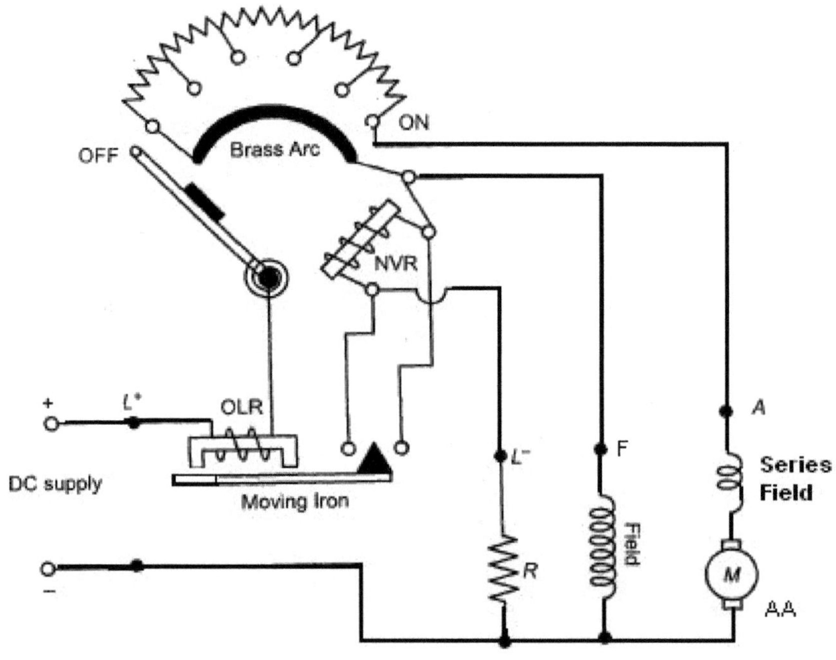

Four Point Starter

The starter terminals are

L+ or L_1 – Terminal that is connected to supply (Line)

L- or L_2 – Terminal that is connected to the No volt coil (NVR or NVC)

F – Terminal that is connected to shunt field winding

A – Terminal that is connected to the armature of the motor

Function of over load release (OLR) or Over Current magnet (OC)

When the load on motor increases above the rated limit then the armature takes high current. When the motor is left unprotected from this high current, then it is damaged, the over current magnet is used for this protection. When there is high current due to over load or due to short circuit the over current magnet is energized and attracts soft iron rod H. *As* a result, the soft, iron rod H closes the switch S. When the switch S is closed, it short circuits the No-Volt magnet. As a result No Volt magnet is de-energized and release the starter handle to the Off position. So the motor is switched off' and protected from the over current or high current.

Function of No volt release (NVR) or No volt coil (NVC)

The No Volt magnet keeps starter handle at run position against the control spring. The No-Volt magnet attracts the soft iron bar placed in the handle. The No-Volt magnet is energized by the .current flowing through the field circuit. If there is no No-Volt magnet the starter handle is pulled back the Off position by the control spring and the motor Point Starter is switched Off.

Conventional Speed Control of DC Motors:

The nature of the speed control requirement for an industrial drive depends upon its type. Some drives may require continuous variation of speed for the whole of the range i.e from zero to full speed, or over a portion of this range, while others may require two or more fixed speeds. Some machines may require a creeping speed for adjusting or setting up the work. For most of the drives, however, a control of speed is within the range of ±20% may be suitable.

Factors Controlling Motor Speed

The speed of a d.c. motor is given by: $N \alpha E_b / \phi = (V - I_a R/\phi)$

where $R = R_a$ for shunt motor

$= R_a + R_{se}$ for series motor

There are three main methods of controlling the speed of a dc motor,

(i) By varying the flux per pole (f). This is known as flux control method.

(ii) By varying the resistance (R) in the armature circuit. This is known as armature control method.

(iii) By varying the applied voltage V. This is known as voltage control method.

These methods as applied to shunt, series and compound motors

Field Control Method

Field control is the most common method. In this method speed can be varied above the rated or base speed of the motor. The speed is inversely proportional to the field current. In this method of speed control back emf kept constant and varying field current so, flux can be varied and hence the speed can be varied.

$N \alpha 1 / \phi$ or $N \alpha 1 / I_f$ (since $\phi \alpha I_f$)

The advantages of this method are:

1. Good working efficiency
2. Accurate speed control
3. Speed control can be performed effectively even at light loads
4. Inexpensive
5. Provides smooth and stepless control of speed
6. Very less losses
7. Speeds above rated speed an be obtained by this method
8. Since voltage across the motor remains constant, it continues to deliver constant output. This characteristics, makes this method more suitable for fixed output loads.

The drawbacks of this method are listed below:

1. Inability to obtain speeds below the basic speed.
2. Instability at high speeds because of-armature reaction.
3. The highest speed is limited electrically by the effects of armature reaction under weak field conditions in causing motor instability and poor commutation. There is possible commutator damage at high speeds.

Armature Rheostatic Control

This method consists of obtaining reduced speeds by including external series resistance in the armature circuit. It can be used with series, shunt and compound motor. This method is used when speeds below the no load speed is required. It is common method of speed control for series motors and is analogous in action to wound rotor induction motor control by series rotor resistance. In this method of speed control flux or field kept constant and the armature resistance is varied.

Advantages

1. Ability to achieve speeds below basic speed.
2. Simplicity and ease of connection.
3. The possibility of combining the functions of motor starting with speed control.

Disadvantages

1. Speed changes with every change in load, because speed variations depend not only on controlling resistance but on load current also. This double dependence makes it impossible to keep the speed sensibly constant on fastly changing loads.
2. Large amount of power is wasted in the controller resistance. Loss of power is directly proportional to the reduction in speed. So, efficiency is decreased.
3. Maximum power developed is diminished in the same ratio as speed.
4. It needs expensive arrangement for dissipation of heat produced in the controller resistance.
5. It gives speeds below the normal, not above it, because armature voltage can be decreased (not increased) by the controller resistance.
6. Poor speed regulation for any given no load speed setting.
7. Difficulty in obtaining stepless control of speed in high power ratings.

Speed control of DC Series Motor

1. Field control method

a. Armature diverter
b. Field diverter
c. Grouping of field coils (Series and Parallel Connection)
d. Tapped field control
e. Series – Parallel control

1. Armature Resistance or Rheostatic control
2. Armature voltage control

Field or Flux control methods

a.Field diverter control

In this method, a variable resistance (called field diverter) is connected in parallel with series field winding as shown in Fig. Its effect is to shunt some portion of the line current from the series field winding, thus weakening the field and increasing the speed ($N \alpha 1 / \phi$). The lowest speed obtainable is that corresponding to zero current in the diverter (i.e., diverter is open). Obviously, the lowest speed obtainable is the normal speed of the motor. Consequently, this method can only provide speeds above the normal speed. The series field diverter method is often employed in traction work. (R_d – diverter resistance)

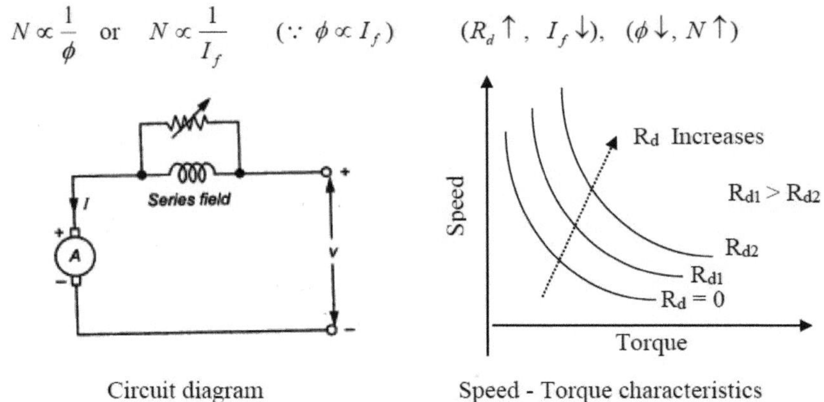

Field diverter control

b. Armature diverter control

In order to obtain speeds below the normal speed, a variable resistance (called armature diverter) is connected in parallel with the armature as shown in Fig.The diverter shunts some of the line current, thus reducing the armature current. Now for a given load, if I_a is decreased, the flux ϕ must increase ($T\alpha\phi I_a$).Since,$N\alpha$ 1 / ϕ the motor speed is decreased. By adjusting the armature diverter, any speed lower than the normal speed can be obtained.

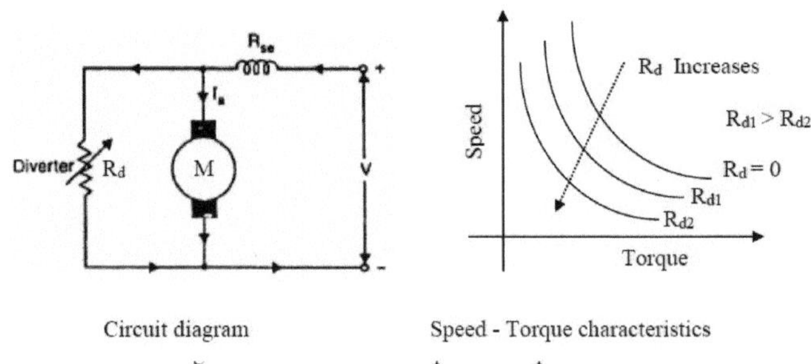

Armature diverter control

C.Tapped field control

In this method, the flux is reduced (and hence speed is increased) by decreasing the number of turns of the series field winding as shown in Fig. The switch S can short circuit any part of the field winding, thus decreasing the flux and raising the speed. With full turns of the field winding, the motor runs at normal speed and as the field turns are cut out, speeds higher than normal speed are achieved. This method is often employed in electric traction.

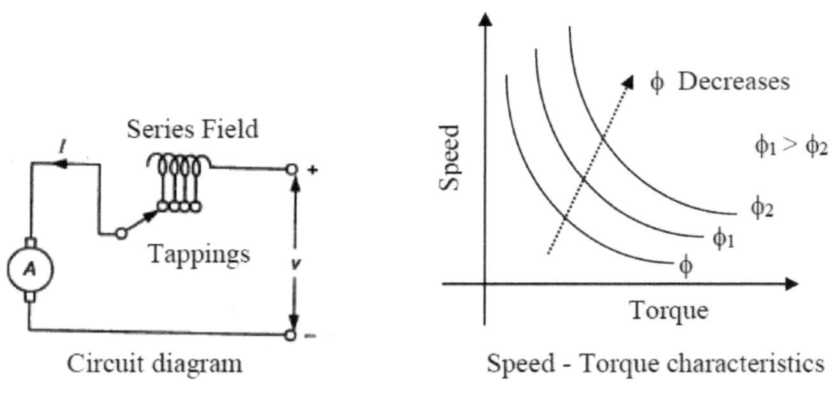

Tapped Field Control

d. Series – Parallel grouping of field coils.

This method is usually employed in the case of fan motors. By regrouping the field coils as shown in Fig. several fixed speeds can be obtained.

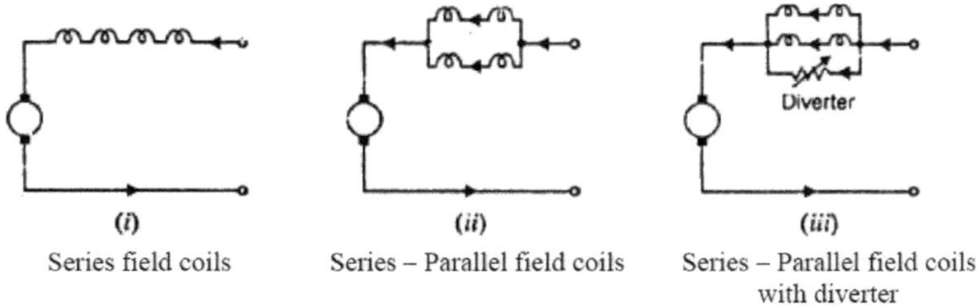

Series-Parallel grouping of Field Coils

Series-Parallel Control

Another method used for the speed control of d.c. series motors is the series parallel method. In this system which is widely used in traction system, two (or more) similar d.c. series motors are mechanically coupled to the same load.

When the motors are connected in series [See Fig. (i)], each motor armature will receive one-half the normal voltage. Therefore, the speed will be low. When the motors are connected in parallel, each motor armature receives the normal voltage and the speed is high [See Fig. (ii)]. Thus we can obtain two speeds. Note that for the same load on the pair of motors, the system would run approximately four times the speed when the machines are in parallel as when they are in series.

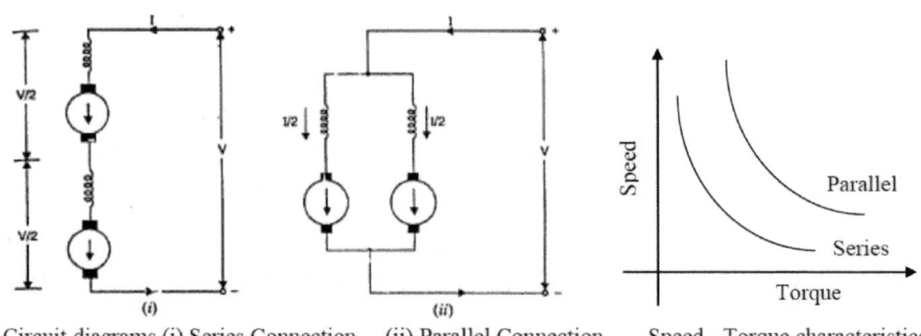

Circuit diagrams (i) Series Connection (ii) Parallel Connection Speed - Torque characteristics

Series-Parallel Control

2. Armature Resistance Control

In this method, a variable resistance is directly connected in series with the supply to the complete motor as shown in Fig. This reduces the voltage available across the armature and hence the speed falls.

By changing the value of variable resistance, any speed below the normal speed can be obtained. This is the most common method employed to control the speed of d.c. series motors. Although this method has poor speed regulation, this has no significance for series motors because they are used in varying speed applications. The loss of power in the series resistance for many applications of series motors is not too serious since in these applications, the control is utilized for a large portion of the time for reducing the speed under light-load conditions and is only used intermittently when the motor is carrying full-load.

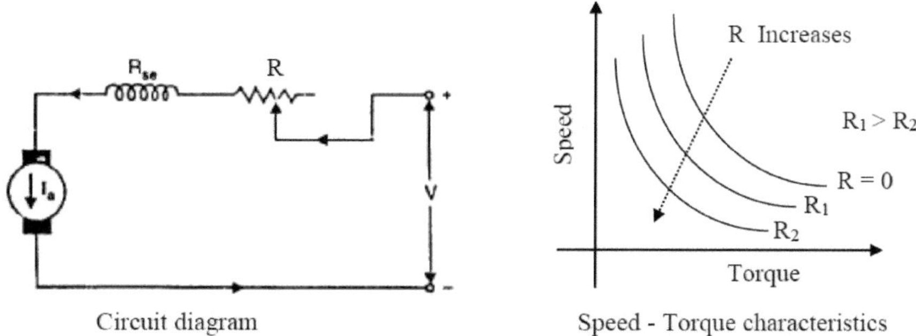

Circuit diagram

Speed - Torque characteristics

Armature Resistance Control

3.Armature Voltage Control

In this method voltage applied to the motor is varied by suitable arrangement and motor speed is decreases as shown in fig.

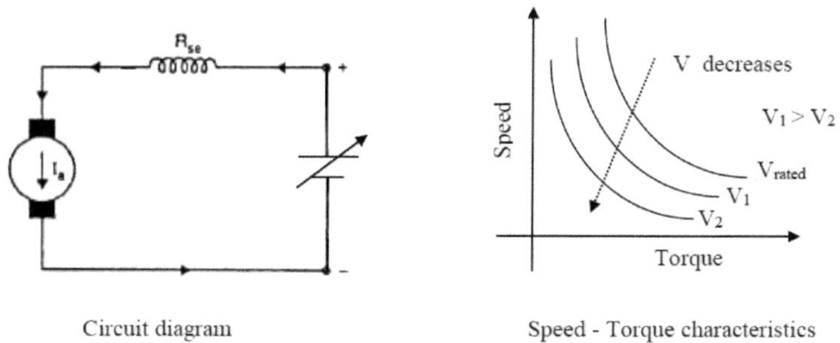

Circuit diagram

Speed - Torque characteristics

Armature voltage control

Speed control of DC Shunt Motor

The speed of a shunt motor can be changed by (i) flux control method (ii) armature control method (iii) voltage control method. The first method (i.e. flux control method) is frequently used because it is simple and inexpensive.

1. Flux control method

It is based on the fact that by varying the flux f, the motor speed (Nα 1 / ϕ) can be changed and hence the name flux control method. In this method, a variable resistance (known as shunt field rheostat) is placed in series with shunt field winding as shown in Fig.

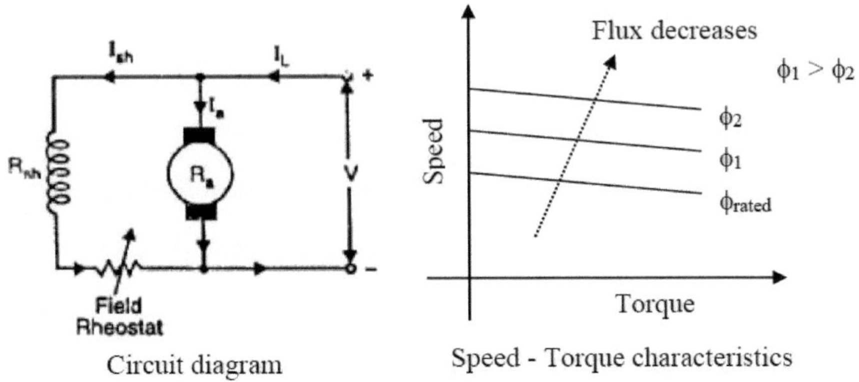

Circuit diagram

Speed - Torque characteristics

Flux control method

The shunt field rheostat reduces the shunt field current I_{sh} and hence the flux ϕ. Therefore, we can only raise the speed of the motor above the normal speed (See Fig.). Generally, this method permits to increase the speed in the ratio 3:1. Wider speed ranges tend to produce instability and poor commutation.

Advantages

(i) This is an easy and convenient method.

(ii) It is an inexpensive method since very little power is wasted in the shunt field rheostat due to relatively small value of I_{sh}.

(iii) The speed control exercised by this method is independent of load on the machine.

Disadvantages

(i) Only speeds higher than the normal speed can be obtained since the total field circuit resistance cannot be reduced below R_{sh} - the shunt field winding resistance.

(ii) There is a limit to the maximum speed obtainable by this method. It is because if the flux is too much weakened, commutation becomes poorer.

2. Armature control method

This method is based on the fact that by varying the voltage available across the armature, the back e.m.f and hence the speed of the motor can be changed. This is done by inserting a variable resistance R_{ex} in series with the armature as shown in Fig.

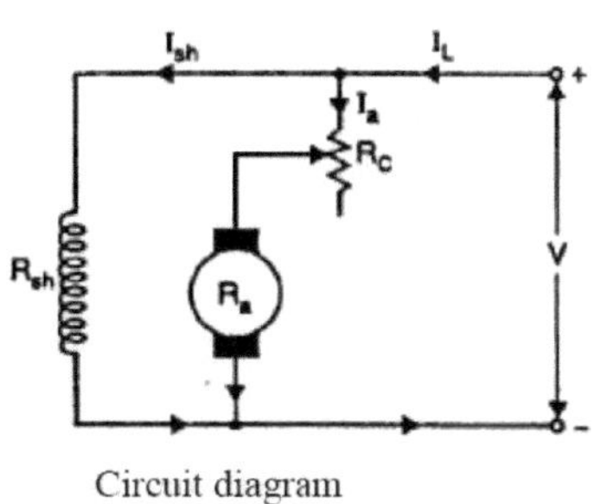

Circuit diagram

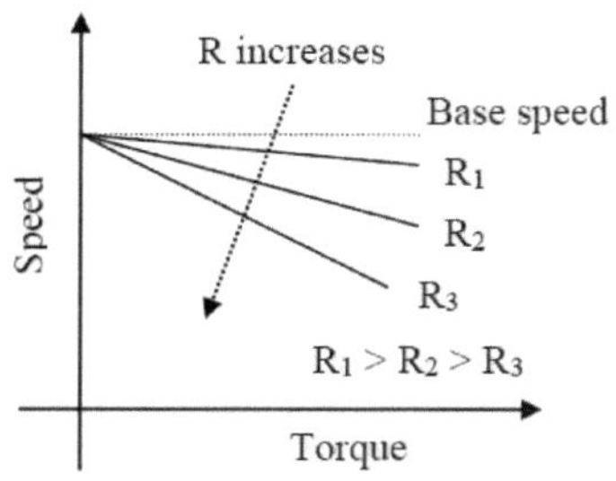

Speed - Torque characteristics

$N \propto V - I_a(R_a + R_{ex})$ where R_{ex} = external resistance or R_c = controller resistance

Armature Voltage Control Method

Due to voltage drop in the controller resistance, the back e.m.f. (E_b) is decreased. Since,N is proportional to E_b, the speed of the motor is reduced. The highest speed obtainable is that corresponding to $R_c = 0$ i.e., normal speed. Hence, this method can only provide speeds below the normal speed (See Fig.).

Advantages

i. Easy and smooth speed control below the base speed is possible
ii. The rheostat in the armature act as a. starter during the starting. So the high current during starting can be avoided.

Disadvantages

i. A large amount of power is wasted in the controller resistance since it carries full armature current I_a.
ii. The speed varies widely with load since the speed depends upon the voltage drop in the controller resistance and hence on the armature current demanded by the load.
iii. The output and efficiency of the motor are reduced.
iv. This method results in poor speed regulation.

Due to above disadvantages, this method is seldom used to control tie speed of shunt motors.

***Note**. The armature control method is a very common method for the speed control of d.c. series motors. The disadvantage of poor speed regulation is not important in a series motor which is used only where varying speed service is required.*

3. Voltage control method

In this method, the voltage source supplying the field current is different from that which supplies the armature. This method avoids the disadvantages of poor speed regulation and low efficiency as in armature control method. However, it is quite expensive. Therefore, this method of speed control is employed for large size motors where efficiency is of great importance.

Multiple voltage control

In this method, the shunt field of the motor is connected permanently across a-fixed voltage source. The armature can be connected across several different voltages through suitable switchgear. In this way, voltage applied across the armature can be changed. The speed will be approximately proportional to the voltage applied across the armature. Intermediate speeds can be obtained by means of a shunt field regulator.

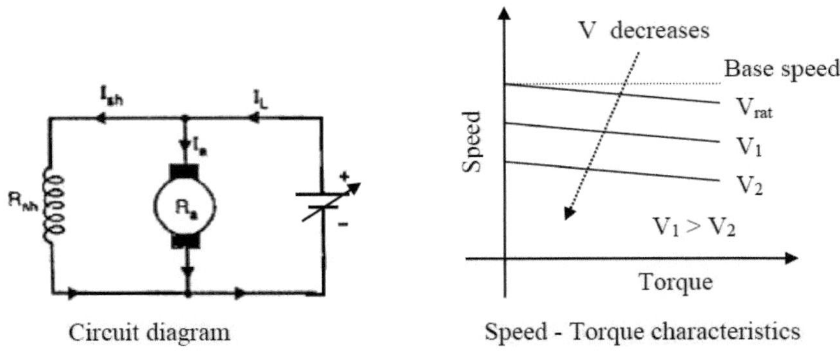

Circuit diagram

Speed - Torque characteristics

Multiple Voltage Control

Universal Motor

A universal motor is a special type of motor which is designed to run on either DC or single phase AC supply. These motors are generally series wound (armature and field winding are in series), and hence produce high starting torque . That is why, universal motors generally comes built into the device they are meant to drive. Most of the universal motors are designed to operate at higher speeds, exceeding 3500 RPM. They run at lower speed on AC supply than they run on DC supply of same voltage, due to the reactance voltage drop which is present in AC and not in DC. There are two basic types of universal motor : (i)compensated type and (ii) uncompensated type.

Construction

It is very similar to the construction of a DC machine. It consists of a stator on which field poles are mounted. Field coils are wound on the field poles. However, the whole magnetic path (stator field circuit and also armature) is laminated. Lamination is necessary to minimize the eddy currents which induce while operating on AC. The rotary armature is of wound type having straight or skewed slots and commutator with brushes resting on it. The commutation on AC is poorer than that for DC. because of the current induced in the armature coils. For that reason brushes used are having high resistance.

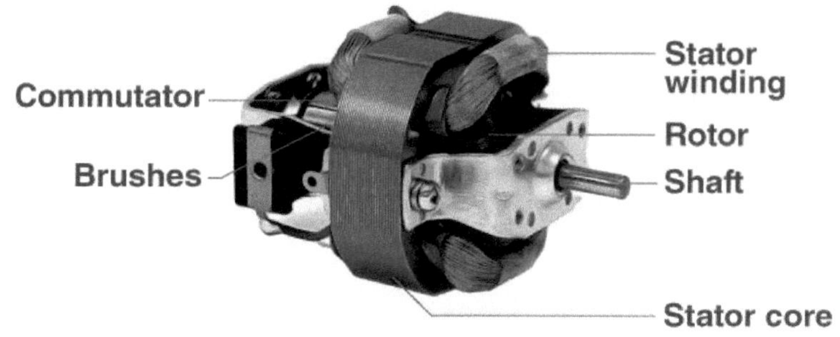

Universal Motor

Working of universal motor

A universal motor works on either DC or single phase AC supply. When the universal motor is fed with a DC supply, it works as a DC series motor. When current flows in the field winding, it produces an electromagnetic field. The same current also flows from the armature conductors. When a current carrying conductor is placed in an electromagnetic field, it experiences a mechanical force. Due to this mechanical force, or torque, the rotor starts to rotate. The direction of this force is given by Fleming's left hand rule. When fed with AC supply, it still produces unidirectional torque.

Because, armature winding and field winding are connected in series, they are in same phase. Hence, as polarity of AC changes periodically, the direction of current in armature and field winding reverses at the same time. Thus, direction of magnetic field and the direction of armature current reverses in such a way that the direction of force experienced by armature conductors remains same. Thus, regardless of AC or DC supply, universal motor works on the same principle that DC series motor works.

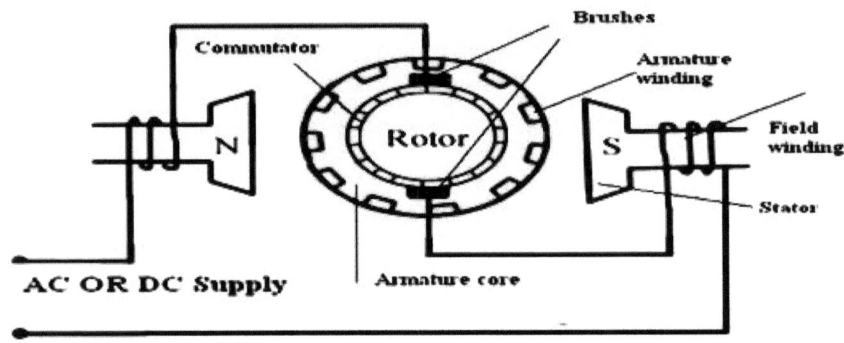

Working of Universal Motor

Speed or Load characteristics

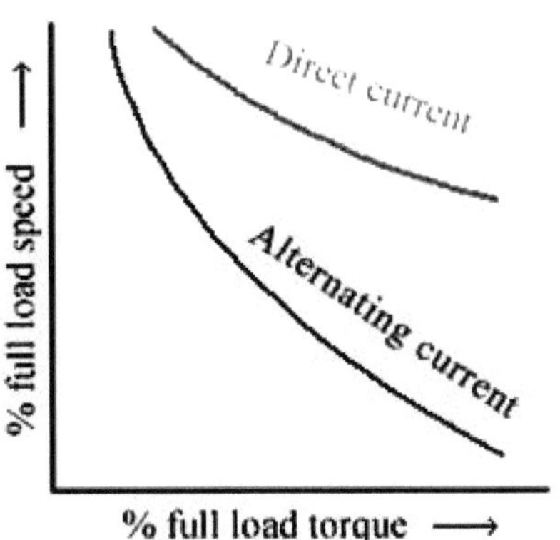

Speed Characteristics

Speed or load characteristics of a universal motor is similar to that of DC series motor. The speed of a universal motor is low at full load and very high at no load. Usually, gears trains are used to get the required speed on required load. The speed/load characteristics are (for both AC as well as DC supply) are shown in the figure.

Applications of universal motor

- Universal motors find their use in various home appliances like vacuum cleaners, drink and food mixers, domestic sewing machine etc.
- The higher rating universal motors are used in portable drills, blenders etc.

STEPPER MOTORS

A stepper motor rotates by a specific number of degrees in response to an input electrical pulse.Typical step sizes are 2°, 2.5^{o}, 5°, 7.5^{o}, and 15° for each electrical pulse. The stepper motor is an electromagnetic incremental actuator that can convert digital pulse inputs to analog output shaft motion. It is therefore used in digital control systems. A train of pulses is made to turn the shaft of the motor by steps. Neither a position sensor nor a feedback system is normally required for the stepper motors to make the output response follow the input command.Typical applications of stepper motors requiring incremental motion are printers, tape drives,disk drives, machine tools, process control systems, X–Y recorders, and robotics. Figure illustrates a simple application of a stepper motor in the paper drive mechanism of a printer.The stepper motor is directly coupled to the platen so that the paper is driven a certain incremental distance whenever the controller receives a digital command pulse.

Typical resolution of commercially available stepper motors ranges from several steps per revolution to as many as 400 steps per revolution and even higher. Stepper motors have been built to follow signals as rapid as 1200 pulses per second with power ratings up to several horsepower.

Two types of stepper motors are widely used: (1) the variable-reluctance type and (2) the permanent magnet type.

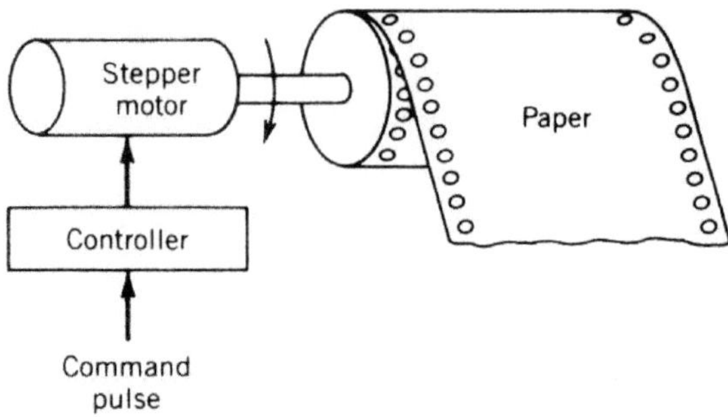

Paper drive using stepper motor

VARIABLE-RELUCTANCE STEPPER MOTOR

A variable-reluctance stepper motor can be of the single-stack type or the multiple-stack type.

Single-Stack Stepper Motor

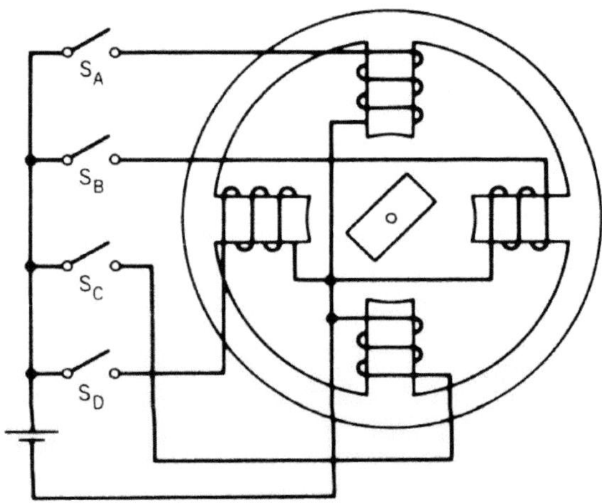

Four Phase Two Pole Stepper Motor

A basic circuit configuration of a four-phase, two-pole, single-stack, variable-reluctance stepper motor is shown in Figure. When the stator phases are excited with dc current in proper sequence, the resultant air gap field steps around and the rotor follows the axis of the air gap field by virtue of reluctance torque. This reluctance torque is generated because of the tendency of the ferromagnetic rotor to align itself along the direction of the resultant magnetic field.

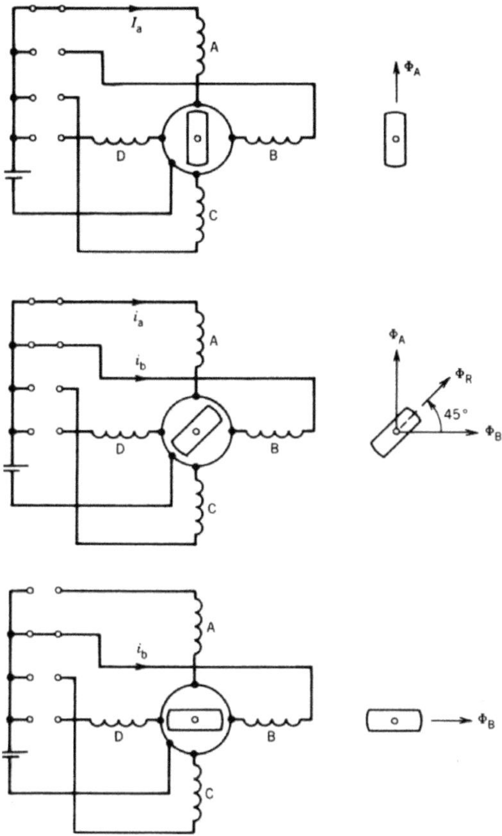

Operating modes of stepper motor for 45°

Figure shows the mode of operation for a 45° step in the clockwise direction. The windings are energized in the sequence A, A + B, B, B + C, and so forth, and this sequence is repeated. When winding A is excited, the rotor aligns with the axis of phase A. Next, both windings A and B are excited, which makes the resultant mmf axis move 45° in the clockwise direction. The rotor aligns with this resultant mmf axis. Thus, at each transition the rotor moves through 45° as the resultant field is switched around. The direction of rotation can be reversed by reversing the sequence of switching the windings—that is, A, A + D, D, D +C, etc.

Multistack Stepper Motor

Multistack variable-reluctance-type stepper motors are widely used to give smaller step sizes.The motor is divided along its axial length into magnetically isolated sections ("stacks"), and each of these sections can be excited by a separate winding ("phase"). Three-phase arrangements are most common, but motors with up to seven stacks and phases are available.

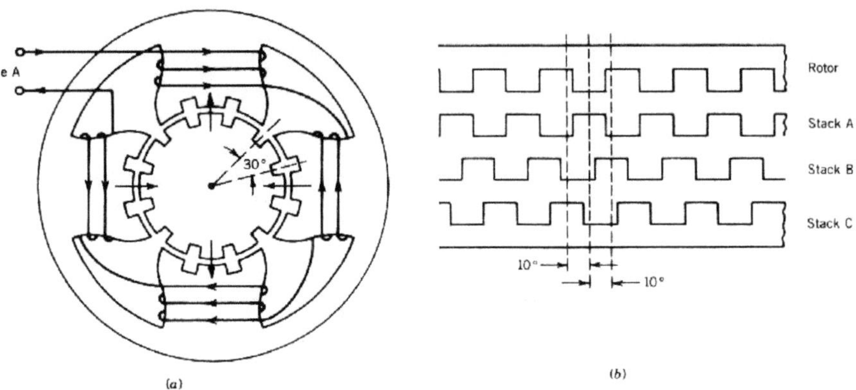

Teeth position in a four-pole,three-stack, variable-reluctance stepper motor. (a) Phase A excited. Rotor and stator teeth are aligned. (b) Developed diagram for rotor and stator teeth for phase A excitation.

Figure shows an example with four poles. Adjacent poles are wound in the opposite sense, and this produces four main flux paths, as shown in Figure. Both stator and rotor have the same number of teeth (12 in Figure a). Therefore, when a particular phase is excited, the position of the rotor relative to the stator in that stack is accurately defined, as shown in Figure a. The rotor teeth in each stack are aligned, whereas the stator teeth have a different orientation between stacks, as shown in the developed diagram of rotor and stator teeth in Figure b. Therefore, when stack A is energized, the rotor and stator teeth in stack A are aligned but those in stacks B and C are not aligned, as shown in Figure b. Next, if excitation is changed from stack A to stack B, the stator and rotor teeth in stack B are aligned. This new alignment is made possible by a rotor movement in the clockwise direction; that is, the motor moves one step as a result of changing excitation from stack A to stack B. Another step motion in the clockwise direction can be obtained if excitation is changed from stack B to stack C. Another change of excitation from stack C to stack A will once more align the stator and rotor teeth in stack A. However, during this process (A - B -C -A) the rotor has moved one rotor tooth pitch, that is, the angle between adjacent rotor teeth. Let x be the number of rotor teeth and N the number of stacks or phases. Then

Tooth pitch $\tau_p = \dfrac{360^\circ}{x}$

Step size $\Delta\theta = \dfrac{360^\circ}{xN}$

Number of steps per revolution is

$$n = \frac{360}{\Delta\theta} = xN$$

For the motor illustrated in Fig.

$$\tau_p = \frac{360^\circ}{12} = 30^\circ$$

$$\Delta\theta = \frac{360^\circ}{12 \times 3} = 10^\circ$$

$$n = \frac{360}{10} = 36$$

Typical step sizes for the multistack variable-reluctance stepping motor are in the range 2 to 15°

PERMANENT MAGNET STEPPER MOTOR

The permanent magnet stepper motor has a stator construction similar to that of the singlestack variable-reluctance type, but the rotor is made of a permanent magnet material. Figure shows a two-pole, permanent magnet stepper motor. The rotor poles align with two stator teeth (or poles) according to the winding excitation. Figure shows the alignment if phase A winding is excited. If the excitation is switched to phase B, the rotor moves by a step of 90°.

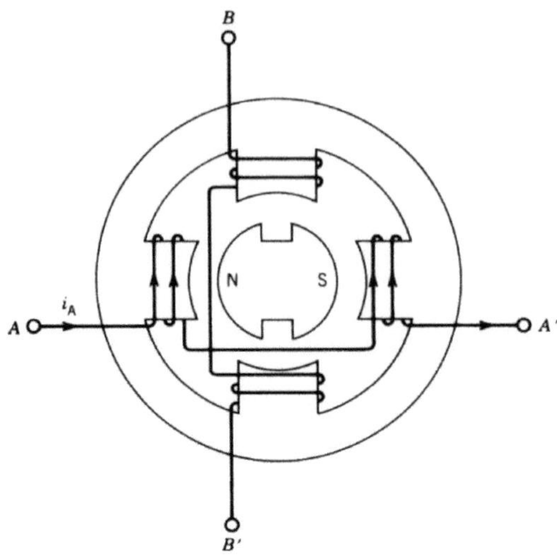

Permanent Magnent Stepper Motor

Note that current polarity is important in the permanent magnet stepper motor, because it decides the direction in which the motor will move. Figure illustrates the rotor position for positive current in phase A. A switch over to positive current in phase B winding will produce a clockwise step, whereas a negative current in phase B winding will produce an anticlockwise step. It is difficult to make a small permanent magnet rotor with a large number of poles, and therefore stepper motors of this type are restricted to larger step sizes in the range 30 to 90º.

Permanent magnet stepper motors have higher inertia and therefore slower acceleration than variable-reluctance stepper motors. The maximum step rate for permanent magnet stepper motors is 300 pulses per second, whereas it can be as high as 1200 pulses per second for variable-reluctance stepper motors. The permanent magnet stepper motor produces more torque per ampere stator current than the variable-reluctance stepper motor.

Hybrid stepper motors are also commercially available in which the rotor has an axial permanent magnet at the middle and ferromagnetic teeth at the outer sections. Smaller step sizes can be obtained from these motors, but they are more expensive than the variable-reluctance-type stepper motors.

Brushless D.C motor:

A synchronous motor with a permanent magnet in the rotor and operated in self-controlled mode—using a rotor position sensor and an inverter to control current in the stator windings—is generally known as a brushless dc motor. The BLDC is an inside-out brushed dc motor, because the armature is in the stator and the magnets are in the rotor, and its operating characteristics are similar to those of the conventional brushed dc motor. The position sensor and the solid-state switches in the inverter perform the role of the brushes and the mechanical commutator of the conventional dc motor. The BLDC motor operates in a manner similar to the self-controlled synchronous motor of Figure. The thyristors in the inverter controlling the motor current are commutated by the back emf of the motor. At low speed, the back emf may not be sufficient to commute the thyristors. In such a situation, the dc link current is to be reduced to zero by operating the supply-end converter in the inversion mode. However, an inverter can be used that employs self-commutating devices, such as BJTs, IGBTs, MOSFETs, and GTOs. The on–off state of these switches can be controlled by their gate signals, which are obtained from the rotor position sensors.

A typical transistor (BJT) inverter configuration fed from a dc current source, as shown in Fig, can be used for a BLDC drive system. The rotor position sensor will control the turn-on and turn-off instants for the switches such that the angle between the rotor field and the stator field is regulated at 90°, similar to the conventional brushed dc motor. The idealized waveforms of the stator currents are also shown in Fig. Theswitches of the inverter are turned on every 60 electrical degrees, and the switches are numbered in the sequence in which they are turned on. If the inverter is fed from a dc voltage source (voltage source inverter), pulse-width modulation of the individual switches can provide the regulation of the motor current. There are two basic types of BLDC motors: trapezoidal type and sinusoidal type. In the trapezoidal type the back emf is of trapezoidal shape and, for ripple-free torque operation, the phase current required is a 120° quasi-square wave. In the sinusoidal type, the back emf is sinusoidal and, for ripple-free torque operation, the phase current required is sinusoidal.

BLDC motors have the following advantages compared with conventional brushed dc motors:

- Small rotor size and high-power density, because of the absence of mechanical commutators, brushes, and field windings.
- Lower inertia and faster dynamic response.
- Higher speed and torque capability, due to the absence of brushes and sparking.
- Lower maintenance cost.
- High torque/inertia ratio.
- Better heat dissipation, due to the stationary armature winding.
- Better overall reliability and life.

BLDC motors have the following advantages compared with induction motors:

- High efficiency, because of no slip power losses.
- High power and torque density, because of high air gap flux density.
- Lower operating temperature, because of low losses.

These motors are being extensively used in computer disk drives, servo drives, robotics, machine tools, electric vehicles, battery-powered applications, windmills, and many other applications.

Problems

1. A 4 pole generator with wave wound armature has 51 slots each having 24 conductors. The flux per pole is 0.01 weber. At what speed must the armature rotate to give an induced emf of 250 V. what will be voltage developed, if the winding is lap connected and the armature rotates at the same speed.

Solution:

$Z = 51 \times 24 = 1224$ conductors, $E_g = 250$ V, P = 4

For wave wound A = 2, $\phi = 0.01$ wb

$$E_g = \frac{P\phi ZN}{60A}$$

$$N = \frac{E_g\ 60A}{P\phi Z} = \frac{250 \times 60 \times 2}{4 \times 0.01 \times 1224}$$

$$\boxed{N = 612.74 \text{ rpm}}$$

For lap connection, A = P Speed N = 612.74 rpm

$$E_g = \frac{P\phi ZN}{60A} = \frac{4 \times 0.01 \times 1224 \times 612.74}{60 \times 4}$$

$$\boxed{E_g = 125 \text{ V}}$$

2. An 8-pole, wave connected armature has 600 conductors and is drives at 625 rev/men. If the flux perpole is 20 mwb, determine the generated emf.

Given data :

Number of poles P = 8, Total number of conductors Z = 600

Flux per pole $\phi = 20$ wb for wave wound A = 2

$$\text{Induced armature voltage } E_g = \frac{P\phi ZN}{60A} = \frac{8 \times 20 \times 10^{-3} \times 600 \times 625}{60 \times 2}$$

$$\boxed{E_g = 500 \text{ V}}$$

3. A 4 pole, 500 V dc shunt motor has 700 wave connected conductors on its armature The full load armature current is 60 A and fluxper pole is 30 mwb. Calculate the full load speed if the motor armature resistance is 0.2 Ω and the brush drop is 1 volt per brush.

Given data :

Number of poles P = 4, Supply Voltage V = 500 V,

Number of conductors Z = 700, Full load armature current I_a = 60 A,

Flux per pole ϕ = 30 mwb Armature resistance R_a = 0.

Brush drop = 1 V per brush = 2 × 1 = 2 V, for wave connection A = 2

To find:

Full load speed (N)

Solution:

Back emf $E_b = V - I_aR_a - \text{brush drop}$

$= 500 - 60 \times 0.2 - 2 = 486$ V

$$E_b = \frac{P\phi ZN}{60A}$$

$$N = \frac{E_b\ 60A}{P\phi Z} = \frac{486 \times 60 \times 2}{4 \times 30 \times 10^{-3} \times 700}$$

$$\boxed{N = 694.28\text{rpm}}$$

4. A 4pole DC motor takes an armature current of 50 A. the armature has 480 lap connected conductors. The fluxper pole is 20 mwb. Calculate the gross torque developed by the motor.

Given data :

Number of poles P = 4, Armature Current I_a = 50 A, Flux per pole ϕ = 20 mwb

Number of conductors Z = 480, for lap connection A = P

To find: Gross Torque (T_a)

Solution:

Gross Torque $T_a = 0.159\,\phi\, I_a \frac{PZ}{A} N-m$

$$= 0.159 \times 20 \times 10^{-3} \times \frac{50 \times 4 \times 480}{4} N\ \ m$$

$$\boxed{T_a = 76.32\ \text{N-m}}$$

5. Determine developed torque, shaft torque and lost torque of a 220 V, 4 pole series motor with 800 conductors wave connected supplying a load of 8.2kW by taking 45 A from the mains. The flux per pole is 25 mwb and its armature resistance is 0.6 Ω.

Given data :

No. of poles P = 4, Supply Voltage V = 220 V,

No. of conductors Z = 800. current I_a = 45 A.

Flux per pole ϕ = 25mwb Armature resistance R_a = 0.6 Ω

Output power P_{out} = 8200W, wave connected ie., A = 2

Solution:

i) Armature torque T_a

$$T_a = 0.159\,\phi\, I_a \frac{PZ}{A} = 0.159 \times 25 \times 10^{-3} \times 45 \times \frac{4 \times 800}{2}$$

$$\boxed{T_a = 286.32 \text{ N-m}}$$

ii) Shaft torque T_{sh}

$$E_b = V - I_a R_a = 220 - 45 \times 0.6 = 193 \text{ V}$$

$$N = \frac{E_b\, 60A}{P\phi Z} = \frac{193 \times 60 \times 2}{4 \times 25 \times 10^{-3} \times 800}$$

N = 289.5 rpm

$$T_{sh} = 9.55 \frac{P_{out}}{N} = 9.55 \times \frac{8200}{289.5}$$

$$\boxed{T_{sh} = 270.5 \text{ N-m}}$$

iii) Lost torque T_f

$$T_f = T_a - T_{sh} = 286.2 - 270.5$$

$$\boxed{T_f = 15.7 \text{ N-m}}$$

CHAPTER THREE

AC ROTATING MACHINES

Three Phase Induction Motor

The most common type of AC motor being used throughout the work today is the "Induction Motor". Applications of three-phase induction motors of size varying from half a kilowatt to thousands of kilowatts are numerous. They are found everywhere from a small workshop to a large manufacturing industry.

The advantages of three-phase AC induction motor are listed below:

- Simple design
- Rugged construction
- Reliable operation
- Low initial cost
- Easy operation and simple maintenance
- Simple control gear for starting and speed control
- High efficiency.

Induction motor is originated in the year 1891 with crude construction (The induction machine principle was invented by *NIKOLA TESLA* in 1888.). Then an improved construction with distributed stator windings and a cage rotor was built.

The slip ring rotor was developed after a decade or so. Since then a lot of improvement has taken place on the design of these two types of induction motors. Lot of research work has been carried out to improve its power factor and to achieve suitable methods of speed control.

Types and Construction of Three Phase Induction Motor

Three phase induction motors are constructed into two major types:

1. Squirrel cage Induction Motors
2. Slip ring Induction Motors

Squirrel cage Induction Motors

Stator Construction

The induction motor stator resembles the stator of a revolving field, three phase alternator. The stator or the stationary part consists of three phase winding held in place in the slots of a laminated steel core which is enclosed and supported by a cast iron or a steel frame as shown in Fig: (a).

The phase windings are placed 120 electrical degrees apart and may be connected in either star or delta externally, for which six leads are brought out to a terminal box mounted on the frame of the motor. When the stator is energized from a three phase voltage it will produce a rotating magnetic field in the stator core.

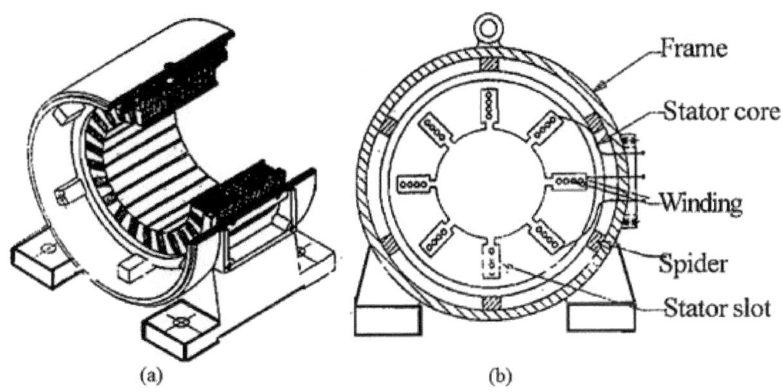

Construction of Squirrel cage induction motor

Rotor Construction

The rotor of the squirrel cage motor shown in Fig.(b) contains no windings. Instead it is a cylindrical core constructed of steel laminations with conductor bars mounted parallel to the shaft and embedded near the surface of the rotor core.

These conductor bars are short circuited by an end rings at both end of the rotor core. In large machines, these conductor bars and the end rings are made up of copper with the bars brazed or welded to the end rings shown in

Fig.(b).In small machines the conductor bars and end rings are sometimes made of aluminium with the bars and rings cast in as part of the rotor core. Actually the entire construction (bars and end-rings) resembles a squirrel cage, from which the name is derived.

The rotor or rotating part is not connected electrically to the power supply but has voltage induced in it by transformer action from the stator. For this reason, the stator is sometimes called the primary and the rotor is referred to as the secondary of the motor since the motor operates on the principle of induction and as the construction of the rotor with the bars and end rings resembles a squirrel cage, the squirrel cage induction motor is used.

The rotor bars are not insulated from the rotor core because they are made of metals having less resistance than the core. The induced current will flow mainly in them. Also the rotor bars are usually not quite parallel to the rotor shaft but are mounted in a slightly skewed position. This feature tends to produce a more uniform rotor field and torque. Also it helps to reduce some of the internal magnetic noise when the motor is running.

End Shields

The function of the two end shields is to support the rotor shaft. They are fitted with bearings and attached to the stator frame with the help of studs or bolts attention.

Slip ring Induction Motors

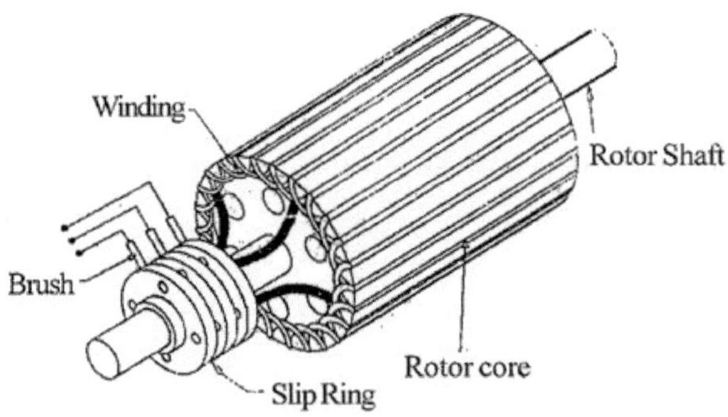

Slipring induction motor

Stator Construction

The construction of the slip ring induction motor is exactly similar to the construction of squirrel cage induction motor. There is no difference between squirrel cage and slip ring motors.

Rotor Construction

The rotor of the slip ring induction motor is also cylindrical or constructed of lamination.

Squirrel cage motors have a rotor with short circuited bars whereas slip ring motors have wound rotors having "three windings" each connected in star.

The winding is made of copper wire. The terminals of the rotor windings of the slip ring motors are brought out through slip rings which are in contact with stationary brushes as shown in Fig.

THE ADVANTAGES OF THE SLIPRING MOTOR ARE

- It has susceptibility to speed control by regulating rotor resistance.
- High starting torque of 200 to 250% of full load value.
- Low starting current of the order of 250 to 350% of the full load current.

Hence slip ring motors are used where one or more of the above requirements are to be met.

Sl.No	Property	*Squirrel cage motor*	*Slip ring motor*
1.	**Rotor Construction**	*Bars are used in rotor.* *Squirrel cage motor is very simple, rugged andlong lasting.* *No slip rings and brushes*	*Winding wire is to beused.* *Wound rotor requiredattention.* *Slip ring and brushes are needed also need frequent maintenance.*
2.	**Starting**	*Can be started by D.O.L., star-delta, auto transformer starters*	*Rotor resistance starteris required.*
3.	**Startingtorque**	*Low*	*Very high*
4.	**StartingCurrent**	*High*	*Low*
5.	**Speed variation**	*Not easy, but could be varied in large steps bypole changing or through smaller incremental steps through thyristors or byfrequency variation.*	*Easy to vary speed.* *Speed change is possibleby inserting ro resistance using thyristors or using frequency variationinjecting emf in rotor circuit cascading.*
6.	**Maintenance**	*Almost Zero maintenance*	*Requires frequentmaintenance*
7.	**Cost**	*Low*	*High*

Comparison of Squirrel cage and slip ring induction motor

Principle of Operation

The operation of a 3-phase induction motor is based upon the application of Faraday Law and the Lorentz force on a conductor. The behaviour can readily be understood by means of the following example.

Consider a series of conductors of length l, whose extremities are short-circuited by two bars A and B (Fig. a). A permanent magnet placed above this conducting ladder, moves rapidly to the right at a speed v, so that its magnetic field B sweeps across the conductors. The following sequence of events then takes place:

1. A voltage E = Blv is induced in each conductor while it is being cut by the flux (Faraday law).
2. The induced voltage immediately produces a current I, which flows down the conductor underneath the pole face, through the end-bars, and back through the other conductors.
3. Because the current carrying conductor lies in the magnetic field of the permanent magnet, it experiences a mechanical force (Lorentz force).
4. The force always acts in a direction to drag the conductor along with the magnetic field. If the conducting ladder is free to move, it will accelerate toward the right. However, as it picks up speed, the conductors will be cut less rapidly by the moving magnet, with the result that the induced voltage E and the current I will diminish. Consequently, the force acting on the conductors wilt also decreases. If the ladder were to move at the same speed as the magnetic field, the induced voltage E, the current I, and the force dragging the ladder along would all become zero.

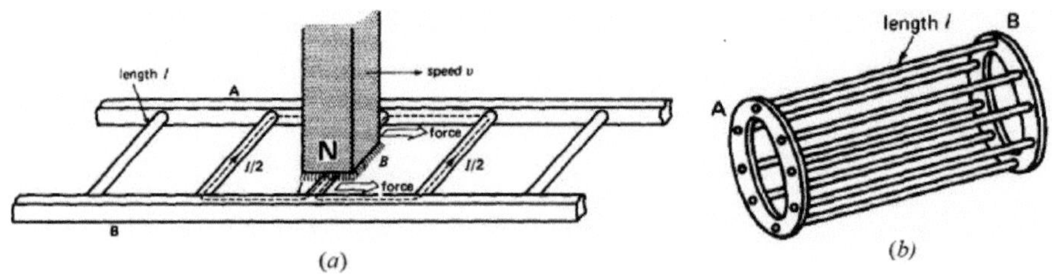

Operation of 3 phase induction motor

In an induction motor the ladder is closed upon itself to form a squirrel-cage (Fig.b) and the moving magnet is replaced by a rotating field. The field is produced by the 3-phase currents that flow in the stator windings.

Equivalent Circuit of Three Phase Induction Motor

Figure shows the equivalent circuit per phase of the rotor at slip s. The rotor phase current isgiven by;

$$I'_2 = \frac{s E_2}{\sqrt{R_2^2 + (s X_2)^2}}$$

Mathematically, this value is unaltered by writing it as:

$$I'_2 = \frac{E_2}{\sqrt{(R_2/s)^2 + (X_2)^2}}$$

As shown in Fig. (ii), we now have a rotor circuit that has a fixed reactance X_2 connected in series with a variable resistance R2/s and supplied with constant voltage E_2. Note that Fig. (i) transfers the variable to the resistance without altering power or power factor conditions.

The quantity R_2/s is greater than R_2 since s is a fraction. Therefore, R_2/s can be divided into a fixed part R_2 and a variable part $(R_2/s - R_2)$ i.e.,

$$\frac{R_2}{s} = R_2 + R_2\left(\frac{1}{s} - 1\right)$$

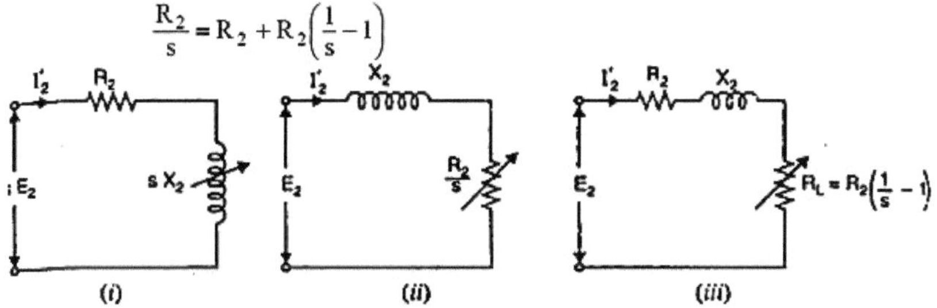

Figure :Equivalent circuit per phase of the rotor at slip

1. The first part R_2 is the rotor resistance/phase,and represents the rotor copper loss.
2. The second part R_2 [(1/s)-1] is a varaible resistance load.The power deleivered to this load represents the total mechanical power developed in the rotor. The mechanical load on the induction motor can be repalced by the varaible resistance load value R_2 [(1/s)-1].This is $R_L = R_2$ [(1/s)-1]

Fig. (iii) shows the equivalent rotor circuit along with load resistance RL.

The circuit shown in Figure is similar to the equivalent circuit of a transformer with secondary load equal to R2 given by equation $R_L = R_2 [(1/s)-1]$. Note that mechanical load on the motor has been replaced by an equivalent electrical resistance R_L given by; The rotor e.m.f. in the equivalent circuit now depends only on the transformation ratio K (= E_2/E_1).

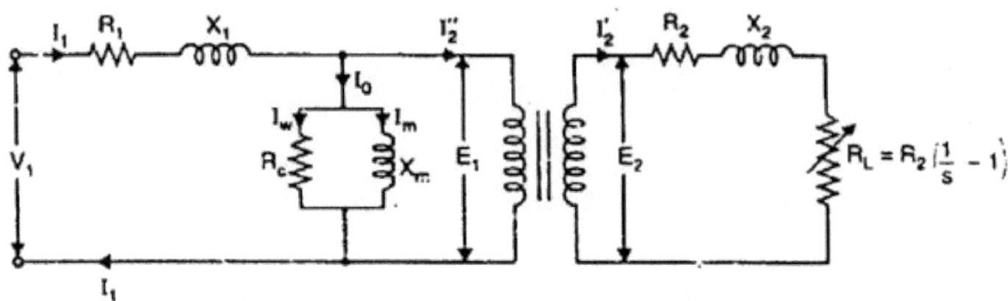

Equivalent circuit of a transformer with secondary load equal to R2

Therefore; induction motor can be represented as an equivalent transformer connected to a variable-resistance load RL given by eq. (i). The power delivered to RL represents the total mechanical power developed in the rotor. Since the equivalent circuit of Figure is that of a transformer, the secondary (i.e., rotor) values can be transferred to primary (i.e., stator) through the appropriate use of transformation ratio K. Recall that when shifting resistance/reactance from secondary to primary, it should be divided by K2 whereas current should be multiplied by K. The equivalent circuit of an induction motor referred to primary is shown in Fig.

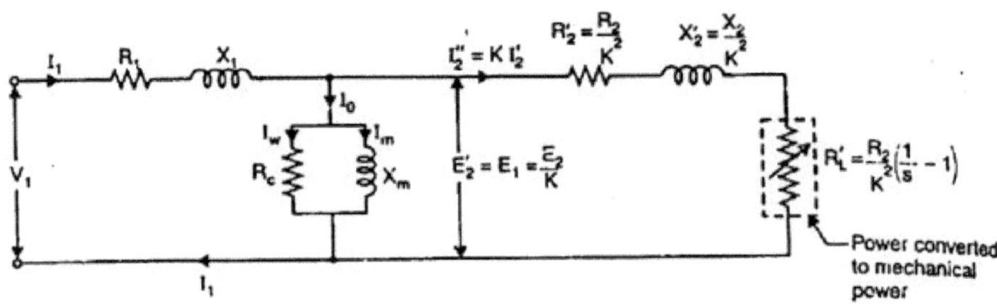

Equivalent circuit of an induction motor referred to primary

Note that the element (i.e., R'L) enclosed in the dotted box is the equivalent electrical resistance related to the mechanical load on the motor. The following points may be noted from the equivalent circuit of the induction motor:

i. At no-load, the slip is practically zero and the load R'L is infinite. This condition resembles that in a transformer whose secondary winding is open-circuited.
ii. At standstill, the slip is unity and the load R'L is zero. This condition resembles that in a transformer whose secondary winding is short-circuited.

iii. When the motor is running under load, the value of R'L will depend upon the value of the slip s. This condition resembles that in a transformer whose secondary is supplying variable and purely resistive load.

iv. The equivalent electrical resistance R'L related to mechanical load is slip or speed dependent. If the slip s increases, the load R'L decreases and the rotor current increases and motor will develop more mechanical power. This is expected because the slip of the motor increases with the increase of load on the motor shaft.

Speed control of Three Phase Induction Motors

The induction machine, when operating from mains is essentially a constant speed machine. Many industrial drives, typically for fan or pump applications, have typically constant speed requirements and hence the induction machine is ideally suited for these. However, the induction machine, especially the squirrel cage type, is quite rugged and has a simple construction. Therefore it is good candidate for variable speed applications if it can be achieved.

Speed control by changing applied voltage

From the torque equation of the induction machine we can see that the torque depends on the square of the applied voltage. The variation of speed torque curves with respect to the applied voltage is shown in Figure. These curves show that the slip at maximum torque ?^ remains same, while the value of stall torque comes down with decrease in applied voltage. The speed range for stable operation remains the same.

Further, we also note that the starting torque is also lower at lower voltages. Thus, even if a given voltage level is sufficient for achieving the running torque, the machine may not start. This method of trying to control the speed is best suited for loads that require very little starting torque, but their torque requirement may increase with speed.

Figure also shows a load torque characteristic — one that is typical of a fan type of load. In a fan (blower) type of load, the variation of torque with speed is such that ? ? ?^{2}.

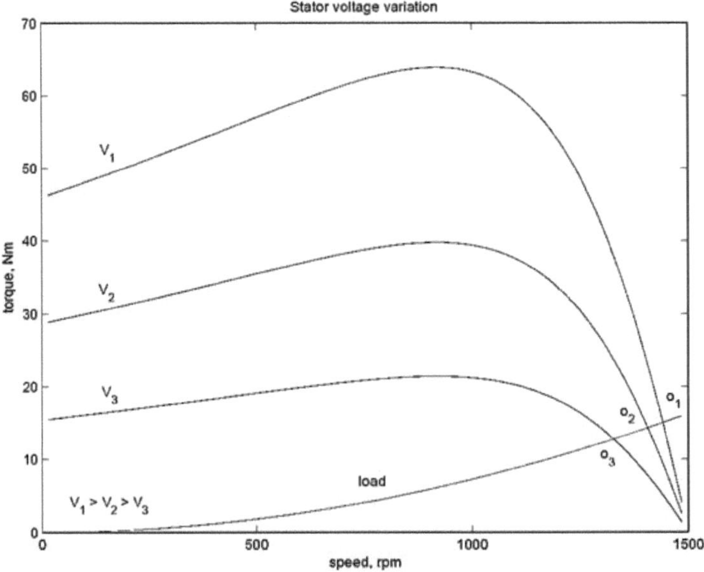

Load Characteristics

Here one can see that it may be possible to run the motor to lower speeds within the range ns to (1 – ˆs) ns. Further, since the load torque at zero speed is zero, the machine can start even at reduced voltages. This will not be possible with constant torque type of loads.

One may note that if the applied voltage is reduced, the voltage across the magnetising branch also comes down. This in turn means that the magnetizing current and hence flux level are reduced. Reduction in the flux level in the machine impairs torque production which is primarily the explanation for Figure. If, however, the machine is running under lightly loaded conditions, then operating under rated flux levels is not required. Under such conditions,reduction in magnetizing current improves the power factor of operation. Some amount of energy saving may also be achieved.

Voltage control may be achieved by adding series resistors (a lossy, inefficient proposition), or a series inductor / autotransformer (a bulky solution) or a more modern solution using semiconductor devices. A typical solid state circuit used for this purpose is the AC voltage controller or AC chopper.

Rotor resistance control

The expression for the torque of the induction machine is dependent on the rotor resistance. Further the maximum value is independent of the rotor resistance. The slip at maximum torque is dependent on the rotor resistance. Therefore, we may expect that if the rotor resistance is changed, the maximum torque point shifts to higher slip values, while retaining a constant torque. Figure shows a family of torque-speed characteristic obtained by changing the rotor resistance.

Note that while the maximum torque and synchronous speed remain constant, the slip at which maximum torque occurs increases with increase in rotor resistance, and so does the starting torque. Whether the load is of constant torque type or fan-type, it is evident that the speed control range is more with this method. Further, rotor resistance control could also be used as a means of generating high starting torque.

For all its advantages, the scheme has two serious drawbacks. Firstly, in order to vary the rotor resistance, it is necessary to connect external variable resistors (winding resistance itself cannot be changed). This, therefore necessitates a slip-ring machine, since only in that case rotor terminals are available outside. For cage rotor machines, there are no rotor terminals. Secondly, the method is not very efficient since the additional resistance and operation at high slips entails dissipation.

The resistors connected to the slip-ring brushes should have good power dissipation capability. Water based rheostats may be used for this. A 'solid-state' alternative to a rheostat is a chopper controlled resistance where the duty ratio control of the chopper presents a variable resistance load to the rotor of the induction machine.

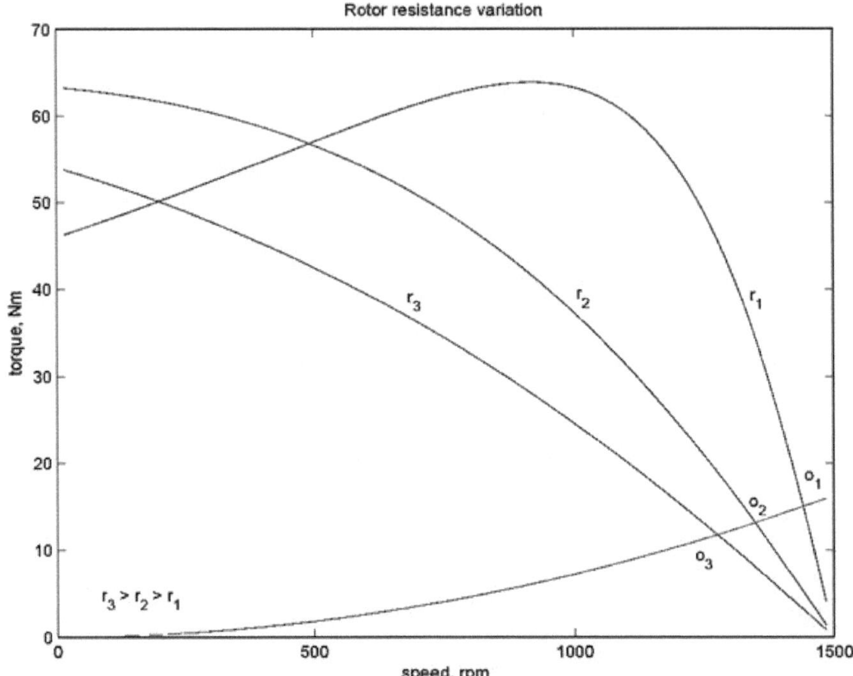

Torque-speed characteristics

Cascade control

The power drawn from the rotor terminals could be spent more usefully. Apart from using the heat generated in meaning full ways, the slip ring output could be connected to another induction machine. The stator of the second machine would carry slip frequency currents of the first machine which would generate some useful mechanical power. A still better option would be to mechanically couple the shafts of the two machines together. This sort of a connection is called cascade connection and it gives some measure of speed control.

Let the frequency of supply given to the first machine be *f*1, its number poles be p1, and its slip of operation be S1. Let *f*2, p2 and S2 be the corresponding quantities for the second machine. The frequency of currents flowing in the rotor of the first machine and hence in the stator of the second machine is S1 $f1$. Therefore $f2$ = S1 $f1$. Since the machines are coupled at the shaft, the speed of the rotor is common for both. Hence, if n is the speed of the rotor in radians,Note that while giving the rotor output of the first machine to the stator of the second, the resultant stator mmf of the second machine may set up an air-gap flux which rotates in the same direction as that of the rotor, or opposes it.

$$n = \frac{f_1}{p_1}(1 - s_1) = \pm\frac{s_1 f_1}{p_2}(1 - s_2).$$

$$n = \frac{f_1}{p_1 + p_2} \quad or \quad n = \frac{f_1}{p_1 - p_2} \quad (s_2\ negligible)$$

$$sE_1 I_2' \cos\phi_2 = I_2' R_2' + P_r.$$

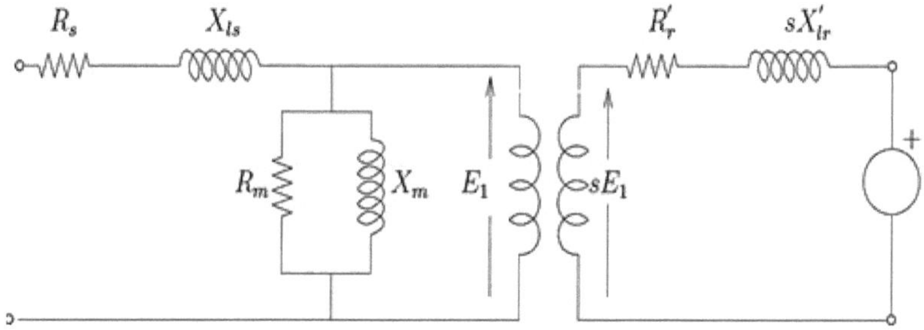

Figure:Induction machine equivalent circuit

The later expression is for the case where the second machine is connected in opposite phase sequence to the first. The cascade connected system can therefore run at two possible speeds.

Speed control through rotor terminals can be considered in a much more general way. Consider the induction machine equivalent circuit of Figure, where the rotor circuit has been terminated with a voltage source Er.

If the rotor terminals are shorted, it behaves like a normal induction machine. This is equivalent to saying that across the rotor terminals a voltage source of zero magnitude is connected. Different situations could then be considered if this voltage source Er had a non-zero magnitude. Let the power consumed by that source be Pr. Then considering the rotor side circuit power dissipation per phase.

Clearly now, the value of s can be changed by the value of Pr. for Pr = 0, the machine is like a normal machine with a short circuited rotor. As Pr becomes positive, for all other circuit conditions remaining constant, *s* increases or in the other words, speed reduces. As Pr becomes negative, the right hand side of the equation and hence the slip decreases. The physical interpretation is that we now have an active source connected on the rotor side which is able to supply part of the rotor copper losses. When Pr = −I′22 R2 the entire copper loss is supplied by the external source. The RHS and hence the slip is zero. This corresponds to operation at synchronous speed. In general the circuitry connected to the rotor may not be a simple resistor or a machine but a power electronic circuit which can process this power requirement. This circuit may drive a machine or recover power back to the mains. Such circuits are called static Kramer drives.

Pole changing method

Sometimes induction machines have a special stator winding capable of being externally connected to form two different number of pole numbers. Since the synchronous speed of the induction machine is given by ns = *fs*/p (in rev. /s) where p is the number of pole pairs, this would correspond to changing the synchronous speed. With the slip now corresponding to the new synchronous speed, the operating speed is changed. This method of speed control is a stepped variation and generally restricted to two steps.

If the changes in stator winding connections are made so that the air gap flux remains constant, then at any winding connection, the same maximum torque is achievable. Such winding arrangements are therefore referred to as constant-torque connections. If however such connection changes result in air gap flux changes that are inversely proportional to the synchronous speeds, then such connections are called constant-horsepower type.

Now, for a given direction of current flow at terminal A1, say into terminal A1, the flux directions within the poles are shown in the figures. In case (a), the flux lines are out of the pole A (seen from the rotor) for and into pole C, thus establishing a two-pole structure. In case (b) however, the flux lines are out of the poles in A & C. The flux lines will be then have to complete the circuit by flowing into the pole structures on the sides. If, when seen from the rotor, the pole emanating flux lines is considered as North Pole and the pole into which they enter is termed as south, then the pole configurations produced by these connections is a two-pole arrangement in Fig: (a) and a four-pole arrangement Fig: (b).

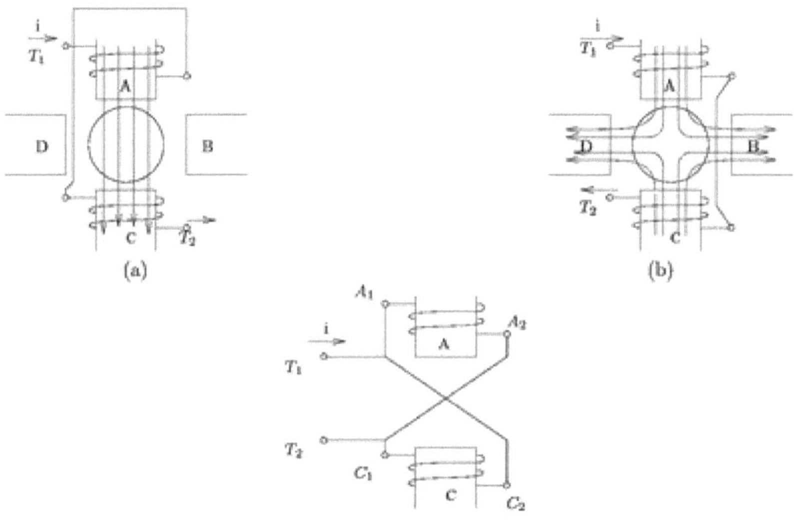

Pole Changing Method

Thus by changing the terminal connections we get either a two pole air-gap field or a four- pole field. In an induction machine this would correspond to a synchronous speed reduction in half from case (a) to case (b). Further note that irrespective of the connection, the applied voltage is balanced by the series addition of induced emf s in two coils. Therefore the air-gap flux in both cases is the same. Cases (a) and (b) therefore form a pair of constant torque connections.

Stator frequency control

The expression for the synchronous speed indicates that by changing the stator frequency also it can be changed. This can be achieved by using power electronic circuits called inverters which convert dc to ac of desired frequency. Depending on the type of control scheme of the inverter, the ac generated may be variable-frequency-fixed-amplitude or variable-frequency-variable- amplitude type. Power electronic control achieves smooth variation of voltage and frequency of the ac output. This when fed to the machine is capable of running at a controlled speed. However, consider the equation for the induced emf in the induction machine.

$$V = 4.44N\phi_m f$$

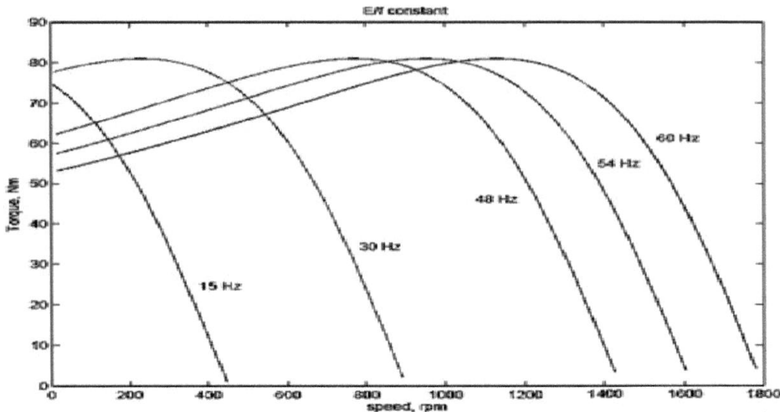

Stator frequency control

Where, N is the number of the turns per phase, ?? is the peak flux in the air gap and *f* is the frequency.

Note that in order to reduce the speed, frequency has to be reduced. If the frequency is reduced while the voltage is kept constant, thereby requiring the amplitude of induced emf to remain the same, flux has to increase. This is not advisable since the machine likely to enter deep saturation. If this is to be avoided, then flux level must be maintained constant which implies that voltage must be reduced along with frequency. The ratio is held constant in order to maintain the flux level for maximum torque capability.

Actually, it is the voltage across the magnetizing branch of the exact equivalent circuit that must be maintained constant, for it is that which determines the induced emf. Under conditions where the stator voltage drop is negligible compared the applied voltage. In this mode of operation, the voltage across the magnetizing inductance in the 'exact' equivalent circuit reduces in amplitude with reduction in frequency and so does the inductive reactance. This implies that the current through the inductance and the flux in the machine remains constant. The speed torque characteristics at any frequency may be estimated as before. There is one curve for every excitation frequency considered corresponding to every value of synchronous speed. The curves are shown in figure. It may be seen that the maximum torque remains constant.

SINGLE PHASE INDUCTION MOTORS

The majority of single phase motors are of induction type. The power rating is in terms of fractional horse power. They are classified according to the starting methods, employed.

They are

1. Resistance start (split- phase)
2. Capacitor start induction motor
3. Capacitor run induction motor
4. Capacitor start And run motor
5. Shaded pole induction motor

CONSTRUCTION OF SINGLE PHASE INDUCTION MOTORS

The construction of a Single phase induction motors is similar to three phase squired cage induction motor. The rotor is the same as that of a three -phase induction motor, but the stator has only a single phase distributed winding. It consists of two parts. One is stator and another one is rotor. The air gap between stator and rotor is uniform. There is no external connection between stator and rotor.

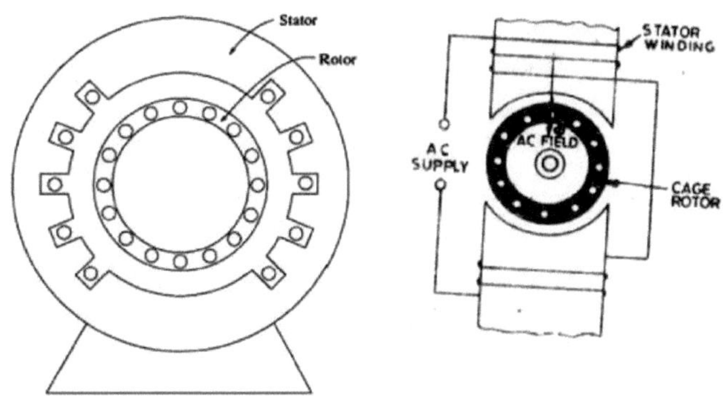

Single Phase Induction motor

OPERATION OF SINGLE-PHASE INDUCTION MOTOR

The stator winding of a single phase induction motor is connected to single phase AC supply. Then a magnetic field is developed in the stator whose axis is always along the axis of stator windings. With alternating current in the fixed stator coil the mmf wave is s tationary in space but pulsates in magnitude and varies sinusoidally with time.

Due to the transformer action, currents are induced in the rotor conductors. The direction of the current is to oppose the stator mmf.

Thus the axis of rotor mmf wave coincides with the axis of stator mmf wave.Therefore the torque angle is zero and no starting torque is developed in the motor. However if rotor is initially given a starting torque by some means, the motor will pick up the speed and continue to rotate in the same direct ion. Thus the single phase induction motor is not a selfstarting motor. The starting torque can be produced by some external arrangement.

STARTING OF SINGLE-PHASE INDUCTION MOTOR

The starting method of single phase induction motor is very simple . An auxiliary winding in the stator is provided in addition to the main winding. Then the induction motor starts as a two phase motor.

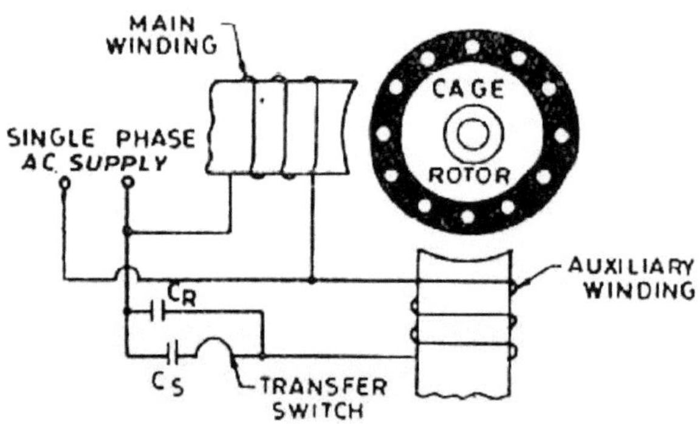

Starting of Single Phase Induction Motor

The main winding axis and auxiliary winding axis are displaced by 90 electrical degrees. The impedance of the windings differs and currents in the main and auxiliary winding are phase shifted from each other.As a result of this, a rotating stator field is produced and the rotor rotates.

When the motor speed is about 75% of synchronous speed, the auxiliary winding is disconnected from the circuit. This is done by connecting a centrifugal switch in the auxiliary winding which is used for starting purpose only. That is why it is c alled starting winding. Under running condition, a single phase induction motor can develop torque only with main winding. That is why it is called running winding.

TYPES OF SINGLE-PHASE INDUCTION MOTOR

The single phase induction motors can be class ified according to the phase difference produced between the current in the main and auxiliary windings. The classifications are

1. Split-phase motors
2. Capacitor Start motors
3. Capacitor run motors
4. Capacitor Start and Run motors
5. Capacitor Pole motors

Split-phase motors

It consists of two stator windings. One is the main winding or running winding and another is auxiliary winding or starting winding. These two winding axes are displaced by 90 electrical degrees. The auxiliary winding has high resistan ce and low reactance and main winding has low resistance and high reactance. Ir is the current flowing through the running winding and Is is the current flowing through the starting winding. These two currents are out of phase.

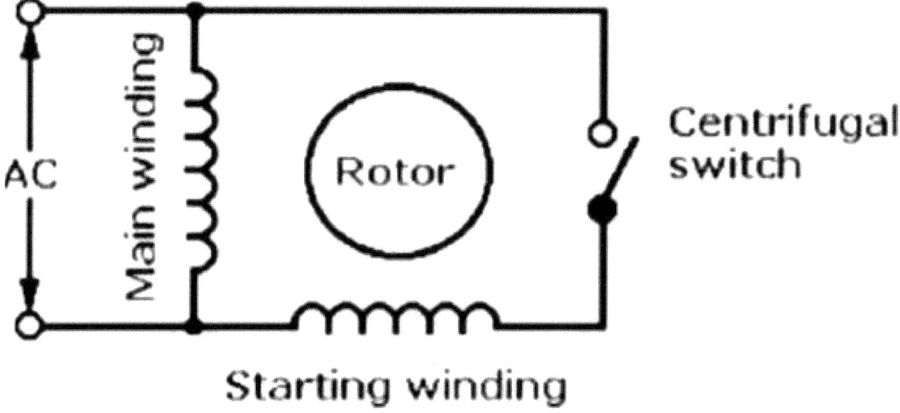

Split Phase Motor

The auxiliary winding is used only for starting period. When the motor is about 75% of synchronous speed, the auxiliary winding is disconnected from the circuit. This is done by connecting a centrifugal switch in the auxiliary c ircuit. After this, motor runs because of main winding only.

Upto 75% of speed, main and auxiliary windings are present in the circuit and after 75% of the speed is attained, only the main winding is present in the circuit. The starting torque of the motor can be increased by connecting a resistance in series with the au xiliary winding. Split-phase induction motor is also called resistance start induction motor.

It is mainly used for loads that require low or medium starting torque. The applications are
i) Fans
ii) Blowers
iii) Centrifugal pu mps
iv) Washing machines

The characteristics of this motor are

1. The starting torque is 100% to 250% of the rated value.
2. The breakdown torque is upto 300%.
3. The power factor of the motor is 0.5 to 0.65.
4. The efficiency of the motor is 55% to 65%.
5. The power rat ing of this motor is in the range of ½ to 1 HP.

Capacitor start single phase induction motor

It is one type of single phase induction motor. Here, a capacitor is connected in series with the auxiliary winding. It is also used to get higher starting torque. Single - phase supply is applied to the windings. The starting current Is leads the line voltage, Because of the capacitor present in the auxiliary winding. The running current Ir lags line voltage. The phase displacement between the two currents is approximately equal to 90° during starting.Again the auxiliary wind ing is disconnected from the circuit by centrifugal switch at 75% of the synchronous speed. i.e., the capacitor is using during starting period only. The direction of rotation of the motor can be changed by changing the connections of one of the windings.
Its is mainly used for hard starting loads, such as

1. Compressors
2. Pumps
3. Conveyors
4. Refrigerators
5. Air conditioning equip ments
6. Washing machines

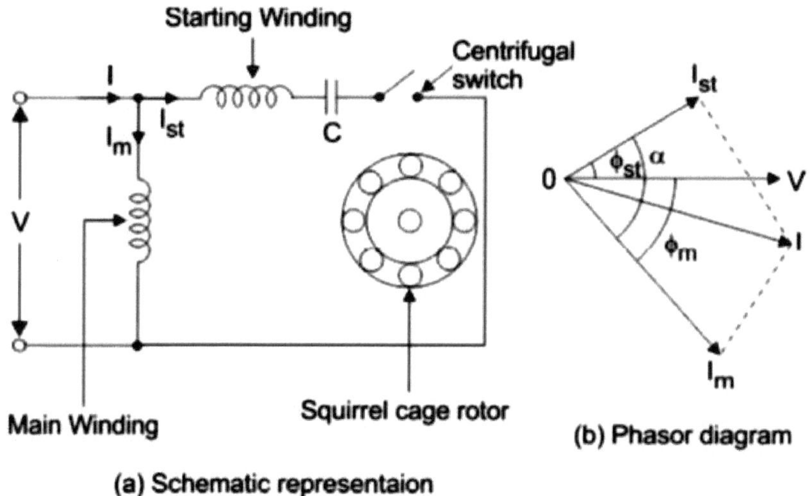

Capacitor start single phase induction motor

Characteristics of these motors are

1. The starting torque is 250% to 400% of the rated value.
2. The breakdown torque is upto 350%.
3. Power factor of the motor is 0.5 to 0.65.T
4. he power rat ing of the motor is 1/ 8 to 1 HP.
5. The efficiency of the motor is 55% to 65%.

Capacitor Run motor

In this motor, a capacitor is permanently connected in series with the auxiliary winding. Here, the centrifugal switch is not needed and therefore the cost of the motor is less.

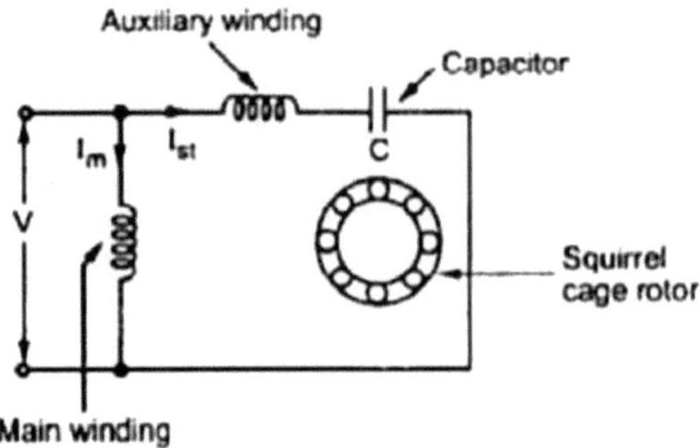

Capacitor Run Motor

Advantages

1. High power factor at full- load
2. High fu ll-load efficiency
3. Increased pull-out torque
4. Low fu ll-load line current

Applications

1. Fans
2. Blowers
3. Centrifugal pu mps

Characteristics

1. The starting torque is 100% to 200% of the rated value.
2. The breakdown torque is upto 250%.
3. The power factor of the motor is in the range of 0.75 to 0.9.
4. The efficiency of the motor is 60% to 70%.
5. The power rating of the motor is 1/8 to 1 HP.

Capacitor-start Capacitor-run motor

Here two capacitors are used. One capacitor Cs is used for starting purpose and another capacitor Cr is used for running purpose. In this motor, we can get high starting torque, because of two capacitors.The value of a starting capacitor Cs is large and the value of running capacitor Cr is small. The running capacitor Cr is permanently connected in series with auxiliary winding. When the motor speed picks up to 75% of synchronous speed, the centrifugal switch is opened and the starting capacitor Cs is disconnected from the circuit.

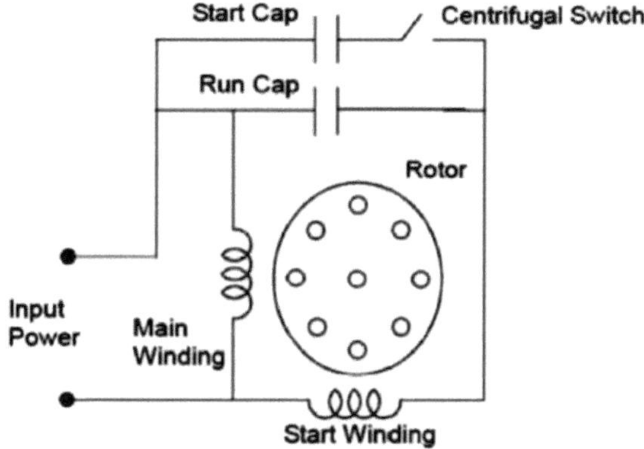

Capacitor-start Capacitor-run motor

The capacitor Cs is used for developing high starting torque and capacitor Cr is used to improve the power factor.

Advantages

1. High starting torque
2. High efficiency
3. High power factor

They are mainly used fo r low noise and high starting torque applications, such as

1. Compressors
2. Pumps
3. Conveyors
4. Refrigerators

Characteristics

1. The starting torque is 200% to 300% of the rated value.
2. The breakdown torque is upto 250%.
3. The power factor of the motor is in the range of 0.75 to 0.9.
4. The efficiency of the motor is 60% to 70%.
5. The power rat ing of the motor is 1/8 to 1 HP.

Shaded Pole Motor

Construction

Shaded pole motor is a split phase type single phase induction motor. It has salient poles on the stator exc ited by single phase supply and a squirrel cage rotor. A portion of each pole is surrounded by a short circuited turn of copper strip called shading coil. It has no commutator, brushes, collector rings, contactors, capacitors or moving switch parts and so it is relatively cheaper, simpler and extremely rugged in construction and reliable .

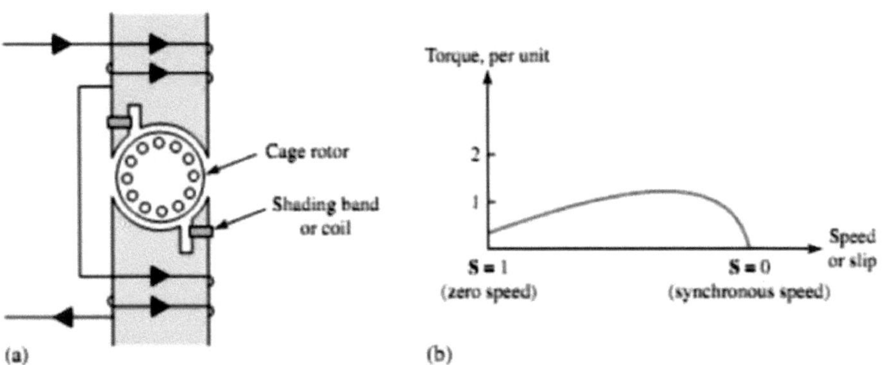

Figure Shaded-pole motor. (a) Schematic diagram. (b) Typical torque–speed characteristic.

Shaded Pole Motor

Operation

The operation of the motor can be understood by referring to which shows one pole of the motor with a shading coil.

a) During the position OA of the alternating current cycle the flu x begins to increase and an emf is induced in the shading coil. The resulting current in the shading coil will be in such a direction as to oppose the change in flux. Thus the flux in the shaded portion of the pole is weakened wh ile that in the un shaded portion in strengthened.

b) During the position AB of the alternating current cycle the flux has reached almost ma ximu m value and is not changing consequently the flux d istribution across the pole is uniform since no current is flowing in the shading.

c) As the flux decreases i.e., portion BC of the alternating current cycle, current is induced in the shading coil so as to oppose the decrease in current. Thus the flux in the shaded portion of the pole is strengthened while that in the un shaded portion in weakened.

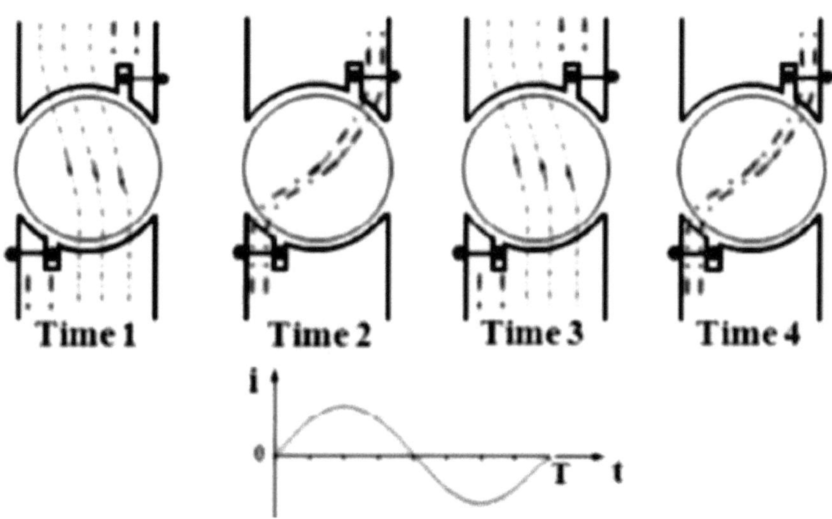

Operation of the shaded pole motor

The effect of the shaded coil is to cause the field flux to shift across the pole face from the unshaded to the shaded portion. This shifting of flux is like a rotating weak field moving in the direction fro m unshaded portion to the shaded portion of the pole.

The rotor is of squirrel cage type and is under the influence of this moving field.Consequently, a small starting torque is developed. As soon as this torque starts to revolve the rotor, additional torque is produced by single phase induction motor action. The motor accelerates to a speed slightly below the synchronous speed and runs as a single phase induction motor. Torque speed characteristics of shaded pole motor.

The main disadvantage of these motors are

1. Low effic iency
2. Low power factor
3. Very low starting torque

The main applications of these motors are for loads requiring low starting torque such as

1. Fans
2. Blowers
3. Turn tables
4. Hair drivers
5. Motion picture projectors

The characteristics of these motors are

1. The starting torque is 40% to 60%.
2. The breakdown torque is upto 140%.
3. The power factor of the motor is in the range of 0.25 to 0.4.
4. The efficiency of the motor is 25% to 40%.
5. The power rat ing of the motor range upto 40W.

SYNCHRONOUS MACHINES INTRODUCTION

The machine which produces three phase power from mechanical power is called an alternator or synchronous generator or AC generator.

Alternator

An alternator works on the princip le of electro magnetic induction.
Like a DC generator, an alternator a lso has an armature winding and a field winding. But there is one important difference between the two. In a DC generator, the armature winding is placed on the rotor in order to provide a way of converting alternating voltage generated in the winding to a direct voltage at the terminals through the use of a rotating commutator. The field poles are placed on the stationary part of the machine. In alternator, the armature winding is placed on the stationary part called stator and field windings are placed on the rotating part called rotor.

ADVANTAGES OF STATIONARY ARMATURE

1. Better insulation
2. Ease of current collection
3. Increased armature tooth strength
4. More rigid construction
5. Reduced armature lea kage reactance
6. Lesser number of slip rings
7. Lesser rotor we ight and inertia
8. Improved ventilation and heat dissipation

CONSTRUCTION OF ALTERNATOR

An alternator has 3 phase winding on the stator and a D.C field winding on the rotor.

Stator

It is the stationary part of the machine and is built up of sheet - steel laminations having slots on its inner periphery. A 3phase winding is placed in these slots serves as the armature winding of the alternator. The alternator winding is a lways connected in star and the neutral is connected to ground.

Rotor

The rotor carries a field winding which is supplied with direct current through two slip rings by a separate d.c. source. Rotor construction is two types, namely,

1. Salient (or) projecting pole type
2. Non- Salient pole (or) cylindrical type

Salient (or) projecting pole type

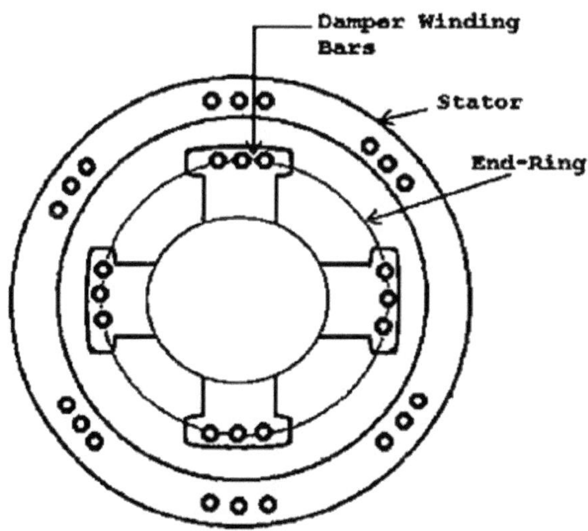

Salient (or) projecting pole type

The rotor of this type is used almost entirely for slow and moderate speed alternators, since it is least expensive and provides ample space for the field ampere -turns. Salient poles cannot be employed in high speed generators on account of very high peripheral speed and the difficulty of obtaining sufficient mechanical strength.

The salient poles are made of thick steel lamination riveted together and are fixed to rotor by a dove-tail jo int. The pole faces are usually provided with slots for damper windings. These dampers are useful in preventing hunting. The pole faces are so shaped that the radial air gap length increases from the pole centre to the pole tips so that the flu distribution over the armature is sinusoidal. The field coils are placed on the pole-pieces and connected in series. The ends of the field windings are connected to a d.c. source through slip-rings carrying brushes and mounted on the shaft of the field structure.

Smooth cylindrical or non salient pole type

The rotors of this type are used in very high speed alternators driven by st eam turbines. To reduce the peripheral velocity, the diameter of the rotor is reduced and axial length is increased. Such rotors have two or four poles.

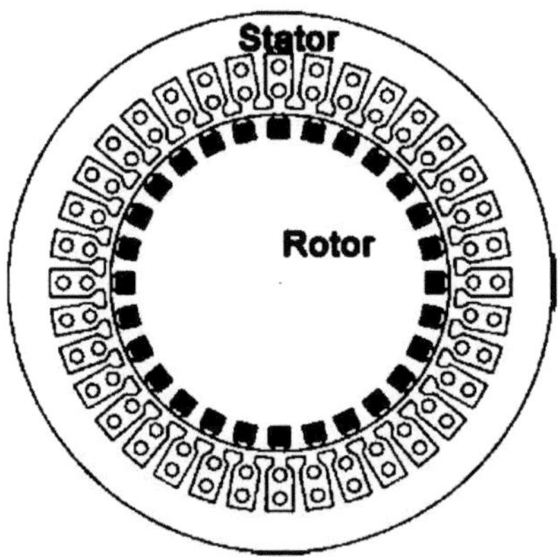

Smooth cylindrical or non salient pole type

It consists of a cylindrical steel forg ing which is suitably fabricated mechanically and treated therma lly. The forg ing has radial slots in which the field copper, usually in strip from is placed. The coils are held in place by steel or bronze wedges and the coil ends are fastened by metal rings. The slots over certain portions of the core are o mitted to form pole faces.

WORKING OF ALTERNATOR

The field magnets are magnetized by applying 125 Vo lts or 250Vo lts through slip rings. The field windings are connected such that, alternate N and S poles are produced. The rotor and hence the field magnets are driven by the prime mover. As the rotor rotates, the armature conductor are cut by the magnetic poles are alternately N and S pole, this emf acts in one direction and then in the other direction. Hence an alternating emf is induced in the stator conductors. The frequency of induced emf depend on the number of N and S poles moving pas an armature conductor in one second. The direction of induced emf can be found by right hand rule and frequency is given by

f=PN/120

Where N = speed of rotor in r.p.m,

P = Number of rotor poles.

TYPES OF ALTERNATOR

Alternators are two types

i) Rotating armature type

ii) Rotating field and stationary armature type.

EMF EQUATION OF AN ALTERNATOR

Let Z = number o f conductors or coil sides in series/phase

Z = 2T, where T is the number of coils or turns per phase

P = number of poles; F = frequency of induced emf in Hz

φ= flux/pole in webers; K_d = distribution factor =sin(mβ/2)/msin(β/2)

K_c or K_p= pitch factor (o r) coil span factor = cosα/ 2

K_f= form factor = 1.11 if emf is assumed sinusoidal

N = rotor speed in r.p.m

For one revolution of the rotor each stator conductor is cut by a flux of φP webers

d φ = φP and dt = 60/N second

Average emf induced per conductor = dϕ/dt ....(1)

Substituting, dϕ=ϕ*p and dt=60/N in equation (1) gives =ϕ*p/(60/N)

Average emf induced per conductor =ϕNp/60 volts

We know that f =PN/120 or N=(120f/P)

Substituting this value of N, we get average emf per conductor=ϕp/ 60*120f/P = 2fϕ Volt

If there are Z conductors in series / phase, then Average e.m.f/phase = 2fϕz volts = 4fϕT volts

The above equation is true only, if the winding is concentrated in one slot. But practically it is not true, as the winding for each phase under each pole is distributed and for such cases K_p and K_d must be considered.

Actually available voltage/phase = 4.44 K_pK_d fϕT volts

If the alternator is tar connected, then the line voltage is √3 times the phase voltage.

VOLTAGE REGULATION

The voltage regulation of an alternator is defined as the increase in terminal voltage when full load is thrown off, assuming field current and speed remaining the same. The percentage regulation is defined as the ratio of change in terminal voltage from full load to no load rated terminal voltage.

Percentage regulation = $\{(E_o\text{-}V)/V\}$x100

Where, E_o = No load Terminal voltage

V = Full load rated terminal voltage

Voltage characteristics of an alternator are shown

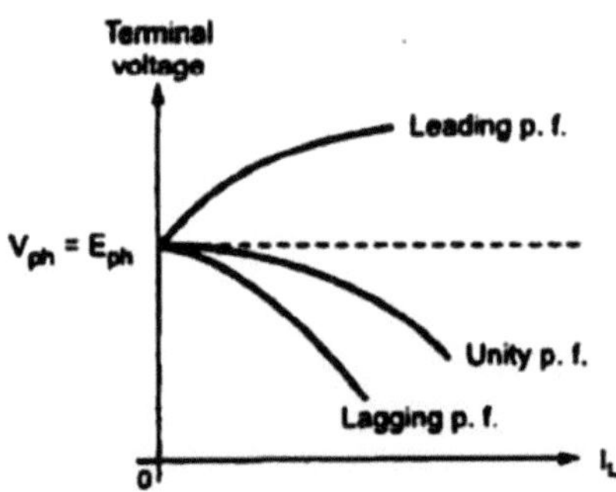

Voltage Characteristics of an alternator

To determine the regulation of an alternator, open circuit and short circuit tests are performed, which give open circuit characteristic and short circuit characteristic.

1. Open circu it test

2. Short circu it test
3. Measurement of armature resistance per phase.

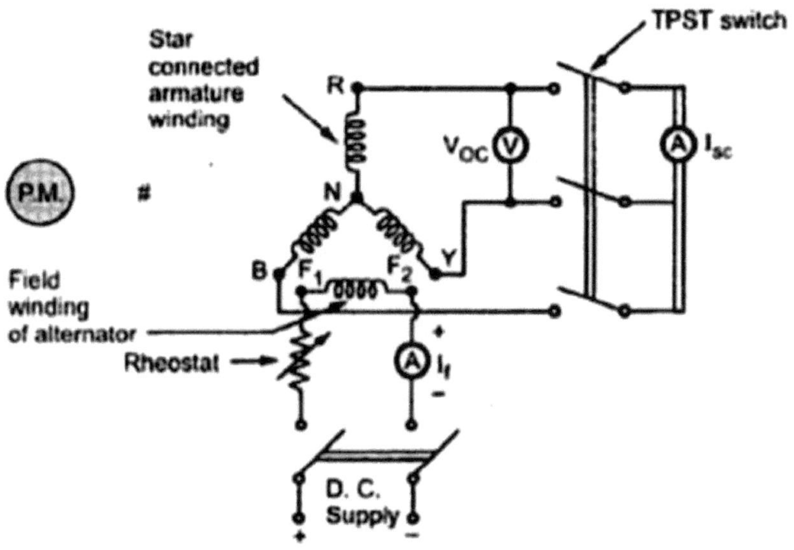

Open circuit and short circuit tests

Open circuit test

The alternator is driven at its rated speed and this speed is kept constant throughout the test. The field excitation is gradually increased and for different values of the fie ld current, corresponding values of the no-load induced emf are noted. Field excitation is increased until the alternator builds up the rated voltage. From the on data no -load test, a graph of the open circuit voltage per phase against the field current is plotted. This graph is known as open circuit characteristic (or OCC).

Short circuit test

The alternator is driven at its rated speed on no load. The field excitation is kept minimum. The field current is adjusted such that the rated current flows through the short -circuited armature. The value of the field current which causes the rated current to flow through the short circuited armature windings is noted. From the data obt ained the short circuit characteristic (or S.C.C) which is the graph of Ia Vs Ir is drawn.

Measurement of armature resistance per phase

The d.c resistance/phase of the armature winding is measured by Ammeter- Voltmeter method (or using Wheatstone Bridge).A s mall direct current is passed through one phase (or winding) of the armature and the voltage drop across it is noted.

D.C resistance of armature/phase = Voltmeter reading/Ammeter reading

$$Z_s = \frac{AC(in\ volts)}{AB(inamps)} \text{ at constant } I_f$$

$$\text{Synchronous reactance } X_s = \sqrt{Z_s^2 - R_a^2}$$

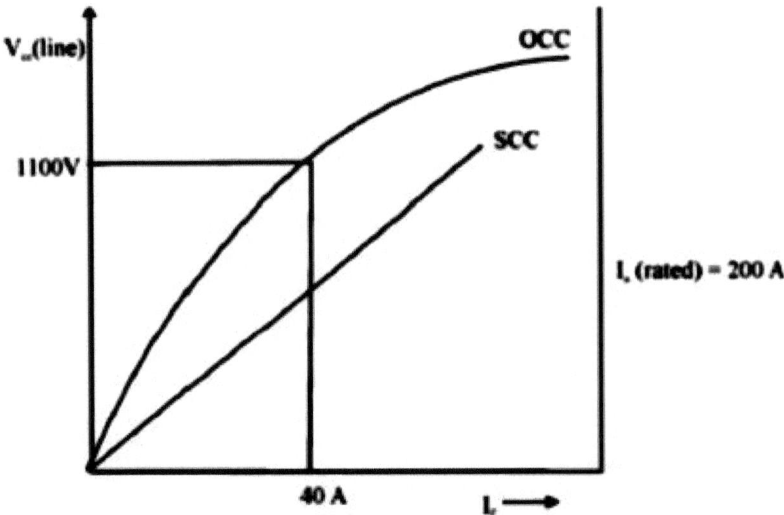

Open Circuit and Short CircuitCharactersitics

SYNCHRONOUS MOTOR

The synchronous motor is one type of 3 phase A.C motors which operate at a constant speed fro m no load to full load.

PRINCIPLE OF OPERATION OF SYNCHRONOUS MOTOR

When a sinusoidal (single phase) voltage is applied to winding, the magnetic field produced by the resultant current flow will a lso be sinusoidally varying with respect to time. This means that the field is pulsating. Now when a three -phase voltage is applied to a three phase winding, the flux produced will be the resultant of all three pulsating fields. It can be shown that the resultant field has a magnitude of 1.5 φm where φm is the maximum value of the flux due to single phase current. Further it can also be shown that the direction of the field changes continuously, i.e., the field is rotating in space at a speed given by.

N_s=(120f/P)

Where f is the frequency of supply and P is the number of poles. This speed is called the synchronous speed. Hence it it to be remembe red that when a three-phase supply is given to a three-phase winding a magnetic field of constant magnitude but rotating at a constant speed, N_s is produced.

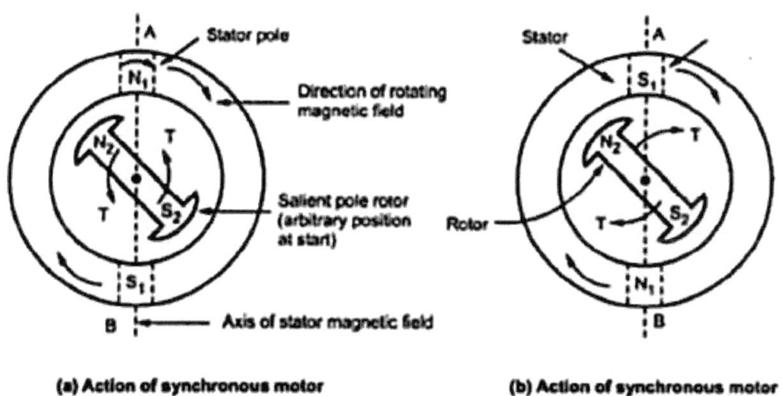

Working of synchronous motor

The two fictitious stator poles marked N_s and S_s assumed to rotate clockwise at a synchronous speed N_s. The rotor poles (assumed to be only 2 in number), N_R and S_R are formed y the d.c excitation. When N_s and N_R are together (and simila rly S_s and S_R) like poles repel each other; since N_s and S_s are moving in the clockwise direction, N_R and S_R tend to figure. Half a cycle later, the stator poles have moved, whereas the rotor poles have moved significantly. This situation is shown figure. N_s and S_R and similarly S_s and N_R get attracted and the rotor tries different to rotate in the clockwise direction. This implies that the rotor experiences torque in different directions every half cycle. As a result, the rotor is at standstill due to its large inertia.

This explains why a synchronous motor has no starting torque and cannot start by itself. However; if the rotor is now rotated separately by prime mover in the same direction as the synchronously rotating stator field, and at a speed near Ns then it is possible that at some instant of time, N_s and S_R and similarly S_s and N_R (i.e., The stator and rotor poles) get attracted and locked to one another.

Hence a synchronous motor, through not self starting, starts working as a motor if it is started up by some means. It needs two separate supplies one a d.c source for excitation of the rotor and other, a three-phase supply for the stator. Because of the interlocking between the stator and rotor poles, the motor runs only at one speed, the synchronous speed.

STARTING METHODS OF SYNCHRONOUS MOTOR

From Dc Source

When dc supply and dc compound motor are availab le, the synchronous motor is coupled and started by means of a dc co mpound motor.The speed of dc motor is adjusted by the speed regulator.The synchronous motor is then exc ited and synchronized with AC supply mains. At the moment of synchronizing, the synchronous motor is switched on with the AC mains and either the dc motor is disconnected from the dc supply ma ins or the field of the dc machine is strengthened until it begins to function as a generator.

Now the synchronous machine is operating as a motor, fro m ac supply mains and dc machine acts as load on it. The synchronous motor can also be started by the exc iter mounted on an overhung synchronous motor bracket and shaft extension.Here aga in, an available dc source operates the exciter as a motor during the starting period then after the synchronous machine is brought up to speed and synchronized, the exciter assumes its normal function.

By Means of AC Motor

A small direct coupled induction motor called the pony motor, may be used for starting the synchronous motor unless the motor is required to start against full load torque. The induction motor frequently has two poles less than the synchronous motor and so is capable of ra ising the speed of the latter to synchronous speed. Before switching on the AC supply to the synchronous motor, it must be synchronized with the bus bars.

After normal operation is established, the pony motor is sometimes de -coupled from the synchronous motor. This method is not very satisfactory and not suited to industrial needs. Modern machine are usually of the self starting type and are arranged to start as induction motors.

By means of Damper Grids in the pole faces

The synchronous motor is made self starting by providing a special wind ing on the rotor poles, known as damper winding or squirre l cage winding.The damper winding consists of short circuited copper bars embedded in the face of the field poles. AC supply given to the stator produces a rotating magnetic field which causes the rotor to rotate, therefore in the beginning synchronous motor provided with damper winding starts as a squirrel cage induction motor.

The exciter moves along the rotor-when the motor attains about 95% of synchronous speed, the rotor winding is connected to exciter terminals and the rotor is magnetically locked by the rotating field of the stator and the motor runs as a synchronous motor.

ADVANTAGES OF SYNCHRONOUS MOTOR

1. Constant speed
2. Operate at high frequencies
3. Power varies linearly with voltage
4. Better mechanically

DISADVANTAGES OF SYNCHRONOUS MOTOR

1. It cannot be started under load
2. It requires separate DC excitation
3. It has a tendency to hunt
4. Collector rings and brushes are required

APPLICATIONS OF SYNCHRONOUS MOTOR

Used in

1. Fans
2. Dc generators
3. Co mpressors
4. Centrifugal pumps

TORQUE EQUATION OF SYNCHRONOUS MOTOR

$AB = E_b \sin\alpha$ and $\cos\phi = \dfrac{AB}{I_a X_s}$

So $AB = I_a X_s \cos\phi$

$E_b \sin\alpha = I_a X_s \cos\phi \Rightarrow I_a \cos\phi = \dfrac{E_b \sin\alpha}{X_s}$

$P = V I_a \cos\phi$

$P = \dfrac{V E_b \sin\alpha}{X_s}$ $P_{in} = \dfrac{3 E_b V}{X} \sin\alpha$ For 3 phase

Since stator copper loss has been neglected,

P_{in} also represents the gross mechanic power (P_m) developed by the motor.

$$P_m = \frac{3 E_b V}{X_s} \sin\alpha$$

Gross torque developed by the motor $T = \dfrac{P_m}{\omega_m}$

$$T = \frac{3 E_b V}{\omega_m X_s} \sin\alpha \quad \left(\omega_m = \frac{2\pi N}{60}\right)$$

$$T = \frac{9.55 P_m}{N}\ Nm$$

Starting Torque

- It indicates the ability of the motor to accelerate the load. It is also sometimes called breakaway torque.
- It may be as low as 10% in case of reciprocating pumps, and as high 200 or 250% full load torque as in case of reciprocating two-cylinder compressors.

- The synchronous motor processes no self starting torque; yet in modern synchronous motors, by making proper changes in the design of damper windings, almost any reasonable torque can be developed.

Running Torque

- Running torque is the torque developed by the motor under running condition.
- It is determined by the output power and speed of the driven machine.
- Peak output power determines the ma ximu m torque that wou ld be required by the driven machine.
- The breakdown or ma ximu m running torque of a motor must be greater than this value in order to avoid stalling of the machine.

Pull in Torque

- It pertains to the ability of the machine to pull in to synchronous when changing from induction to synchronous motor operation.

Pull out torque

- It is the maximum torque that the synchronous motor will develop without pulling out of synchronous. Its value ranges from 1.25 to 3.5 times the full load torque.

PROBLEMS

1. A 4 pole , 3 phase induction motor operates from a supply of frequency of 50Hz. Calculate the speed at which the magnetic field of the stator is rotating.

Given data

P=4 f=50Hz

To find Ns = ?

Solution

$$Ns = \frac{120f}{P} = \frac{120 \times 50}{4} = 1500 rpm$$

2. A 6pole , 3 phase, 50Hz induction motor has a slip of 3% at full load. Calculate the speed of full load.

Given data

P=6

f=50Hz

s=0.03

To find N= ?

Solution

$$Ns = \frac{120f}{P} = \frac{120 \times 50}{6} = 1000rpm$$

N=Ns(1-s)= 1000(1-0.03)=970rpm

3. A 6pole , 3 phase, 50Hz induction motor runs at 800rpm at full load. Calculate the value of slip at this load conditon.

Given data P=6

f=50Hz

N=800rpm

To find S = ?

Solution

$$Ns = \frac{120f}{P} = \frac{120 \times 50}{6} = 1000rpm$$

$$S = \frac{Ns - N}{Ns} \times 100 = \frac{1000 - 800}{1000} \times 100 = 20\%$$

4. A 3 phase, 50Hz induction motor is operating at 400V supply. If the slip is 4% Calculate the frequency of its rotor induced emf.

Given data

V=400V

f=50Hz

s=0.04

To find fr = ?

Solution fr=sf=0.04×50=2Hz

5. A 6 pole induction motor is fed from 50Hz supply. If the frequency of rotor emf at full load is 2Hz, Calculate the slip and speed

Given data

P=6

f=50Hz

To find S=? N = ?

Solution

fr=sf

s=fr/f=2/50=0.04

$$Ns = \frac{120f}{P} = \frac{120 \times 50}{6} = 1000rpm$$

N=Ns(1-s)= 1000(1-0.04)=960rpm

CHAPTER FOUR

MEASUREMENTS AND INSTRUMENTATION

INTRODUCTION

The measurement of any quantity plays very important role not only in science but in all branches of engineering, medicine and in almost all human day to day activities.

MEASUREMENT

The measurement of a given parameter or quantity is the act or result of a quantitative comparison between a predefined standard and an unknown quantity to be measured.

METHODS OF MEASUREMENT

The methods of measurement are classified as,
1. Direct method
2. Indirect method

1. Direct method

In direct method, the quantity to be measured is used to produce certain effects which directly give the indication on the meter.
Examples: a mmeters, volt meter, wattmeter, oh mmeter etc.

2. Indirect method

In the indirect method of measure ment, the quantity to be measured is not directly measured but other parameters re lated to the quantity are measured. Example is the measurement of resistance. Instead of using ohmmeter for d irect measurement, the voltage across the resistance and the current through the resistance are measured. Then resistance can be calculated using ohms law R=V/I

APPLICATIONS OF MEASURING SYSTEMS

- Monitoring of process and operation.
- Control of process and operation.
- Experimental engineering analysis.

INSTRUMENT

The measuring instrument may be defined as a device for determining the value or magnitude of a quantity or variable.

INSTRUMENT CLASSIFICATION

The instruments are classified as,
1. Active/Passive instruments
2. Null/De flect ion type instruments
3. Monitoring/Control instruments
4. Analog/Digital instruments
5. Absolute/Secondary instruments

FUNCTIONAL ELEMENTS OF AN INSTRUMENT

The functional elements of an instrument are ,
1. Primary Sensing Element
2. Variable Conversion Element
3. Variable Manipulation Element
4. Data Transmission Element
5. Data Presentation Element

1.Primary Sensing Element

The quantity to be measured or measurand is first detected by the primary sensing element. A transducer follo ws primary sensing element which c onverts the measurand into a corresponding electrical signal. A transducer is a device which converts a physical quantity into an electrical quantity. The quantity to be measured is sensed and detected by an element which gives the output in diffe rent analogous form. The output is then converted into an electrical quantity by a transducer. The first stage of measurement system is known as detector transducer stage.

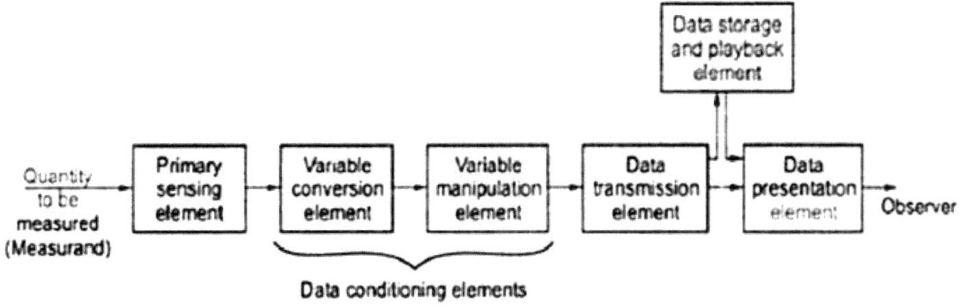

Functional elements of an instrument

2. Variable Conversion Element

The output of the primary sensing element is in electrical fo rm such as voltage, frequency or any other electrical parameters. So met imes this output may not be suitable for actual measurement system. For example the measurement of a system is digital then the analog signal obtained from the primary sensing element is not suitable for the digital systems. In such case analog to digital converter is required. Many instruments do not need any variable conversion element, while others need more than one variable conversion element.

3. Variable Manipulation Element

The function of this element is to manipulate the signal, preserving the original nature of the signal. The manipulat ion means a change in numerical value of the signal. For example an amplifier which just amplifies the magnitude of the input, at its output retaining the original nature of the signal. In some cases the levels of outputs of the previous stage are high and required to be lowered. In such case attenuators are used as variable manipulation element.Sometimes the output of the transducer may be affected due to unwanted signals like noise.Some process like modulation, cliping, clamp ing etc. is done to obtain the signal in pure or acceptable form. Such a process is called signal conditioning.The term signal conditioning
includes many other functions in addition to variable conversion and

variable manipulation. The second stage is called data conditioning or signal conditioning.

4. Data Transmission Element

When the elements of an instrument are physically separated, it is necessary to transmit the data from one stage to the other. This is done by data transmission element. The signal conditioning and data transmission together is called intermediate stage of an instrument.

5. Data Presentation Element

The transmitted data may be used by the syst em, finally for monitoring, controlling and analyzing purpose. The person handling the instrument must get the information in propernform. If the data is to be monitored then visual display devices are used. If the data is to be recorded for analysis purpose then magnetic tape recorders, high speed cameras are used. For control and analysis purpose, microprocessors, computers and microcontrollers are used as data presentation element. This stage may be called terminating stage of an instrument.

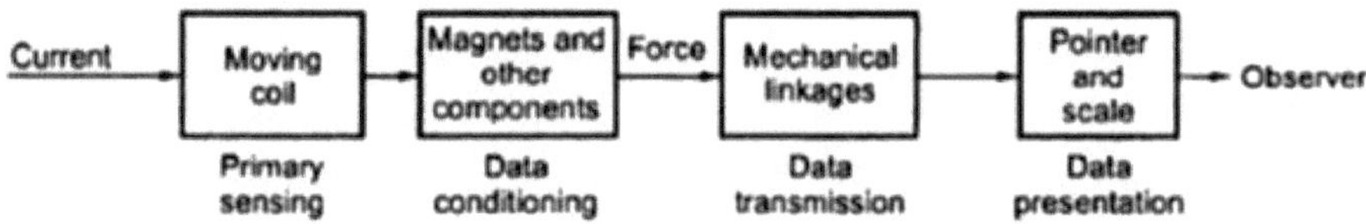

Basic schematic of an ammeter

For example consider a simple analog meter used to measure current or voltage. The moving coil is primary sensing element. The magnets and coil together acts as data conditioning stage to convert current in a coil to a force. This force is transmitted to the pointer through mechanical linkages which acts as data transmission element. The pointer and the scale act as data presentation element.

STANDARDS

A standard is a physical representation of a unit of measurement. A standard means known accurate measure of physical quantity. All the standards are preserved at the international Bureau of Weights and measures at severes, near paris.

The different types of standards of measurement are classified as,

1. International Standards
2. Prima ry Standards
3. Secondary Standards
4. Working Standards

1. International Standards

International Standards are defined on the basis of international agreement.These standards are ma intained at the International Bureau of We ights and measures.It is periodically evaluated and checked by absolute measurements. The international standards are not available to the ordinary users. For improvements it can be replaced by the absolute units in 1948.

2. Primary Standards

Primary Standards are absolute standards of such high accuracy they can be used as the ultimate reference standards. These standards are maintained at National Standard Laboratories in different countries. The fundamental units are calibrated independently by absolute measurements at each of the national laboratories. These are not available for use, outside the national laboratories.The main function of the primary standards is the calibration and verification of secondary standards.

3. Secondary Standards

Secondary Standards are the basic reference standards used in industrial measurement laboratories. The responsibility of maintance and calibration of these standards lies in particular industry. Secondary Standards are periodically send to the National Standard Laboratories for calibration. The National Laboratories sent them back to the industries with the certification comparing them with the primary standards. Each industry has its own standard.

4. Working Standards

The Working Standards are the major tools of a measurement laboratory.These standards are used to check and calibrate laboratory instruments for their accuracy and measurement. For example the resistor manufacturing industry maintains a standard resistor in the laboratory for checking the values of the manufactured resistors. The manufacturers verifies that the value of manufactured resistor are well within the specified accuracy limits.

CALIBRATION:

- Calibration of the measuring instrument is the process in which the readings obtained from the instrument are compared with the sub-standards in the laboratory at several points along the scale of the instrument
- As per the results obtained from the readings obtained of the instrument and the sub-standards, the curve is plotted. If the instrument is accurate there will be matching of the scales of the instrument and the sub-standard
- If there is deviation of the measured value from the instrument against the standard value, the instrument is calibrated to give the correct values
- **Static calibration** refers to the input-output relations obtained when only one input of the instrument is varied at a time, all other inputs being kept constant
- Steps involved in static calibration-

1. Examine the construction of the instrument and identify and list all the possible inputs
2. Decide the best possible input which will be significant to the application for which the instrument is to be calibrated
3. Select the apparatus that will allow to vary all the significant inputs over the range considered necessary
4. By holding some inputs constant, varying others and record the output, develop a desired static input-output relation

CLASSIFICATION OF ERRORS:

Measurement is the foundation of all experimental science and technology. The result of every measurement by any measuring instrument contains some uncertainty. This uncertainty is called error. There are generally two types of error in measurement as

- **STATIC ERROR**

A static error is defined as the difference between the measured value and the true value of the quantity. The true value is the exact value of the measurement which is impossible to obtain. Hence the approximate true value of the measurement should be taken into consideration. The errors mainly occur because of poor design and improper maintenance of the system.

1. **Gross Errors**

- These errors are mainly due to human mistakes in reading or in using instruments or error in recording observations. Error may also occur due to incorrect adjustment of instruments and computational mistakes
- These errors cannot be treated mathematically
- The complete elimination of gross error is not possible, but one can minimize them. Some errors are easily detected while others may be elusive
- One of the basic gross errors that occur frequently is the improper use of an instrument. The error can be minimized by taking proper care in reading and recording the measurement parameter

2. **Systematic Error**

- The systematic errors are those errors that tend to be in one direction, either positive or negative
- Some sources of systematic error are:

    - Errors in the calibration of the measuring instruments.
    - Incorrect measuring technique: For example, one might make an incorrect scale Reading because of parallax error
    - Bias of the experimenter. The experimenter might consistently read an instrument incorrectly, or might let knowledge of the expected value of a result influence the measurements

- There are basically three types of systematic errors:-

    a. Instrumental errors
    b. Environmental errors
    c. Observational errors
    ***a.* Instrumental Errors**

- Instrumental error refers to the combined accuracy and precision of a measuring instrument, or the difference between the actual value and the value indicated by the instrument.
- These errors are inherent in measuring instruments, because of their mechanical structure.

- Instrumental errors can be avoided by:-

- Selecting a suitable instrument for the particular measurement applications.
- Appling correction factors after determining the amount of instrumental error.
- Calibrating the instrument against a standard.

b. Environmental Errors

- An environmental error is an error in calculations that are being a part of observations due to environment. Any experiment performing anywhere in the universe has its surroundings, from which we cannot eliminate our system. The study of environmental effects has primary advantage of being able to justify the fact that environment has impact on experiments and feasible environment will not only rectify our result but also amplify it.
- The environmental errors have different causes, which are widening with the passage of time, as the research works telling us, including; temperature, humidity, magnetic field, constantly vibrating earth surface, wind and improper lightening.
- In high precision laboratories, where a slightest bug can destroy the whole system, removal or at least minimizing the environmental errors proved to be very fruitful.

c. Observational Errors

- Observational errors are error introduced by the observer. The most common error is the parallax error introduced in reading a meter scale, and the error of estimation when obtaining a reading from a meter scale.
- These errors are caused by the habit of individual observers. For example, an observer may always introduce and error by consistently holding his head too far to the left while reading a needle and scale reading.
- In general, systematic errors can also be subdivided into static and dynamic errors. Static errors are caused by limitations of the measuring device or the physical laws governing its behavior.

Dynamic errors are caused by the instrument not responding fast enough to follow the changes in a measured variable.

3. **Random Errors**

- The random errors are those errors, which occur irregularly and hence are random with respect to sign and size. These can arise due to random and unpredictable fluctuations in experimental conditions (e.g. unpredictable fluctuations in temperature, voltage supply, mechanical vibrations of experimental set-ups, etc), personal (unbiased) errors by the observer taking readings, etc.

- Random errorsare errors that remain after gross and systematic errors have been substantially reduced or at least accounted for. Random errors are generally an accumulation of a large number of small effects and may be of real concern only in measurements requiring a high degree of accuracy. Such errors can be analyzed statically.
- These errors are due to unknown causes, not determinable in the ordinary processor making measurements. Such errors are normally small and follow the laws of probability. Random errors can thus be treated mathematically.
- For example, suppose a voltage is being monitored by a voltmeter which is read at 15 minutes intervals. Although the instrument operates under ideal environmental conditions and accurately calibrated before measurements, it still gives that vary slightly over the period of observation. This variation cannot be corrected by any method of calibration or any other known method of control.
- Random error unlike systematic error is not unidirectional. Some of the measured values are greater than true value some are less than true value.
- The errors introduced are sometimes positive and sometimes negative with respect to true value. It is possible to minimize this type of error by repeating measurements and applying statistical technique to get closer value to the true value.
- Another distinguishing aspect of random error is that it is not biased. It is there because of the limitation of the instrument in hand and the limitation on the part of human ability. No human being can repeat an action in exactly the same manner. Hence, it is likely that same person reports different values with the same instrument, which measures the

quantity correctly.

- Sources of Random Errors other than the inability of a piece of hardware to provide true measurements, are as follows:

- Insufficient knowledge of process parameters and design conditions
- Poor design.
- Change in process parameters, irregularities, upsets, etc.
- Poor maintenance.
- Errors caused by person operating the instrument or equipment.
- Certain design limitations

DYNAMIC ERROR

Dynamic error is the difference between the true value of a quantity changing with time and the value indicated by the instrument.

LIMITING ERROR:

- In most indicating instruments the accuracy is guaranteed to a certain percentage to a full scale reading. The limits of this deviation from the specified value are known as limiting errors or guarantee errors.
- For example, if the resistance of a resistor is given as 500Ω ± 10%, the manufacture guarantees that the resistance full between the limits 450Ω and 550Ω.
- The limited deviation of the measured value from the true value is known as the **limiting error or guarantee error**. Such type of error is fixed on the instrument.
- The magnitude of the limiting error depends on the design, material and the workmanship used for the instrument. The manufacturer already knew about the limiting error of the instrument.
- The actual value of the instrument along with the **limiting error** is expressed as $\mathbf{A_a = A_s \pm \delta A}$

Where A_a – actual value, A_s – specified or rated value, δ_A – limiting error or tolerance

- **Relative Limiting Error = (actual value – nominal value) / nominal value**

PROBABLE ERROR:

The error associated with providing estimates for a sample that is from a normal distribution. It is the product of the standard error and 0.6745.

PERMANENT MAGNET MOVING COIL INSTRUMENT (PMMC)

Basic range: 10 μA-100 mA, **Coil resistance:** 10 Ω-1 kΩ

Usage: dc PMMC ammeters and voltmeters,

ac PMMC ammeters and voltmeters (with rectifiers)

Principle of Operation

The principle on which a Permanent Magnet Moving Coil (PMMC) instrument operates is that a torque is exerted on a current-carrying coil placed in the field of a permanent magnet. A PMMC instrument is shown below.

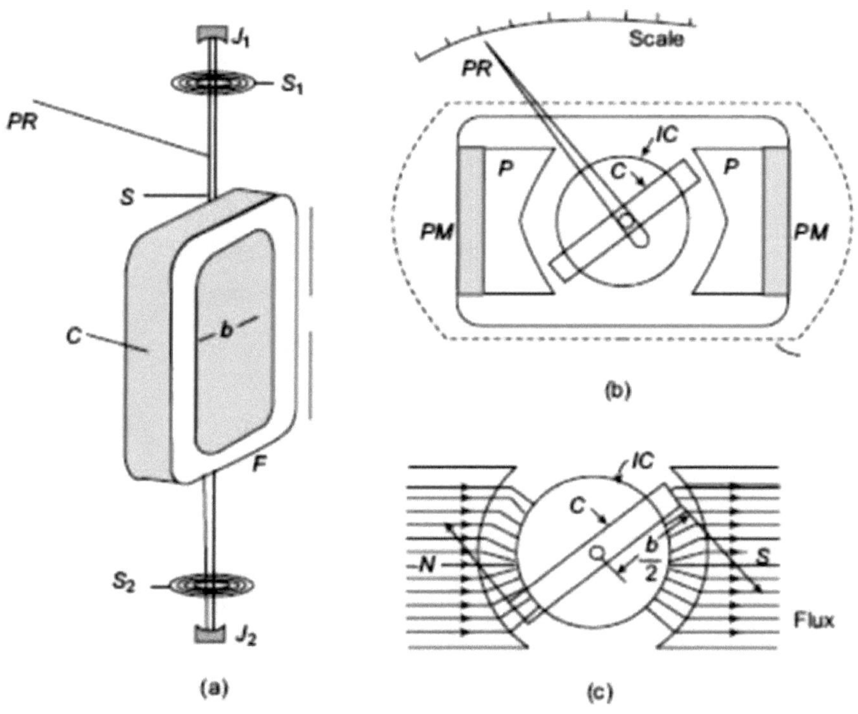

PMMC construction

The coil C has a number of turns of thin insulated wires wound on a rectangular aluminium former F. The frame is carried on a spindle S mounted in jewel bearings J1, J2. A pointer PR is attached to the spindle so that it moves over a calibrated scale. The whole of the moving system is made as light in weight as possible to keep the friction at the bearing to a minimum.

The coil is free to rotate in air gaps formed between the shaped soft-iron pole piece (pp) of a permanent magnet PM and a fixed soft-iron cylindrical core IC.

The core serves two purposes;

(a) it intensifies the magnetic field by reducing the length of the air gap, and

(b) it makes the field radial and uniform in the air gap.Thus, the coil always moves at right angles to the magnetic field. Modern permanent magnets are made of steel alloys which are difficult to machine. Soft-iron pole pieces (pp) are attached to the permanent magnet PM for easy machining in order to adjust the length of the air gap. The following figure shows the schematic of internal parts of a moving-coil instrument.

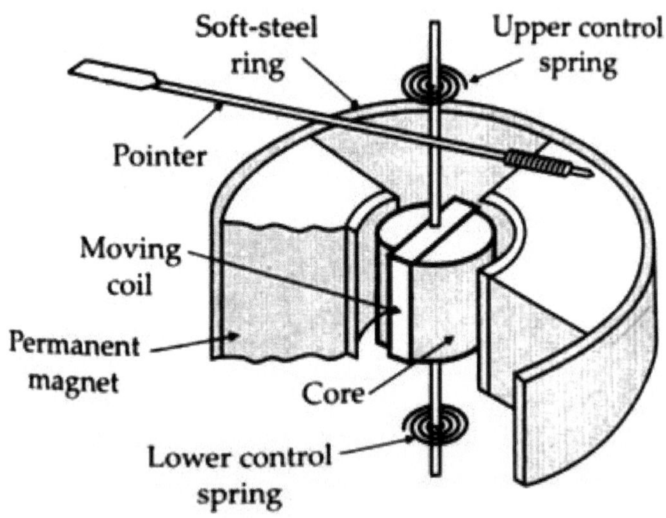

Internal parts of Moving Coil instrument

A soft-iron yoke (Y) is used to complete the flux path and to provide shielding from stray external fields.

Torque Equation, The above Figure shows the dimensions that enter the torque equation of a galvanometer.

let l= length of vertical side of coil; m,

d=length of horizontal side (width) of coil ; m

N=number of turns in: the coil, .

B =flux density in the air gap at the coil position; Wb/m2,

i=current ; A

K=spring constant of suspension; Nm/rad,

Θ_F= final steady deflection; rad.

Force on each side of coil =$NBil$ sinα

α=angle between direction of magnetic field and the conductor.

The field is radial and, therefore, α=90·

Hence, force on each side =$NBil$

Deflecting torque T_d=force X distance=NBild

=$NBAi$ newton metre

Where A=ld - area of coil; m^2

Where N, B, A are constants for a galvanometer.

. ‘. Deflecting torque T_d=Gi newton meter .

where . $G=NBA=NBld$

G is called the displacement constant of the galvanometer

Controlling torque provided by spring and id proportional to angular deflection of the pointer

$Tc= K\Theta$

For final steady deflection, $Tc = T_d$ or $K\Theta= Gi$

$\Theta = Gi/K$ radian

Or i= (K/G) Θ

Swamping Resistor

The coil of the instrument is made of copper. Its resistance varies with temperature. A resistor of low temperature coefficients, called the swamping resistor, is connected in series with the coil. Its resistance practically remains constant with temperature. Hence the effect of temperature on coil resistance is swamped by this resistor.

Advantages of PMMC Instruments

1. Sensitive to small current
2. Very accurate and reliable
3. Uniform scale up to 270° or more
4. Very effective built in damping
5. Low power consumption, varies from 25 μW to 200 μW

6. Free from hysteresis and not effected by external fields because its permanent magnet shields the coil from external magnetic fields
7. Easily adopted as a multirange instrument.

Disadvantages of PMMC Instruments

1. This type of instrument can be operated in direct current only. In alternating current, the instrument does not operate because in the positive half, the pointer experiences a force in one direction and in the negative half the pointer experiences the force in the opposite direction. Due to the inertia of the pointer, it retains it's zero position.
2. The moving system is very delicate and can easily be damaged by rough handling.
3. The coil being very fine, cannot withstand prolonged overloading.
4. It is costlier.
5. The ageing of the instrument (permanent magnet and control spring) may introduce some errors.

MOVING IRON INSTRUMENTS

Basic range: 10 mA-100 A. **Usage:** dc MI ammeters and voltmeters, ac MI ammeters and voltmeters

Moving-Iron or MI instruments can be classified as

- Attraction-type moving-iron instruments
- Repulsion-type moving-iron instruments

The current to be measured, in general, is passed through a coil of wire in the moving iron instruments. In case of voltage measurement, the current which is proportional to the voltage is measured. The number of turns of the coil depends upon the current to be passed through it. For operation of the instrument, a certain number of ampere turns is required. These ampere turns can be produced by the product of few turns and large current or reverse.

Attraction-type Moving-Iron Instruments

The attraction type of MI instrument depends on the attraction of an iron vane into a coil carrying current to be measured. A soft iron vane IV is attached to the moving system. When the current to be measured is passed through the coil C, a magnetic field is produced. This field attracts the eccentrically mounted vane on the spindle towards it. The spindle is supported at the two ends on a pair of jewel bearings. Thus, the pointer

PR, which is attached to the spindle S of the moving system is deflected. The pointer moves over a calibrated scale. The control torque is provided by two hair springs S1 and S2 in the same way as for a PMMC instrument; but in such instruments springs are not used to carry any current. Gravity control can also be used for vertically mounted panel type MI meters. The damping torque is provided by the movement of a thin vane V in a closed sector-shaped box B, or simply by a vane attached to the moving system. Eddy current damping can not be used in MI instruments owing to the fact that any permanent magnet that will be required to produce Eddy current damping can distort the otherwise weak operating magnetic field produced by the coil.

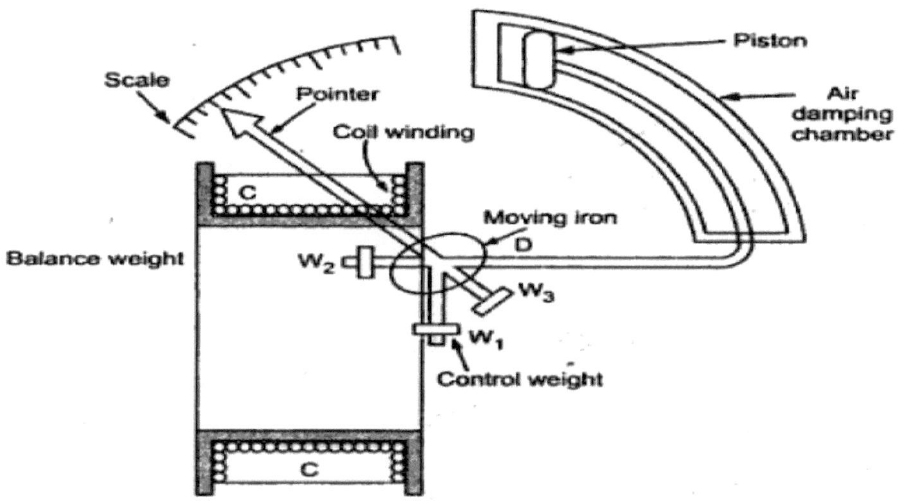

Attraction-type Moving-Iron Instruments

If the current in the fixed coil is reversed, the field produced by it also reverses. So the polarity induced on the vane reverses. Thus whatever be the direction of the current in the coil the vane is always be magnetized in such a way that it is attracted into the coil. Hence such instrument can be used for both direct current as well as alternating current.

Repulsion-type Moving-Iron Instruments

In the repulsion type, there are two vanes inside the coil. One is fixed and the other is movable. These are similarly magnetized when the current flows through the coil and there is a force of repulsion between the two vanes resulting in the movement of the moving vane.

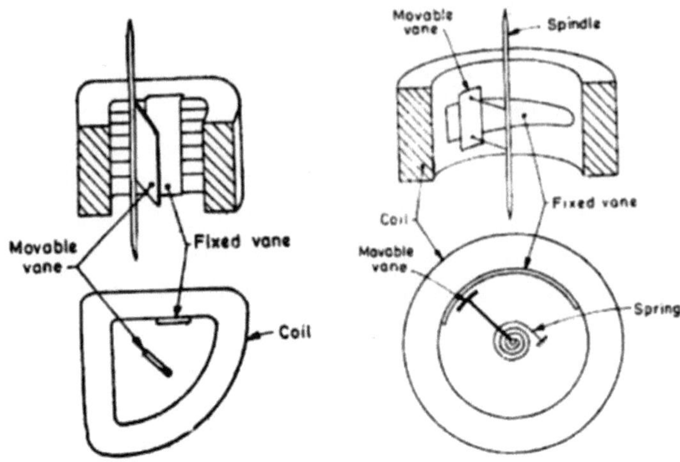

Repulsion types moving iron instruments

Two different designs for moving iron instruments commonly used are as follows:

1. Radial Vane Type In this type, the vanes is radial strips of iron. The strips are placed within the coils. The fixed vane is attached to the coil and the movable one to the spindle of the instrument. The instrument pointer is attached to the moving vane spindle.

As current flows through the coil, the generated magnetic field induces identical polarities on both the fixed and moving vane. Thus, even when the current through the coil is alternating (for AC measurement), there is always a repulsion force acting between the like poles of fixed and moving vane. Hence deflection of the pointer is always in the same direction irrespective of the polarity of current in the coil. The amount of deflection depends on the repulsion force between the vanes which in turn depends on the amount of current passing through the coil. The scale can thus be calibrated to read the current or voltage directly.

2. *Co-axial Vane Type* I In these type of instruments, the fixed and moving vanes are sections of coaxial cylinders. Current in the coil magnetizes both the vanes with similar polarity. Thus the movable vane rotates along the spindle axis due to this repulsive force. Coaxial vane type instruments are moderately sensitive as compared to radial vane type instruments that are more sensitive.

Moving iron instruments have their deflection is proportional to the square of the current flowing through the coil. These instruments are thus said to follow a square law response and have non-uniform scale marking. Deflection being proportional to square of the current, whatever be the polarity of current in the coil, deflection of a moving iron instrument is in the same direction. Hence, moving iron instruments can be used for both DC and AC measurements.

General Torque equation of Moving Iron Instruments

An expression for the torque of a moving iron instrument may be derived by considering the Energy relations when there is a small increment in current supplied to the instrument. When this happens there will be a small deflection dΘand some mechanical work will be done.

Let T_d=deflecting torque

:. Mechanical work done = $T_d\ d\Theta$

Alongside there will be a change in the energy stored owing to inductance.Suppose the initial current is I, the instrument inductance Land the deflection Θ.If the current increases by dIthen the deflection changes by dΘ and the inductance by dL.In order to effect an increment dLin the current there must be -an increase in the applied voltage given by

e =d(LI)/dt) = I(dL/dt)+L(dI/dt)

The electrical energy supplied $eIdt=I^2dL+ILdI$

The stored energy changes from=1/2 I^2L to $1/2(I+dl)^2$ (L+dL),

Hence the change in stored energy = ½(I^2 +2IdI+dI^2) (L+dL) -1/2(I^2 L)

Neglecting second and higher order terms in small quantities this becomes ILdI+(1/2)I^2dL

From the principle of conservation of energy

Electrical energy supplied = Increase in stored energy + Mechanical work done

$I^2dL+ILdI = ILdI = (1/2)\ I^2dL+ T_d\ d\Theta$

$T_d\ d\Theta = (1/2)\ I^2dL$

Thus deflecting torque $T_d = (1/2)I^2dL/d\Theta$

T is in newton-metre, *I* in ampere, *L* in henry, and Θ in radian,

The moving system is provided with control springs and it turns the deflecting torque T_d is .

balanced by the controlling torque T_c.

Controlling torque T_c. =*K*Θ

where K=control spring constant; Nm/rad, Θ=deflection; rad,

At equilibrium (or ftnal steady) position, $T_c = T_d$

$K\Theta = \frac{1}{2}(I^2)dL/d\Theta$ or deflection Θ

Hence the deflection is proportional to square of the rms value 'of the operating current.

Advantages and Disadvantages.

(1) ***Universal Use.*** These instruments can be used for both a.c and d.c.

(2) ***Less Friction Errors.*** Errors due to friction are quite small as torque-weight ratio is quite high in these instruments.

(3) ***Cheapness;*** Depending upon tho magnitude of the current to be measured, the coil may have few turns of very heavy section of conductor or many turns of fine wire so that the total mmf is required is the same for given displacement of the moving system irrespective of the instrument range. Hence identical moving system may be used for an entire series of instrument from voltmeter which require a small value of current to the highest range ammeter. Thus in a series of instrument which use an mmf of 200A at full scale the highest range ammeter could be for 200A using one turn while voltmeters of the series could 50mA with 4000 turns for full scale deflection. The .fact that a single type of moving element could cover the entire range is-one reason that moving Iron Instruments, can be built at less cost than some other types.

(4) ***Robustness:*** The instruments are robust, owing to simple construction and also that there are no current carrying moving parts.

(5) ***Accuracy.*** These instruments are capable of giving an accuracy within the limits of both precision and Industrial grades. Modern well designed portable moving iron instruments are expected to have a d.c error of 2 % or less. The initial accuracy of high grade instruments is stated to be 0'75 percent for frequencies between 25 to'135 Hz and they may be expected to be accurate with in 0.2% to 0.3% a.t 50 Hz if carefully designed.

(6)**Scale** Moving iron instruments now available 240 circular scales. The greatly increased scale, length being a certain advantage. The scale of Moving iron instruments is not uniform and is cramped at the lower end and therefor accurate reading is not possible at this end.

(7) **Errors.** These instruments are subjected to serious error due to hysteresis frequency changes and stray magnetic fields.

Errors: There are two types of errors which occur in moving iron instruments errors , which occur with both a,c). and d.c, arid the other which occur only with a.c, only.

Errors with both DC and A.C

(1)Hysteresis error. This error occurs as the value‘ of flux density is different for. the same current when ascending and descending. The value of flex density is higher for descending value of current. And therefore, the instrument tends to read higher for descending values of current (and voltage) than for ascending values . This error ean be minimized by making the iron parts small so that they demagnetize themselves quickly. Another method is to work the iron parts at low values of flux density so that the hysteresis effects are small.

Hysteresis may produce a 2 to 3 percent error. With the use .of nickel iron alloys with narrow hysteresis loops, the error may be brought down to less than 0.05 per cent.

(2) Temperature Error. The effect of temperature changes on moving iron instruments arises chiefly from the temperature coefficient of spring .The error may be 0.02 percent per °C. In volt- meters, errors are caused due to self-heating of coil and series resistance. The temperature of the coil may increase by 10 to 20 C for a power consumption of 1W. Therefore, the resistance increases (by about 4 to 8%), causing a decrease in current for a given voltage. This produces a decreased deflection. Therefore, the series resistance should be made of a material like Manganin which has a small temperature co-efficient. The value of series resistance should be very large as compared with the coil resistance in order to minimize errors due to self-heating. .In the case of switch board instruments, the series resistance is about 10 times the coil resistance.

(3) Stray Magnetic Fields.'The errors due to stray magnetic fields (fields other than the operating magnetic field) may be appreciable as the operating magnetic field is weak (about 0.006 to 0.0075 Wb/m^2 at full scale deflection) and hence can be easily distorted. Such errors depend upon the direction *of* the stray magnetic field relative to the field of the instrument, These errors can be minimized by using an iron case or a thin iron shield over the working parts.

Errors with A.C only

(1) Frequency Error

These error are related to ac operation of the instrument. The change in frequency affects the reactance of the working coil and also affects the magnitude of the eddy currents. This causes error in the instrument.

(2) Eddy current errors

When the instrument is used for ac measurement the eddy currents are produced in the iron parts of the instrument. This eddy current affects the instrument current causing change in deflecting torque. This produces error in the meter reading. As the eddy currents are frequency dependent frequency changes cause eddy current error.

Measurement of Power

A *wattmeter* is an instrument with a potential coil and a current coil so arranged that its deflection is proportional to $VI \cos \theta$, where V is the voltage (rms value) applied across the potential coil, I is the current (rms value) passing through the current coil, and θ is the angle between $\bar{V}$ and $\bar{I}$. By inserting such a single-phase wattmeter to measure the average real power in each phase (with its current coil in series with one phase of the load and its potential coil across the phase of the load), the total real power in a three-phase system can be determined by the sum of the wattmeter readings. However, in practice, this may not be possible due to the nonaccessibility of either the neutral of the wye connection, or the individual phases of the delta connection. Hence it is more desirable to have a method for measuring the total real power drawn by a three-phase load while we have access to only three line terminals.

The three-phase power can be measured by three single-phase wattmeters having current coils in each line and potential coils connected across the given line and any common junction. Since this common junction is completely arbitrary, it may be placed on any one of the three lines, in which case the wattmeter connected in that line will indicate zero power because its potential coil has no voltage across it. Hence, that wattmeter may be dispensed with, and three-phase power can be measured by means of only two single-phase wattmeters having a common potential junction on any of the three lines in which there is no current coil. This is known as the *two-wattmeter method of measuring three-phase power.* In general, m-phase power can be measured by means of $m - 1$ wattmeters. The method is valid for both balanced and unbalanced circuits with either the load or the source unbalanced.

Figure shows the connection diagram for the two-wattmeter method of measuring three-phase power. The total real power delivered to the load is given by the *algebraic sum* of the two wattmeter readings,

$$P = W_A + W_C \qquad (.1)$$

The significance of the algebraic sum will be realized in the paragraphs that follow. Two wattmeters can be connected with their current coils in any two lines, while their potential coils are connected to the third line, as shown in Figure . The wattmeter readings are given by

$$W_A = V_{AB} \cdot I_A \cdot \cos \theta_A \qquad (.2)$$

where θ_A is the angle between the phasors $\bar{V}_{AB}$ and $\bar{I}_A$, and

$$W_C = V_{CB} \cdot I_C \cdot \cos \theta_C \qquad (.3)$$

where θ_C is the angle between the phasors $\bar{V}_{CB}$ and $\bar{I}_C$.

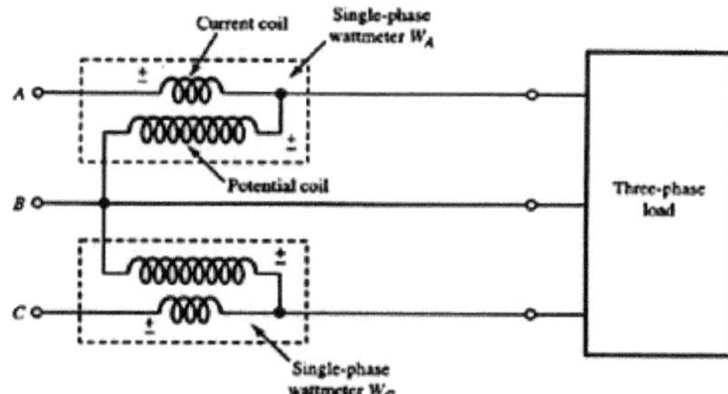

Figure. Connection diagram for two-wattmeter method of measuring three-phase power.

The two-wattmeter method, when applied to the *balanced* loads, yields interesting results. Considering either balanced wye- or delta-connected loads, with the aid of the corresponding phasor diagrams drawn earlier for the phase sequence A–B–C (Figures)..., it can be seen that the angle between $\bar{V}_{AB}$ and $\bar{I}_A$ is $(30° + \phi)$ and that between $\bar{V}_{CB}$ and $\bar{I}_C$ is $(30 - \phi)$, where ϕ is the load power factor angle, or the angle associated with the load impedance. Thus, we have

$$W_A = V_L I_L \cos(30° + \phi) \tag{.4}$$

and

$$W_C = V_L I_L \cos(30° - \phi) \tag{5}$$

where V_L and I_L are the magnitudes of the line-to-line voltage and line current, respectively. Simple manipulations yield

$$W_A + W_C = \sqrt{3}\, V_L I_L \cos\phi \tag{.6}$$

and

$$W_C - W_A = V_L I_L \sin\phi \tag{.7}$$

from which,

$$\tan\phi = \sqrt{3}\,\frac{W_C - W_A}{W_A + W_C} \tag{.8}$$

Energy Meter

Definition: The meter which is used for measuring the energy utilises by the electric load is known as the energy meter. The energy is the total power consumed and utilised by the load at a particular interval of time. It is used in domestic and industrial AC circuit for measuring the power consumption. The meter is less expensive and accurate.

SINGLE PHASE ENERGY METER

The induction type single phase energy meters are universally used for energy measurements in domestic and industrial establishments since they possess some of the very useful features such as :

- Accurate characteristics
- Lower friction
- Higher torque weight ratio
- Cheaper manufacturing methods and
- Ease of maintenance.

Constructional Details :

The energy meter has four main parts. They are the

1. Driving System
2. Moving System
3. Braking System
4. Registering System

The detail explanation of their parts is written below.

1. Driving System – The electromagnet is the main component of the driving system. It is the temporary magnet which is excited by the current flow through their coil. The core of the electromagnet is made up of silicon steel lamination. The driving system has two electromagnets. The upper one is called the shunt electromagnet, and the lower one is called series electromagnet.

The series electromagnet is excited by the load current flow through the current coil. The coil of the shunt electromagnet is directly connected with the supply and hence carry the current proportional to the shunt voltage. This coil is called the pressure coil.

The centre limb of the magnet has the copper band. These bands are adjustable. The main function of the copper band is to align the flux produced by the shunt magnet in such a way that it is exactly perpendicular to the supplied voltage.

2. Moving System – The moving system is the aluminium disc mounted on the shaft of the alloy. The disc is placed in the air gap of the two electromagnets. The eddy current is induced in the disc because of the change of the magnetic field. This eddy current is cut by the magnetic flux. The interaction of the flux and the disc induces the deflecting torque.

When the devices consume power, the aluminium disc starts rotating, and after some number of rotations, the disc displays the unit used by the load. The number of rotations of the disc is counted at particular interval of time. The disc measured the power consumption in kilowatt hours.

3. Braking system – The permanent magnet is used for reducing the rotation of the aluminium disc. The aluminium disc induces the eddy current because of their rotation. The eddy current cut the magnetic flux of the permanent magnet and hence produces the braking torque.

This braking torque opposes the movement of the disc, thus reduces their speed. The permanent magnet is adjustable due to which the braking torque is also adjusted by shifting the magnet to the other radial position.

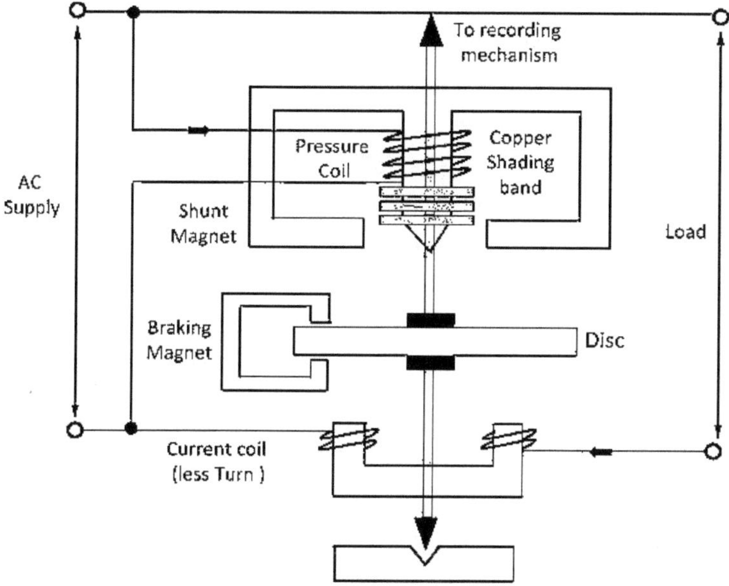

Induction type Energy meter

4. Registration (Counting Mechanism) – The main function of the registration or counting mechanism is to record the number of rotations of the aluminium disc. Their rotation is directly proportional to the energy consumed by the loads in the kilowatt hour.

The rotation of the disc is transmitted to the pointers of the different dial for recording the different readings. The reading in kWh is obtained by multiply the number of rotations of the disc with the meter constant.

Working of the Energy Meter

The energy meter has the aluminium disc whose rotation determines the power consumption of the load. The disc is placed between the air gap of the series and shunt electromagnet. The shunt magnet has the pressure coil, and the series magnet has the current coil.

The pressure coil creates the magnetic field because of the supply voltage, and the current coil produces it because of the current.

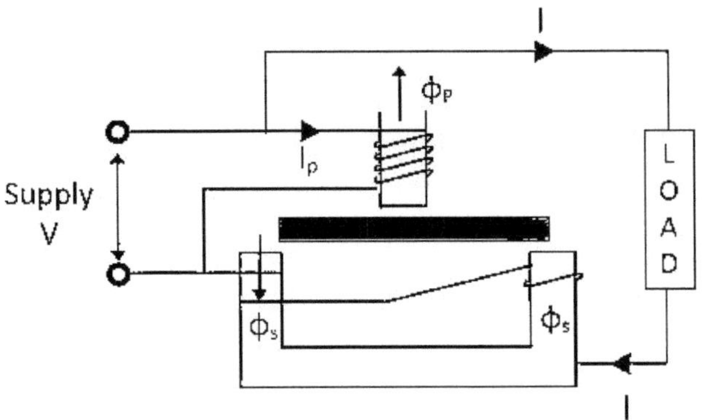

Working of an energy meter

The field induces by the voltage coil is lagging by 90° on the magnetic field of the current coil because of which eddy current induced in the disc. The interaction of the eddy current and the magnetic field causes torque, which exerts a force on the disc. Thus, the disc starts rotating.

The force on the disc is proportional to the current and voltage of the coil. The permanent magnet controls Their rotation. The permanent magnet opposes the movement of the disc and equalises it on the power consumption. The cyclometer counts the rotation of the disc.

Theory of Energy Meter

The pressure coil has the number of turns which makes it more inductive. The reluctance path of their magnetic circuit is very less because of the small length air gap. The current Ip flows through the pressure coil because of the supply voltage, and it lags by 90°

The Ip produces the two Φp which is again divided into Φp1 a.nd Φp2. The major portion of the flux Φp1 passes through the side gap because of low reluctance. The flux Φp2 goes through the disc and induces the driving torque which rotates the aluminium disc.

The flux Φp is proportional to the applied voltage, and it is lagged by an angle of 90º. The flux is alternating and hence induces an eddy current Iep in the disc.

The load current passes through the current coil induces the flux Φs. This flux causes the eddy current Ies on the disc. The eddy current Ies interacts with the flux Φp, and the eddy current Iep interacts with Φs to produce the another torque. These torques are opposite in direction, and the net torque is the difference between these two.

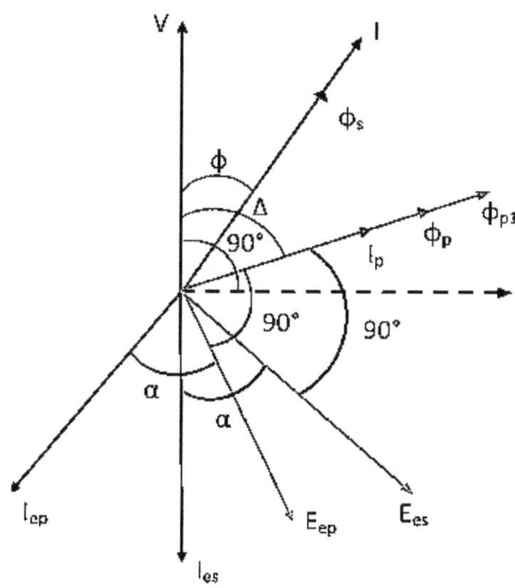

Phasor diagram

Let

V – applied voltage

I – load current

∅ – the phase angle of load current

Ip – pressure angle of load

Δ – the phase angle between supply voltage and pressure coil flux

f – frequency

Z – impedance of eddy current

∝ – the phase angle of eddy current paths

Eep – eddy current induced by flux

Iep – eddy current due to flux

Eev – eddy current due to flux
Ies – eddy current due to flux

The net driving torque of the dis is expressed as

where K1 – constant

Φ1 and Φ2 are the phase angle between the fluxes. For energy meter, we take Φp and Φs.

β – phase angle between fluxes Φp and Φp = (Δ – Φ), therefore

If f, Z and α are constants,

If N is steady speed, braking torque

At steady state, the speed of the driving torque is equal to the braking torque.

If Δ = 90º,

Speed,

The speed of the rotation is directly proportional to the power.

If Δ = 90º, total number of revolutions

The three phase energy meter is used for measuring the large power consumption.

Three Phase Energy Meter

Definition: The meter which is used for measuring the power of three phase supply is known as the three phase energy meter. The three phase meter is constructed by connecting the two single phase meter through the shaft. The total energy is the sum of the reading of both the elements.

Working Principle of Three Phase Energy Meter

The torque of both the elements is added mechanically, and the total rotation of the shaft is proportional to the three phase energy consumption.

Construction of Three Phase Energy Meter

The three phase energy meter has two discs mounted on the common shaft. Both the disc has its braking magnet, copper ring, shading band and the compensator for getting the correct reading. The two elements are used for measuring the three phase power. The construction of the three phase meter is shown in the figure below.

For three phase meter, the driving torque of both the elements is equal. This can be done by adjusting the torque. The torque is adjusted by connecting the current coils of both the elements in the series and their potential coils in parallel. The full load current is passed through the coil due to which the two opposite torque is set up in the coil.

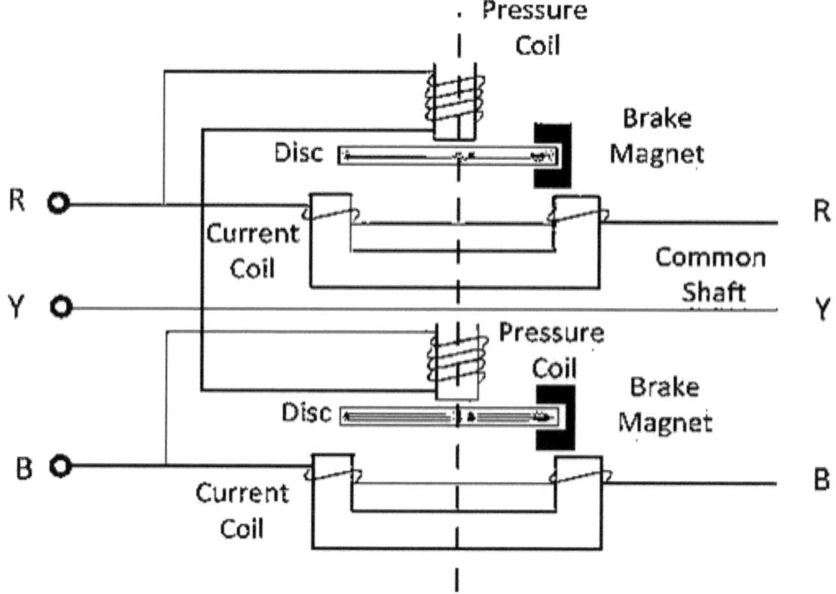

Three phase energy meter

The strength of both the torques are equal, and hence they do not allow the disc to rotate. If the torque becomes unequal and the disc rotates then the magnetic shunt is adjusted. The balance torque is obtained before testing the meter. The position of the compensator and the braking magnet are separately adjusted to each of the element for obtaining the balance torque.

INSTRUMENT TRANSFORMERS

Transformers are used in a c. systems for the measurement of current, voltage, power and energy. They are also used in connection with measurement of power factor, frequency and for indication of synchronism. Transformers find wide application in protection circuits of power systems for the operation of over current, under voltage and various other types of relays. In all the above applications, the transformer is put for measurement purposes the actual measurements being done by measuring instruments. Transformers used in conjunction with measuring instruments for measurement purposes are called "Instrument Transformers". The transformer used for measurement of current is called a "Current Transformer" or simply "C T" Transformers for voltage measurement are called "Voltage Transformers" or "Potential Transformers or simply "P.T." for short.

Instrument Transformers are used in AC system for measurement of electrical quantities i.e. voltage, current, power, energy, power factor, frequency. Instrument transformers are also used with protective relays for protection of power system. Basic function of Instrument transformers is to step down the AC System voltage and current. The voltage and current level of power system is very high. It is very difficult and costly to design the measuring instruments for measurement of such high level voltage and current. Generally measuring instruments are designed for 5 A and 110 V.

The measurement of such very large electrical quantities, can be made possible by using the Instrument transformers with these small rating measuring instruments.Therefore these instrument transformers are very popular in modern power system.

It might appear that extension of range could be conveniently, done by the use of shunts for currents, and multipliers for voltage measurements, as is done in dc, measurements. But, this method, is suitable only for small values of current and voltage. There are certain disadvantages with the use of shunts and multiplier

Disadvantages of Shunts.

i. It is difficult to achieve accuracy, with a shunt on ac, since division of current between a meter and shunt depends upon the reactance and resistance of two paths. For proper measurements, time constants of meter and shunt should be the same. Therefore, a separate shunt would be needed for each instrument. Also since measurements are made over a wide frequency range it becomes difficult to obtain good accuracy with shunts.
ii. The shunt method is limited to capacities of a few hundred ampere at most, since the power consumed by shunts at large currents would be considerable large.
iii. The problem of insulation of instrument and shunt is quite difficult to solve if measurements are done at high voltages of several hundred or thousand volt above ground.
iv. The measuring circuit is not isolated electrically from the power circuit.

Disadvantages of Multipliers. Multipliers for voltage measurements do not present any serious difficulties below 1000 V. But their use above this limit becomes impractical owing to the following reasons.

i. The power consumed by multipliers becomes large as the voltage increases. A power dissipation of about 7.5W is the upper limit for a self-contained instrument.
ii. Care has to be exercised to keep leakage currents to high voltage multipliers down to negligible values. However, insulation of multipliers required to prevent leakage currents and the reduction of distributed capacitance to avoid shunt capacitance currents becomes very difficult above a few thousand volt. Special types of construction are needed to prevent the above effects. Hence the construction of multipliers for use at high voltages is very costly and complicated.
iii. The measuring circuit Is not electrically isolated from the power circuit.

Advantages of Instrument Transformers

i. Using shunts for extension of range on ammeters in ac circuits will require careful designing of the reactance and resistance proportions for the shunt and the meter. Any deviation from the designed time constants of the shunt and the meter may lead to errors in measurement. This problem is not present with CT being used with ammeter.
ii. Shunts cannot be used for circuits involving large current; otherwise the power loss in the shunt itself will become prohibitably high.
iii. Multipliers, once again, due to inherent leakage current, can introduce errors in measurement, and can also result in unnecessary heating due to power loss.
iv. Measuring circuits involving shunts or multipliers, being not electrically isolated from the power circuit, are not only safe for the operator, but also insulation requirements are exceedingly high in high-voltage measurement applications.
v. High voltages can be stepped down by the PT to a moderate level as can be measured by standard instruments without posing much danger for the operator and also not requiring too much insulation for the measuring instrument.
vi. Single range moderate size instruments can be used to cover a wide range of measurement, when used with a suitable multi-range CT or PT.

vii. Clamp-on type or split-core type CT's can be very effectively used to measure current without the need for breaking the main circuit for inserting the CT primary winding.

viii. Instrument transformers can help in reducing overall cost, since various instruments, including metering, relaying, diagnostic, and indicating instruments can all be connected to the same instrument transformer.

Types of Instrument Transformers

Instrument transformers are of two types –

transformer (C.T.)

Potential transformer (P.T.)

Ratios: There are some definitions which must be given here

Transformation Ratio. It is the ratio of the magnitude of the Primary phasor to the secondary phasor Transformation ratio R = | primary phasor| / | secondary phasor |

Transformation ratio R for C T = primary current / secondary current

Transformation ratio R for P T = primary voltage / secondary voltage

Nominal Ratio, .It is the ratio of rated primary current (or voltage) to the rated secondary current (or voltage).

Nominal ratio Kn = rated primary current / rated secondary current for CT = rated primary voltage / rated secondary voltage for PT

Turns Ratio. Turns Ratio for CT is n = Number of turns of secondary winding /

Number of turns of primary winding.

Turns Ratio for PT is n = Number of turns of primary winding / Number of turns of secondary winding

Ratio Correction Factor (RCF) The ratio correction factor of a transformer is the transformation ratio divided by nominal ratio.

Transformation ratio = ratio correction factor x nominal ratio RCF = R/ Kn

The ratio marked on the transformers is their nominal ratio.

Burden: it is convenient to express load across the secondary terminals as the output in volt – ampere at the rated secondary voltage. The rated burden is the volt-ampere loading which is permissible without errors exceeding the limits for the particular class of accuracy.

Total secondary burden = (secondary induced voltage)^2 /(impedance of secondary circuit including impedance of secondary winding

= (secondary current)^2 x (impedance of secondary circuit including secondary winding)

Secondary burden due to load = (secondary terminal voltage)^2 /(impedance of load on secondary winding)

CURRENT TRANSFORMER (C.T.)

Definition: A current transformer is a device that is used for the transformation of current from a higher value into a proportionate current to a lower value. It transforms the high voltage current into the low voltage current due to which the heavy current flows through the transmission lines is safely monitored by the ammeter.

The current transformer is used with the AC instrument, meters or control apparatus where the current to be measured is of such magnitude that the meter or instrument coil cannot conveniently be made of sufficient current carrying capacity.

The primary and secondary current of the current transformers are proportional to each other. The current transformer is used for measuring the high voltage current because of the difficulty of inadequate insulation in the meter itself. The current transformer is used in meters for measuring the current up to 100 amperes.

Construction of Current Transformers

The core of the current transformer is built up with lamination of silicon steel. For getting a high degree of accuracy the Permalloy or Mumetal is used for the making cores. The primary windings of the current transformers carry the current which is to be measured, and it is connected to the main circuit. The secondary windings of the transformer carry the current proportional to the current to be measured, and it is connected to the current windings of the meters or the instruments.

The primary and the secondary windings are insulated from the cores and each other. The primary winding is a single turn winding (also called a bar primary) and carries the full load current. The secondary winding of the transformers has a large number of turns.

The ratio of the primary current and the secondary current is known as a current transformer ratio of the circuit. The current ratio of the transformer is usually high. The secondary current ratings are of the order of 5A, 1A and 0.1A. The current primary ratings vary from 10A to 3000A or more.

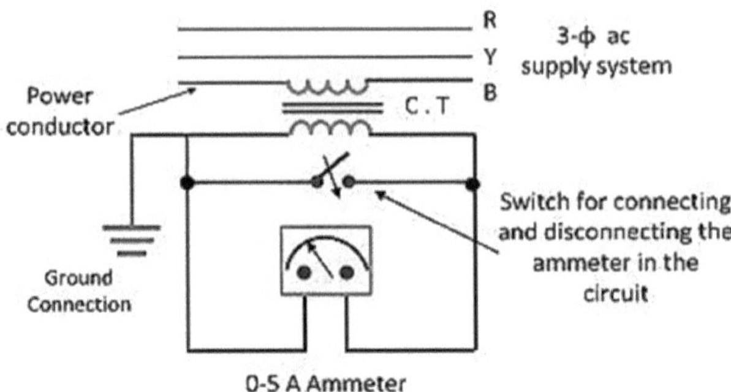

Current Transformer

The working principle of the current transformer is slightly different from the power transformer. In a current transformer, the load's impedance or burden on the secondary has slightly differed from the power transformers. Thus, the current transformer operates on secondary circuit conditions.

Burden on a Load

The burden of a current transformer is the value of the load connected across the secondary transformer. It is expressed as the output in volt-amperes (VA). The rated burden is the value of the burden on the nameplate of the CT. The rated burden is the product of the voltage and current on the secondary when the CT supplies the instrument or relay with its maximum rated value of current.

Effect of Open Secondary Windings of a CT

Under normal operating conditions the secondary winding of a CT is connected to its burden, and it is always closed. When the current flows through the primary windings, it always flows through secondary windings and amperes turns of each winding are subsequently equal and opposite.

The secondary turns will be 1% and 2% less than the primary turns and the difference being used in the magnetising core. Thus, if the secondary winding is opened and the current flows through the primary windings, then there will be no demagnetizing flux due to the secondary current.

Due to the absence of the counter ampere turns of the secondary, the unopposed primary MMF will set up an abnormally high flux in the core. This flux will produce core loss with subsequent heating, and a high voltage will be induced across the secondary terminal.

This voltage caused the breakdown of the insulation and also the loss of accuracy in the future may occur because the excessive MMF leaves the residual magnetism in the core. Thus, the secondary of the CT may never be open when the primary is carrying the current.

Phasor Diagram of Current Transformer

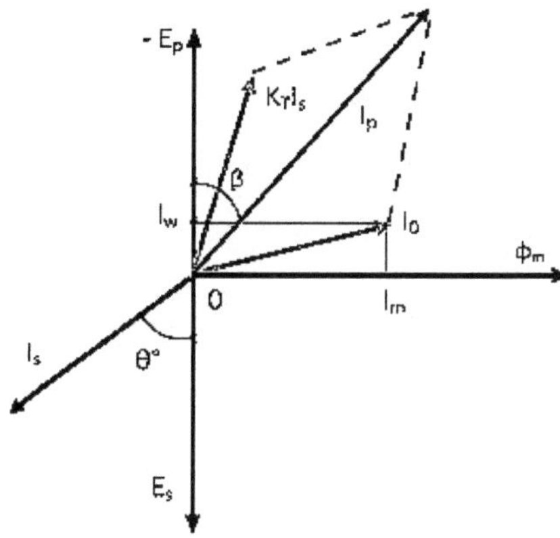

Phasor diagram of CT

The phasor diagram of the current transformer is shown in the figure . The main flux is taken as a reference. The primary and secondary induced voltages are lagging behind the main flux by 90°. The magnitude of the primary and secondary voltages depends on the number of turns on the windings. The excitation current induces by the components of magnetising and working current.

where, Is – secondary current
Es – secondary induced voltage
Ip -primary current
Ep – primary induced voltage
Kt – turn ratio, number of secondary turn/number of primary turn
I0 – excitation current
Im – magnetising current
Iw – working component
Φs – main flux

The secondary current lags behinds the secondary induced voltage by an angle θ°. The secondary current relocates to the primary side by reversing the secondary current and multiply by the turn ratio. The current flows through the primary is the sum of the exciting current I0 and the product of the turn ratio and secondary current Kt Is.

Ratio and Phase Angle Errors of CT

The current transformer has two errors – ratio error and a phase angle error.

Current Ratio Errors – The current transformer is mainly due to the energy component of excitation current and is given as

Ratio Error=(KtIs-Ip)/Ip

Where Ip is the primary current. Kt is the turn ratio and is the secondary current.

Phase Angle Error – In an ideal current transformer the vector angle between the primary and reversed secondary current is zero. But in an actual current transformer, there is a phase difference between the primary and the secondary current because the primary current has also supplied the component of exciting current. Thus, the difference between the two phases is termed as a phase angle error.

Potential Transformer (PT)

Definition – The potential transformer may be defined as an instrument transformer used for the transformation of voltage from a higher value to the lower value. This transformer step down the voltage to a safe limit value which can be easily measured by the ordinary low voltage instrument like a voltmeter, wattmeter and watt-hour meters, etc.

Construction of Potential Transformer

The potential transformer is made with high-quality core operating at low flux density so that the magnetising current is small. The terminal of the transformer should be designed so that the variation of the voltage ratio with load is minimum and the phase shift between the input and output voltage is also minimum.

The primary winding has a large number of turns, and the secondary winding has a much small number of turns. For reducing the leakage reactance, the co-axial winding is used in the potential transformer. The insulation cost is also reduced by dividing the primary winding into the sections which reduced the insulation between the layers.

Connection of Potential Transformer

The potential transformer is connected in parallel with the circuit. The primary windings of the potential transformer are directly connected to the power circuit whose voltage is to be measured. The secondary terminals of the potential transformer are connected to the measuring instrument like the voltmeter, wattmeter, etc.The secondary windings of the potential transformer are magnetically coupled through the magnetic circuit of the primary windings.

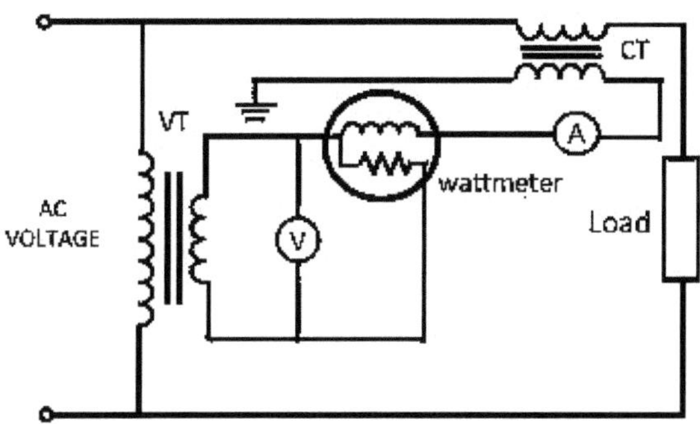

Connection of potential transformer

The primary terminal of the transformer is rated for 400V to several thousand volts, and the secondary terminal is always rated for 400V. The ratio of the primary voltage to the secondary voltage is termed as transformation ratio or turn ratio.

Ratio and Phase Angle Errors of Potential Transformer

In an ideal potential transformer, the primary and the secondary voltage is exactly proportional to the primary voltage and exactly in phase opposition. But this cannot be achieved practically due to the primary and secondary voltage drops. Thus, both the primary and secondary voltage is introduced in the system.

Voltage Ratio Error – The voltage ratio error is expressed in regarding measured voltage, and it is given by the formula as shown below.

Ratio Error=(KtIs-Ip)/Ip

Where Ip is the primary current. Kt is the turn ratio and is the secondary current.

Phase Angle Error – The phase angle error is the error between the secondary terminal voltage which is exactly in phase opposition with the primary terminal voltage.

The increases in the number of instruments in the relay connected to the secondary of the potential transformer will increase the errors in the potential transformers.

Burden of a Potential Transformer

The burden is the total external volt-amp load on the secondary at rated secondary voltage. The rated burden of a PT is a VA burden which must not be exceeded if the transformer is to operate with its rated accuracy.The rated burden is indicated on the nameplate.

The limiting or maximum burden is the greatest VA load at which the potential transformer will operate continuously without overheating its windings beyond the permissible limits. This burden is several times greater than the rated burden.

Phasor Diagram of a Potential Transformer

The phasor diagram of the potential transformer is shown in the figure below.

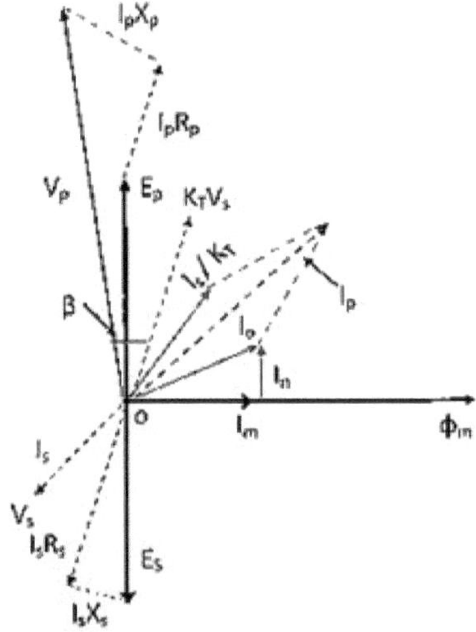

Phasor diagram of the potential transformer

Where, Is – secondary current

Es – secondary induced emf

Vs – secondary terminal voltage

Rs – secondary winding resistance

Xs – secondary winding reactance

Ip – Primary current
Ep – primarily induced emf
Vp – primary terminal voltage
Rp – primary winding resistance
Xp – primary winding reactance
Kt – turn ratio
Io – excitation current
Im – magnetising component of Io
Iw – core loss component of Io
Φm – main flux
B- phase angle errorThe main flux is taken as a reference. In instrument transformer, the primary current is the vector sum of the excitation current Io and the current equal to the reversal secondary current Is multiplied by the ratio of 1/kt. The Vp is the voltage applied to the primary terminal of the potential transformer.

The voltage drops due to resistance and reactance of primary winding due to primary current is given by IpXp and IpRp. When the voltage drop subtracts from the primary voltage of the potential transformer, the primarily induced emf will appear across the terminals.

This primary emf of the transformer will transform into secondary winding by mutual induction and converted into secondary induced emf Es. This emf will drop by the secondary winding resistance and reactance, and the resultant voltage will appear across the secondary terminal voltage, and it is denoted by Vs.

Applications of Potential Transformer

- It is used for a metering purpose.
- For the protection of the feeders.
- For protecting the impedance of the generators.
- For synchronising the generators and feeders.

The potential transformers are used in the protecting relaying scheme because the potential coils of the protective device are not directly connected to the system in case of the high voltage. Therefore, it is necessary to step down the voltage and also to insulate the protective equipment from the primary circuit.

Digital Storage Oscilloscope

Definition: The digital storage oscilloscope is defined as the oscilloscope which stores and analysis the signal digitally, i.e. in the form of 1 or 0 preferably storing them as analogue signals. The digital oscilloscope takes an input signal, store them and then display it on the screen. The digital oscilloscope has advanced features of storage, triggering and measurement. Also, it displays the signal visually as well as numerically.

Working Principle of Digital Storage Oscilloscope

The digital oscilloscope digitises and stores the input signal. This can be done by the use of CRT (Cathode ray tube) and digital memory. The block diagram of the basic digital oscilloscope is shown in the figure below. The digitisation can be done by taking the sample input signals at periodic waveforms.

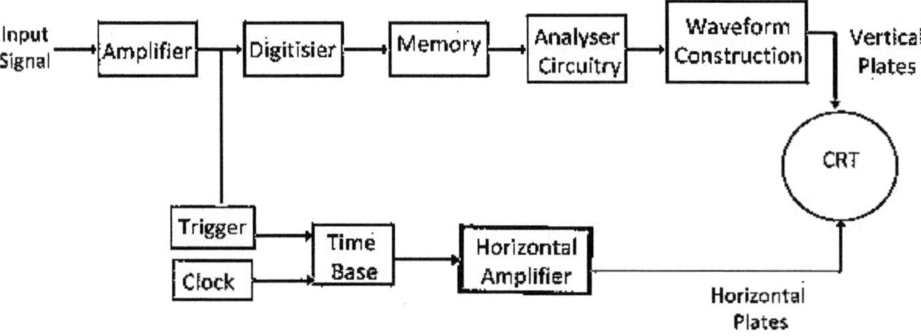

Block Diagram of Digital Storage Oscilloscope or Digital CRO

The maximum frequency of the signal which is measured by the digital oscilloscope depends on the two factors. Theses factors are the

1. Sampling rate
2. Nature of converter.

Sampling Rate – For safe analysis of input signal the sampling theory is used. The sampling theory states that the sampling rate of the signal must be twice as fast as the highest frequency of the input signal. The sampling rate means analogue to digital converter has a high fast conversion rate.

Converter – The converter uses the expensive flash whose resolution decreases with the increases of a sampling rate. Because of the sampling rate, the bandwidth and resolution of the oscilloscope are limited.

The need of the analogue to digital signal converters can also be overcome by using the shift register. The input signal is sampled and stored in the shift register. From the shift register, the signal is slowly read out and stored in the digital form. This method reduces the cost of the converter and operates up to 100 megasample per second.

The only disadvantage of the digital oscilloscope is that it does not accept the data during digitisation, so it had a blind spot at that time.

Waveform Reconstruction

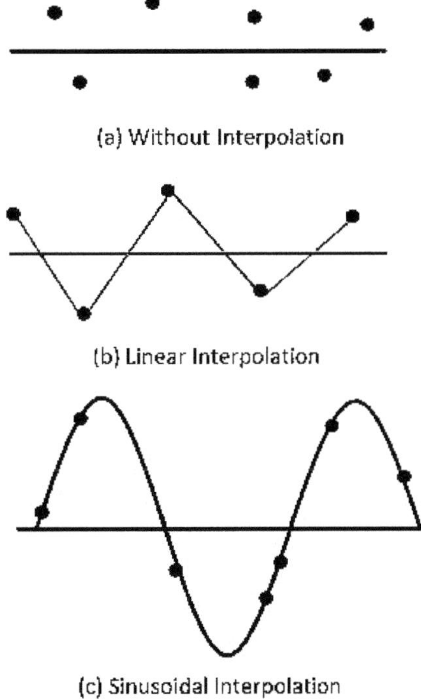

Wave form reconstrution

For visualising the final wave, the oscilloscopes use the technique of inter-polarization. The inter-polarization is the process of creating the new data points with the help of known variable data points. Linear interpolation and sinusoidal interpolation are the two processes of connecting the points together.

In interpolation, the lines are used for connecting the dot together. Linear interpolation is also used for creating the pulsed or square waveform. For sine waveform, the sinusoidal interpolation is utilised in the oscilloscope.

Data acquisition system

Data acquisition system (DAS) is a computerized system that collects data from the real world, converts it into the form of electrical signals and do required processing on it for storage, and presentation on computers.

The complete system is controlled and operated by a software application. This software application is developed by using general-purpose high-level programming languages like C, C++, java, etc.

These systems are used in industrial and commercial fields. They are used for collecting, storing and processing of data.

The data acquisition system can be divided into two types:

- Analog data acquisition system
- Digital data acquisition system

The analog data acquisition system gives an analog output whereas the digital data acquisition system gives a digital output.

Analog DAS is used when wide frequency width is required or when lower accuracies can be tolerated.

Digital DAS is used when physical quantity being monitored has a narrow bandwidth (i.e. when the quantity varies slowly). Also, high accuracy and low per channel cost are required. These are more complex than analog DAS.

The digital data have more advantages over analog data. Some of those are:

- easy and fast processing,
- easy and fast transmission,
- easy display,
- less storage space is required,

- more accurate.

Due to these advantages, mostly the digital data acquisition system is preferred.

Data Acquisition System Block Diagram

A generalized data acquisition system block diagram is shown in Figure.

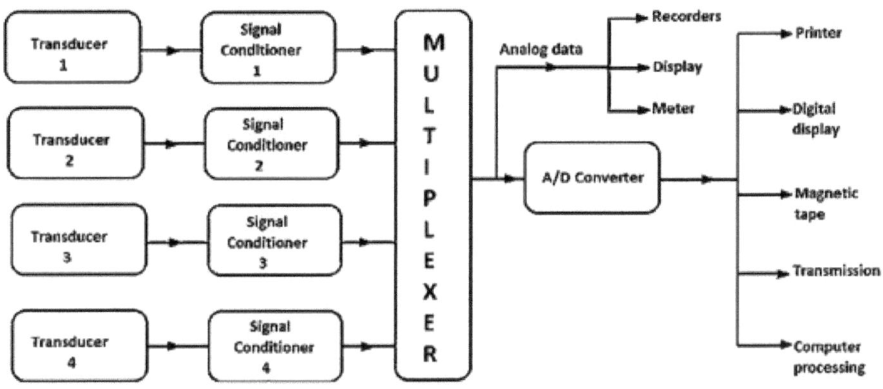

Generalized data acquisition system

The function of each block is as under:

Transducers: They are converting physical quantities (such as temperature, pressure, etc.) into electrical quantities, or measuring electrical quantities directly. They collect data from the physical world.

The most commonly used transducers are:

- RTDs, thermocouples, and thermistors for temperature measurements.
- Photosensors for light measurements.
- Strain gages, piezoelectric transducers for force and pressure measurements.
- Microphone for sound measurements.
- Potentiometer, LVDT, optical encoder for position and displacement measurements.

Signal Conditioning Unit: The signal produced by the transducers may or may not be very suitable for our system to work properly. It may be very weak, very strong or may have some noise.To convert this signal into the most suitable form, amplification, and filtration is done respectively by signal conditioning unit. So the signal conditioning unit converts electrical signals in the most suitable form.

Multiplexer: The multiplexer receives multiple analog inputs and provides a single output signal according to the requirements.If a separate channel is used for each quantity, the cost of installation, maintenance, and periodic replacement becomes high. Therefore, a single channel is used which is shared by various quantities.

Analog to Digital (A/D) Converters: The data is converted into digital form by A/D converters.After the conversion of data into digital form, it is displayed with the help of oscilloscopes, numerical displays, panel meters to monitor the complete system.

Also, the data can be either permanently or temporarily stored or recorded according to the requirement. The data is recorded on optical, ultraviolet, stylus or ink recorders for future use.

Objectives of Data Acquisition System

- It must collect the necessary data at the correct speed.
- It must use all the data efficiently to inform the operator about the state of the system.
- It must monitor the complete system operation to maintain on-line optimum and safe operations.
- It must be able to summarize and store data for the diagnosis of operation and record purpose.
- It must be flexible for future requirements.
- It must be reliable and not have a downtime of more than 0.1%.
- It must provide an effective communication system.

Applications of Data Acquisition System

The data acquisition system is used in industrial and scientific fields like aerospace, biomedical and telemetry industries.

CHAPTER FIVE

BASICS OF POWER SYSTEMS

Structure Of Electrical Power System

Electricity is generated at central power stations and then transferred to loads (i.e, Domestic, Commercial and Industrial) through the transmission and distribution system. A combination of all these systems is collectively known as an Electric Power System.

A power system is a combination of central generating stations, electric power transmission system, Distribution and utilization system.

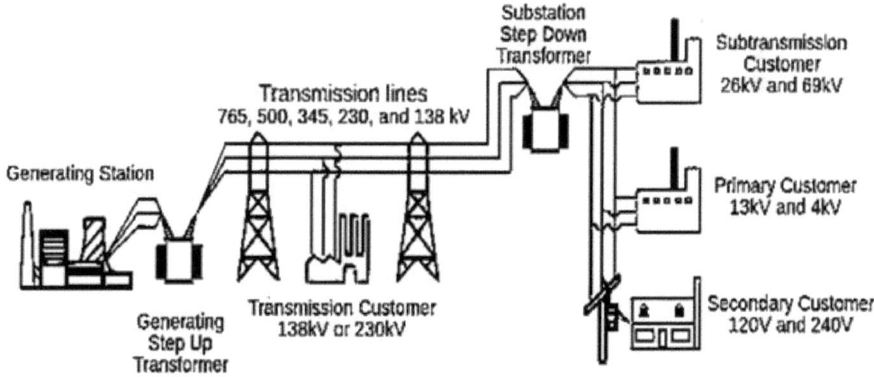

Basic Structure of an Electric Power System(Energy Supply System)

An electric supply system consists of three principal components viz., the power station, the transmission lines and the distribution system.

Electric power is produced at the power stations which are located at favourable places, generally quite away from the consumers. It is then transmitted over large distances to load centres with the help of conductors known as transmission lines. Finally, it is distributed to a large number of small and big consumers through a distribution network, supply system can be broadly classified into (i) d.c. or a.c. system (ii) overhead or underground system.

Nowadays, 3-phase, 3-wire AC system is universally adopted for generation and transmission of electric power as an economical proposition. However, distribution of electric power is done by 3-phase, 4-wire a.c. system. The underground system is more expensive than the overhead system. Therefore, the overhead system is mostly adopted for transmission and distribution of electric power.

Typical AC Power Supply in a Power System

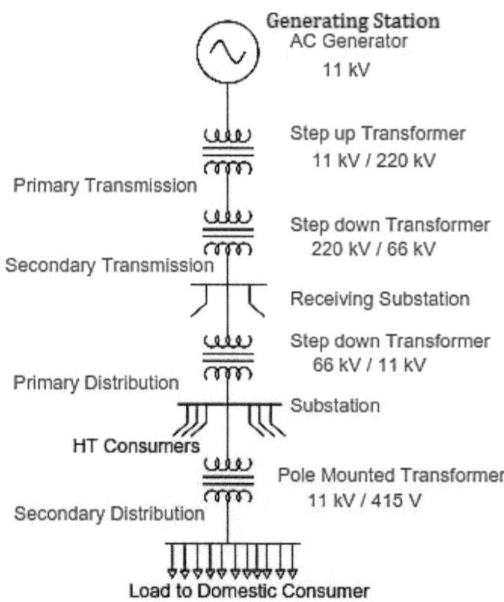

Single Line Diagram of Power Supply System

The large network of conductors between the power station and the consumers can be broadly divided into two parts viz., transmission system and distribution system. Each part can be further sub-divided into two—primary transmission and secondary transmission and primary distribution and secondary distribution. In Figure the layout of a typical AC power supply scheme in a power system is shown by a single line diagram. It may be noted that it is not necessary that all power schemes include all the stages shown in the figure. For example, in a certain power scheme, there may be no secondary transmission and in another case, the scheme may be so small that there is only distribution and no transmission.

Generating Stations

Energy is generated (transformed from one to another) at the generating stations. Generating stations are of different type, for example, thermal, hydel, solar power sations, nuclear. The generated electricity is stepped up through the transformer and then transferred over transmission lines to the load centres.

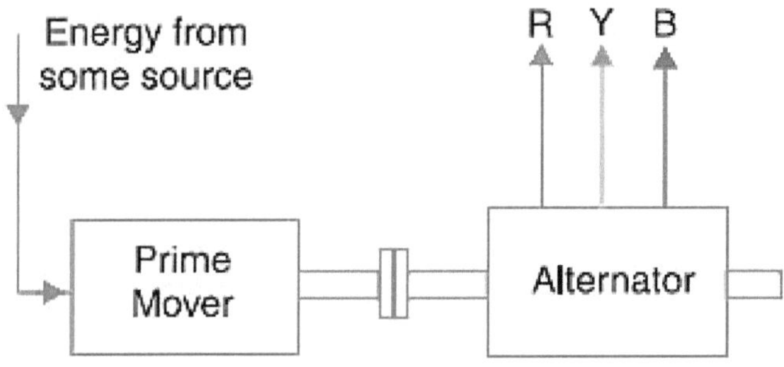

Energy Conversion Process

In Fig. , Generating Station represents the generating station where electric power is produced by 3-phase alternators operating in parallel. The usual generation voltage is †11 kV. For economy in the transmission of electric power, the generation voltage (i.e., 11 kV) is stepped upto 132 kV at the generating station with the help of 3-phase transformers. The transmission of electric power at high voltages has several advantages including the saving of conductor material and high transmission efficiency.

It may appear advisable to use the highest possible voltage for transmission of electric power to save conductor material and have other advantages. But there is a limit to which this voltage can be increased. It is because the increase in transmission voltage introduces insulation problems as well as the cost of switchgear and transformer equipment is increased. Therefore, the choice of proper transmission voltage is essentially a question of economics. Generally, the primary transmission is carried at 66 kV, 132 kV, 220 kV or 400 kV.

Primary transmission

The electric power at 132 kV is transmitted by 3-phase, 3-wire overhead system to the outskirts of the city. This forms the primary transmission.

Secondary transmission

The primary transmission line terminates at the receiving station (RS) which usually lies atthe outskirts of the city. At the receiving station, the voltage is reduced to 33kV by step-down transformers. From this station, electric power is transmitted at 33kV by 3-phase, 3-wire overhead system to various sub-stations (SS) located at the strategic points in the city. This forms the secondary transmission.

Primary distribution

The secondary transmission line terminates at the sub-station (SS) where voltage is reduced from 33 kV to 11kV, 3-phase, 3-wire. The 11 kV lines run along the important road sides of the city. This forms the primary distribution. It may be noted that big consumers (having demand more than 50 kW) are generally supplied power at 11 kV for further handling with their own sub-stations.

Secondary distribution

In the last stage in a Power System, the electric power from primary distribution line (11 kV) is delivered to distribution sub-stations (DS) or Distribution Transformer. These sub-stations are located near the consumers' localities and step down the voltage to 400 V, 3-phase, 4-wire for secondary distribution. The voltage between any two phases is 400 V and between any phase and neutral is 230 V. The single-phase residential lighting load is connected between any one phase and neutral, whereas 3-phase, 400 V motor load is connected across 3-phase lines directly. It may be worthwhile to mention here that secondary distribution system consists of feeders, distributors and service mains.

Voltages in Power Transmission Lines or Transmission Voltages

In electrical generating power stations, electrical power is generated at medium voltage level that ranges from 11 kV to 25 kV.

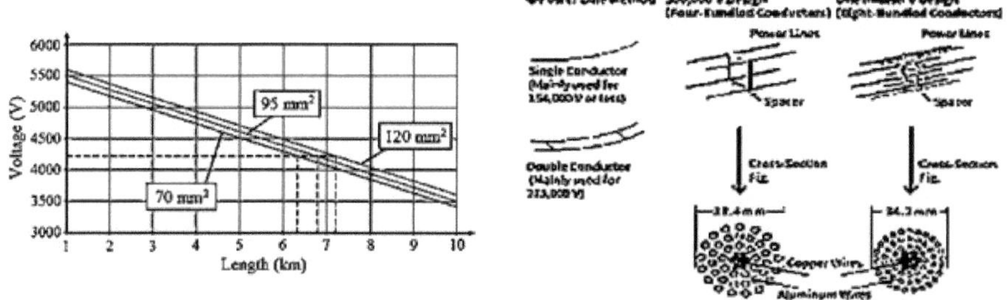

Voltages in Power transmission lines

This generated power is sent to the generating step up transformer to make the voltage level higher. From this point to the user end voltage level varies in different levels. We can realize this voltage level variation step by step.

- At 11 kV or more than that up to 25 kV voltage level is maintained at alternator stator terminals to generate electrical power in the generating station.
- This generated power is fed to the generating step up transformer to make this medium voltage level to higher level, i.e. up to 33 kV.
- Power at 33 kV is sent to the generating substation. There the transformer increases the voltage level to 66 kV or 132 kV.
- From this generating substation power is sent to the nearer substation to increase the voltage level higher than previous. This level of voltage is increased at different suitable levels, it may be at 400 kV or 765 kV or 1000 kV. This high voltage or extra high voltage level is maintained to transmit the power to a long distant substation. It is called primary transmission of power.
- At the end point of primary transmission of power, in the substation, the step down transformers are used to step down the voltage level to 132 kV. Secondary transmission of power starts from this substation.
- Power transformer at the end of the secondary transmission, just makes 132 kV voltage level steps down to 33 kv or 11 kV as per requirement. From this point, the primary distribution of power starts to distribute power to different distribution stations.

- At the end of the primary distribution, the distribution stations receive this power and step down this voltage level of 11 kV or 33 kV to 415 V (Line Voltage). From these distribution stations to consumer ends, 415 V is kept to sustain for utilization purpose.

From the very beginning of power generation to the user end transmission lines are broadly classified based on different voltage levels

Voltage Level	Value Level Mark	System	Valid Section
Low Voltage Level	Below 1000V	AC	Secondary distribution
Medium Voltage Level	1000V to 69kV	AC	Primary distribution
High voltage Level	Below 100kV	AC	Secondary transmission
Extra High Voltage level	230kV to 800kV	AC, DC both	Primary Transmission
Ultra High Voltage Level	800kV to 1000kV	AC, DC both	Primary transmission
	Over 1000kV	HVDC is preferable	Primary Transmission

Various Voltage levels

Why High Voltage is used for Long Transmission Line?

Generally long distant transmission lines are designed to operate at high voltage, extra high or ultra high voltage level. It is because of line power loss reduction purpose.

$P=\sqrt{3}V_LI_L\cos\Theta$ (1)

$P_{Loss}=I_L^2R=(P^2R/V_L^2\cos^2\Theta)$ (2)

Practically long distant transmission line resistance is comparatively more than medium and short transmission line. Due to this higher valued transmission line resistance considerable amount of power is lost. So we need to decrease the amount of current through each conductor by making the operating voltage very high for same amount of power transmission.
We know that the power in AC system to transmit is

Total power loss PLoss = $3I_L^2R$, considering three phases altogether.R is the resistance in ohm per phase of the transmission line.
Now, rearranging Equation (1) we get,

$P_L=(P^2R/V_L^2)$ (3)

Again in DC system, there is no phase difference between voltage and current, i.e. $\cos\Theta = 1$, and only two conductors (positive and negative) are used. So, in DC system transmitted power P = VI, and power loss

From equation (2) and (3), it is clear that power loss in transmission line is inversely proportional to the square of line voltage. The higher value of line voltage the lesser amount of power loss occurs. Hence transmission line conductor is used with less diameter, hence savings of conductor material.

Why HVAC is Used for Long Transmission Line?

Now-a-days electrical energy is generated, transmitted and distributed in AC form. Especially for long distant transmission line high voltage AC is transmitted for several reasons, they are:

- AC voltage can be stepped up or down as per requirement easily by transformer.
- Maintenance of AC substation is easy and cheaper.
- Throughout electrical power system AC voltage is handled. So no extra hazard of rectification or inversion like DC voltage transmission.

Why HVDC is Used for Long Transmission Line?

High Voltage DC is used at extra or ultra high voltage level. HVDC transmission is used at fixed level of voltage in primary transmission only as it cannot be stepped up or down by transformer. Only in long distant transmission line it is used only, because:

- Only two conductors (positive and negative) are required as compared to three of AC transmission.
- The absence of inductance, capacitance and phase displacement power loss is very less. Hence better voltage regulation.
- Surge problem never occurs.
- No skin effect.
- Less insulation requires due to less potential stress.
- Less corona discharge (i.e. the corona effect), and hence less power loss.
- Highly stabilized and synchronized.

Why Low and Medium Voltage is Used in Distribution Line?

In primary distribution, power is handled at 11 kV or 33 kV. As voltage level gets stepped down from 132 kV to 11 kV or 33 kV, current level gets higher valued. But this high valued current distributed among various local distribution stations (distribution transformers) nearby. These distribution transformers again steps down the voltage to 415 V. It is because; Power at 415 V is used at the user end. Distance between these distribution transformers and the primary distribution stations is very short, hence conductor resistance is not large. Very small amount of power is lost in this section.

Disadvantages of AC or HVAC Transmission

The main disadvantages of AC transmission are

- AC lines require more conductor material than DC.
- AC transmission line construction is more complicated than DC.
- Effective resistance is increased due to skin effect, hence power loss.
- Continuous power loss due to charging current because of line capacitance.

Disadvantages of DC or HVDC Transmission

The main disadvantages of DC transmission are

- Electric power is not generated in HVDC form due to commutation problem. Only HVDC is achieved for transmission from HVAC by rectification. So special arrangement is required for this conversion.
- DC voltage cannot be stepped up or down for transmission.
- DC switches and circuit breakers are expensive and with certain limitations.

Earthing

Earthing is used to protect from an electric shock. It does this by providing a path (a protective conductor) for a fault current to flow to earth. It also causes the protective device (either a circuit-breaker or fuse) to switch off the electric current to the circuit that has the fault.

Methods of Earthing

There are several methods of earthing like wire or strip earthing, rod earthing, pipe earthing, plate earthing or earthing through water mains. Most commonly used methods of earthing are pipe earthing and plate earthing. These methods are explained below in details.

Earthing Mat

Earthing mat is made by joining the number of rods through copper conductors. It reduced the overall grounding resistance. Such type of system helps in limiting the ground potential. Earthing mat is mostly used in a placed where the large fault current is to be experienced. While designing an earth mat, the following step is taken into consideration.

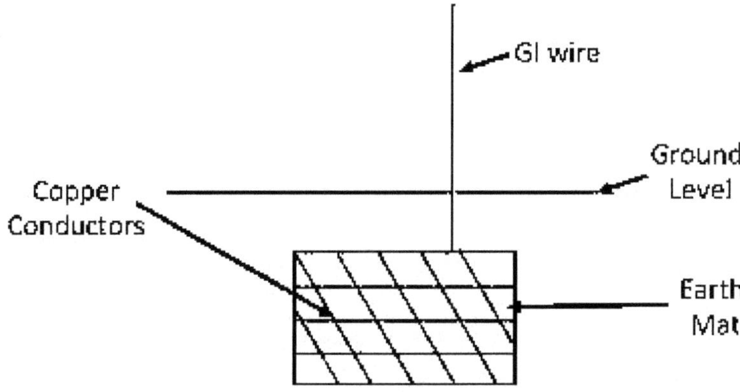

Earthing Mat

- In a fault condition, the voltage between the ground and the ground surface should not be dangerous to a person who may touch the noncurrent-carrying conducting surface of the electrical system.
- The uninterrupted fault current that may flow into the earthing mat should be large enough to operate the protective relay. The resistance of the ground is low to allow the fault current to flow through it.The resistance of the mat should not be of such a magnitude as to permit the flow of fatal current in the live body.
- The design of grounding mat should be such that the step voltage should be less than the permissible value which would depend on the resistivity of the soil and fault required for isolating the faulty plant from the live system.

Earthing Electrode

In this type of earthing any wire, rod, pipe, plate or a bundle of conductors, inserted in the ground horizontally or vertically. In distributing systems, the earth electrode may consist of a rod, about 1 meter in length and driven vertically into the ground. In generating substations, grounding mat is used rather than individual rods.

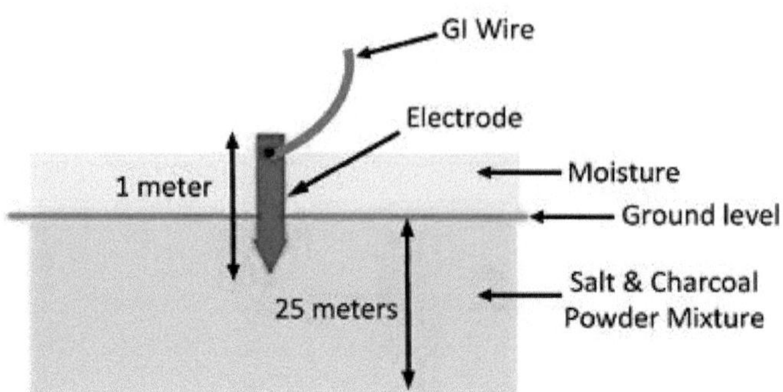

Earthing through Electrode

Pipe Earthing

This is the most common and best system of earthing as compared to other systems suitable for the same earth and moisture conditions. In this method the galvanized steel and perforated pipe of approved length and diameter in place upright in a permanently wet soil, as shown below. The size of the pipe depends upon the current to be carried and type of soil.

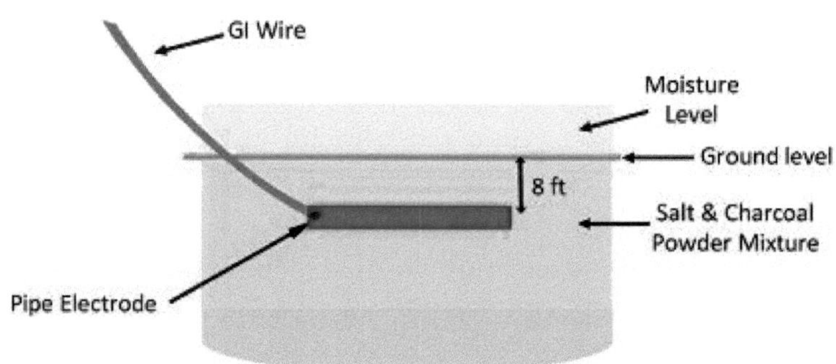

Pipe Earth Electrode

Normally, the size of the pipe uses for earthing is of diameter 40 mm and 2.5 meters in length for ordinary soil or of greater length in case of dry and rocky soil. The depth at which the pipe must be buried depends on the moistures of the ground.

The pipe is placed at 3.75 meters. The bottom of the pipe is surrounded by small pieces of coke or charcoal at a distance of about 15 cm. Alternate layers of coke and salt are used to increase the effective area of the earth and to decrease the earth resistance respectively.

Another pipe of 19 mm diameter and minimum length 1.25 meters is connected at the top of GI pipe through reducing socket.

During summer the moisture in the soil decreases, which causes an increase in earth resistance. So a cement concrete work is done to keep the water arrangement accessible, and in summer to have an effective earth, 3 or 4 buckets of water are put through the funnel connected to 19 mm diameter pipe, which is further connected to GI pipe.

The earth wire either GI or a strip of GI wire of sufficient cross section to carry faulty current safely is carried in a GI pipe of diameter 12 mm at a depth of about 60cm from the ground.

Plate Earthing

In Plate Earthing an earthing plate either of copper of dimension 60cm×60cm×3m of galvanized iron of dimensions 60 cm× 60 cm×6 mm is buried into the ground with its face vertical at a depth of not less than 3 meters from ground level.

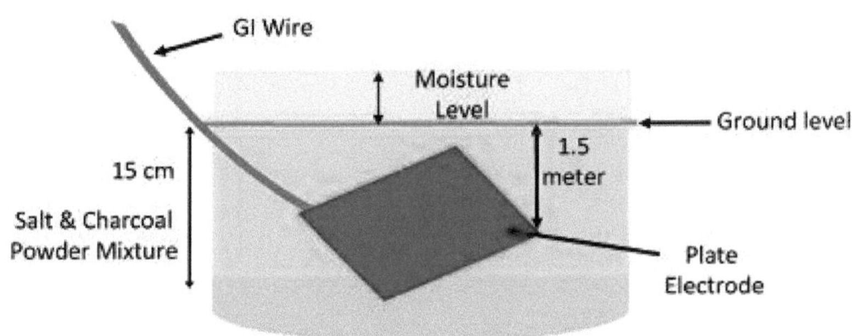

Plate Earth Electrode

The earth plate is inserted into auxiliary layers of coke and salt for a minimum thickness of 15 cm. The earth wire (GI or copper wire) is tightly bolted to an earth plate with the help of nut or bolt. The copper plate and copper wire are usually not employed for grounding purposes because of their higher cost.

Earthing Through Water Mains

In this type of earthing the GI or copper wire are connected to the water mains with the help of the steel binding wire which is fixed on copper lead as shown below.

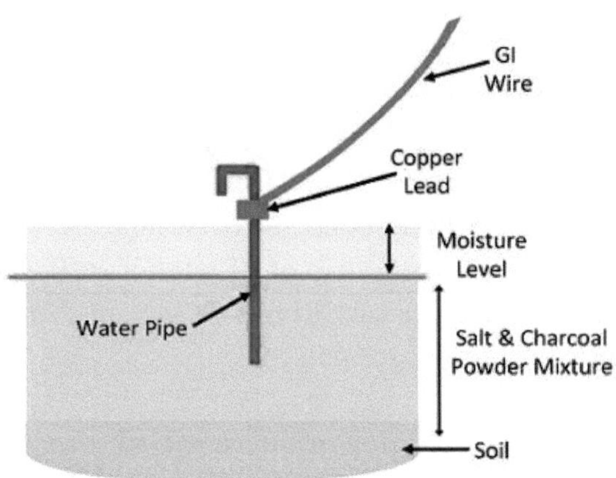

Earthing through water mains

The water pipe is made up of metal, and it is placed below the surface of the ground, i.e. directly connected to earth. The fault current flow through the GI or copper wire is directly get earthed through the water pipe.

Power system protection

It become necessary to protect equipment from various faulty condition like over voltage, lightning surges, insulation failure, resonance, improper earthing, short circuit or open circuit condition and balanced and unbalanced faults.

• Primary protection -designed in such a way that the component of the power system are protected

• Back up protection- secondary defence mechanism which comes into operation when the primary protection scheme fails.

Different protective equipment or devices

- fuses
- circuit breakers
- •protective relays

Switch Fuse Unit (SFU)

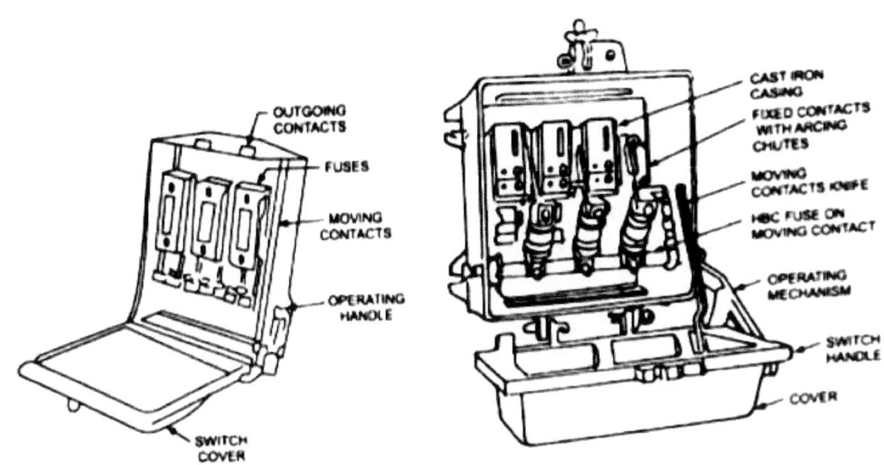

Switch Fuse Unit

Switch fuse is a combined unit and is known as an iron clad switch, being made of iron. It may be double pole for controlling single phase two-wire circuits or triple pole for controlling three-phase, 3-wire circuits or triple pole with neutral link for controlling 3-phase, 4-wire circuits. The respective switches are known as double pole iron clad (DPIC), triple pole iron clad (TPIC), and triple pole with neutral link iron clad (TPNIC) switches.

1. For Two-wire DC Circuits or Single Phase AC Circuits: 240V, 16A, DPIC switch fuse

2. For Three-Wire DC Circuits: 500V, 32A (63/100/150 or higher amperes), IS approved TPIC switch fuse.

3. For Three-Phase Balanced Load Circuits: 415V, 32A (63/100/150 or higher amperes), IS approved TPIC switch fuse.

Miniature Circuit Breaker (MCB)

A device which provides definite protection to the wiring installations and sophisticated equipment against over-currents and short-circuit faults. Thermal operation (overload protection) is achieved with a bimetallic strip, which deflects when heated by any overcurrents flowing through it. In doing so, releases the latch mechanism and causes the contacts to open. Inverse-time current characteristics result. i.e. greater the overload or excessive current, shorter the time required to operate the MCB.

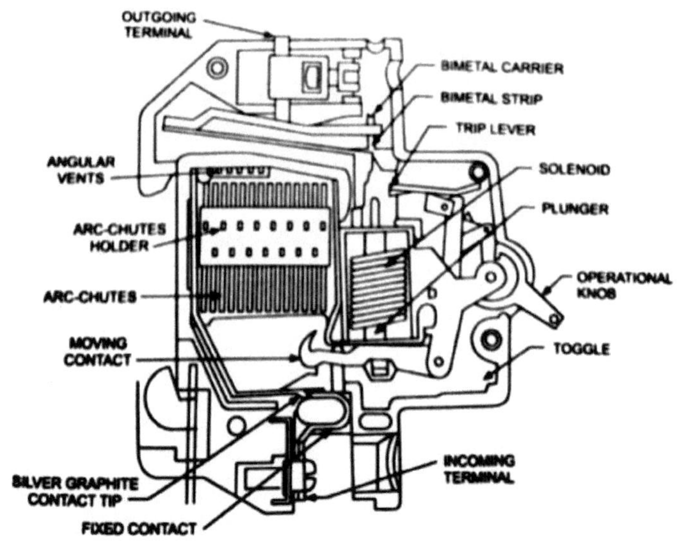

Miniature Circuit Breaker

On occurrence of short circuit, the rising current energizes the solenoid, operating the plunger to strike the trip lever causing immediate release of the latch mechanism. Rapidity of the magnetic solenoid operation causes instantaneous opening of contacts. MCBs are available with different current ratings of 0.5, 1.2, 2.5, 3, 4, 5, 6, 7.5, 10, 16, 20, 25, 32, 35, 40, 63, 100, 125, 160 A and voltage rating of 240/415 V AC and up to 220 V DC. Operating time is very short (less than 5 ms). They are suitable for the protection of important and sophisticated equipment, such as air-conditioners, refrigerators, computers etc.

Molded Case Circuit Breaker (MCCB)

It is a type of electrical protection device that can be used for a wide range of voltages, and frequencies of both 50 Hz and 60 Hz, the main distinctions between molded case and miniature circuit breaker are that MCCB can have current rating up to 2500 amperes, and its trip setting are normally adjustable. MCCBs are much larger than MCBs.

An MCCB has three main functions:

- Protection against overload.
- Protection against electrical faults.
- Switching a circuit ON and OFF.

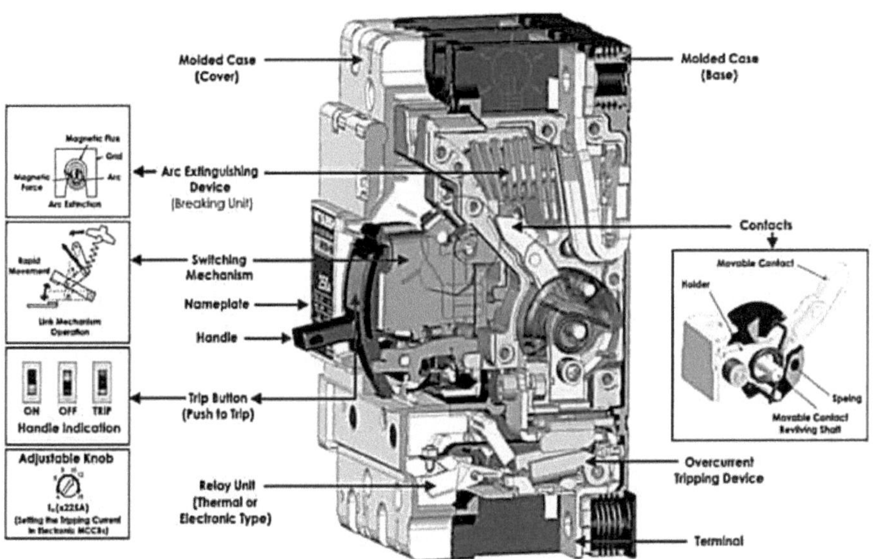

Molded case Circuit Breaker

This is a less common function of circuit breakers, but they can be used for that purpose if there is not an adequate manual switch.

The wide range of current ratings available from molded-case circuit breakers allows them to be used in a wide variety of applications. MCCBs are available with current ratings that range from low values such as 15 amperes, to industrial ratings such as 2500 amperes. This allows them to be used in both low power and high power applications.

Operating Mechanism: At its core, the protection mechanism employed by MCCBs is based on the same physical principles used by all types of thermal-magnetic circuit breakers. • Overload protection is accomplished by means of a thermal mechanism. MCCBs have a bimetallic contact what expands and contracts in response to changes in temperature. Under normal operating conditions, the contact allows electric current through the MCCB. However, as soon as the current exceeds the adjusted trip value, the contact will start to heat and expand until the circuit is interrupted.

The thermal protection against overload is designed with a time delay to allow short duration overcurrent, which is a normal part of operation for many devices. However any over current conditions, that lasts more than what is normally expected represent an overload, and the MCCB is tripped to protect the equipment and personnel.

On the other hand, fault protection is accomplished with electromagnetic induction, and the response is instant. Fault currents should be interrupted immediately, no matter if their duration is short or long. Whenever a fault occurs, the extremely high current induces a magnetic field in a solenoid coil located inside the breaker-this magnetic induction trips a contact and current is interrupted. As a complement to the magnetic protection mechanism, MCCBs have internal arc dissipation measures to facilitate interruption.

Earth Leakage Circuit Breaker (ELCB)

It is a device that provides protection against earth leakage.These are of two types.

1. Current operated earth leakage circuit breaker
2. Voltage operated earth leakage circuit breaker.

1. Current operated earth leakage circuit breaker: It is used when the product of the operating current in amperes and the earth-loop impedance in ohms does not exceed 40. such circuit breakers is used where consumer's earthing terminal is connected to a suitable earth electrode.

A current-operated earth leakage circuit breaker is applied to a 3-phase, 3-wire circuit. In normal condition when there is no earth leakage, the algebraic sum of the currents in the three coils of the current transformers is zero, and no current flows through the trip coil.In case of any earth leakage, the currents are unbalanced and the trip coil is energized and thus the circuit breaker is tripped.

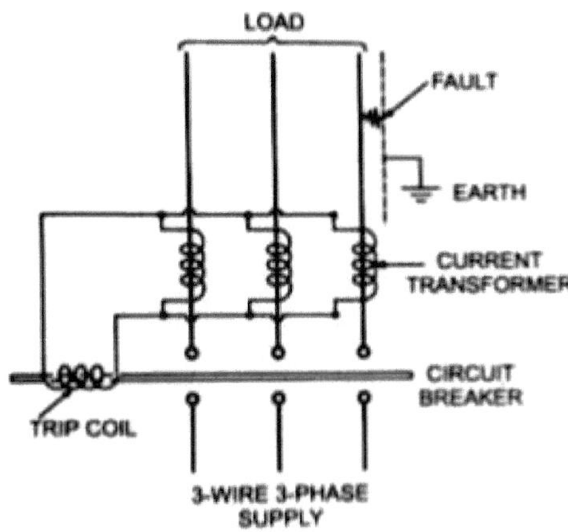

Current operated earth leakage circuit breaker

2. Voltage operated earth leakage circuit breaker

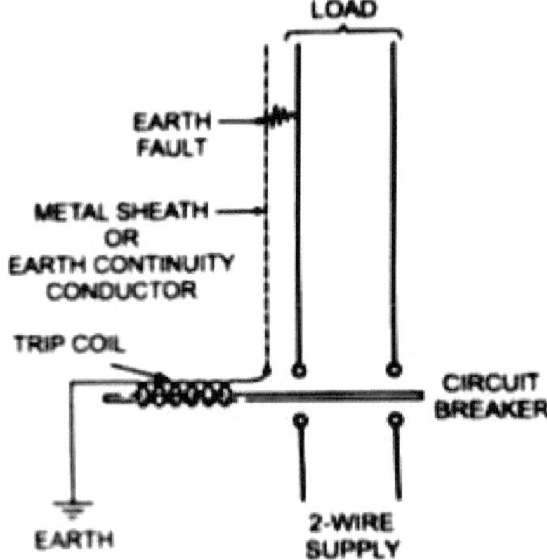

Voltage operated earth leakage circuit breaker

It is suitable for use when the earth –loop impedance exceeds the values applicable to fuses or excess current circuit breaker or to current operated earth leakage circuit breaker. When the voltage between earth continuity conductor (ECC) and earth electrode rises to sufficient value, the trip coil will carry the required current to trip the circuit breaker. With such a circuit breaker the earthing lead between the trip coil and the earth electrode must be insulated; in addition, the earth electrode must be placed outside the resistance area of any other parallel earths which may exist.

In both the above types of ELCB the tripping operation may be tested by means of a finger-operated test button which passes a predetermined current from the line wire through a high resistance to trip the coil and thus to earth. This test operation should be performed regularly.

Safety Precautions for Electrical System

Actual safety requires whole hearted cooperation, from all levels of workers involved in the work. It is need not to say, that all the people engaged in the electrical work should well aware of all safety rules and regulations related to the work they are executing. The workers executing the work should be extremely disciplined. Electrical work should not be done by wearing loose dresses.

Before starting the work, the working place should be made neat and clean. The place should also be sufficiently illuminated before work. All levels of voltage should be considered equally dangerous. Even the voltage levels which cannot produce electrical shock should also not be ignored. We shall first confirm the circuit is dead before touching it for repairing maintenance and any others works.

- We have to switch off, isolate and properly earth the circuit before doing any work with the circuit.
- We shall only execute the work after getting properly issued work permit from the concerned operating personal.
- The work permit can only be issued after making the circuit completely dead, isolated and earthed.
- We must display Danger Board at the place of work.
- We should not allow any unauthorized person to enter in the working place.
- We should not put any new equipment into the service without necessary testing by authority.
- All electrical equipments, bays, circuits, should be identified by properly viewable labels to avoid any mistakes.
- We should not work on electrical circuit during heavy lightning storm.

- We should wear shoes having sewn soles, preferably insulated rubber soles.
- We should not wear suspenders, arm bands, with metal buckets or other metal parts. We also do not wear metal key chain or metal keepers for key rings or watch rings outside the clothing during work. We should always, take extra precaution while work in extra damp area.
- When there is a hurry to do the work, the tired and exhausted workers should be avoided to do so.
- We should not toss the tools or working materials to other person. It is better to deliver the tools and materials hand to hand.
- We should not keep any tools at the edge of equipment cabinet or structure from where these may fall off.
- We should not do anything which may startle the person working in hazardous condition.

Electric shock

An electric shock happens when an electric current passes through your body. This can burn both internal and external tissue and cause organ damage.

Current Levels (Milliamps)	**Probable Effect on Human Body**
1mA	Slight tingling sensation. (Still dangerous under some conditions.)
5mA	Slight shock felt. Disturbing but not painful. Average person can let go.
6mA – 16mA	Painful shock causing some loss of muscle control. Commonly termed "let go" range or freezing current.
17mA- 99mA	Extreme pain, respiratory arrest, severe muscle contractions, individual cannot let go. Death is possible.
100mA – 2000mA	Ventricular fibrillation, muscular contraction and nerve damage. Death is likely.
Over 2000mA	Cardiac arrest. Internal organ damage and severe burns. Death is probable.

Typical effects of electric shocks on humans

First Aid

If you receive an electric shock

- Let go of the electric source as soon as you can.
- If you can, call 911 or local emergency services.
- If you can't, ask for someone else around you to call.
- If the shock feels minor ,See a doctor as soon as you can, even if you don't have any noticeable symptoms. Remember, some internal injuries are hard to detect at first.

In the meantime, cover any burns with sterile gauze.Don't use adhesive bandages or anything else that might stick to the burn.

If someone else has been shocked

- Don't touch someone who has been shocked if they're still in contact with the source of electricity.
- Turn off the flow of electricity if possible.
- Stay at least 20 feet away if they've been shocked by high-voltage power lines that are still on.

Question Bank

UNIT-I – TRANSFORMER

PART-A(Two marks)

1.Define transformer

A transformer is a static piece of apparatus by means of which electric power in one circuit is transferred to another circuit with change in voltage without change in frequency .

2. State the principle of working of a transformer.

Transformer consists of two inductive coils which are electrically separated but magnetically linked through a path of low reluctance. If one coil connected to a source of alternating voltage, an alternating flux is set up in the laminated core, most of which linked with the other coil in which it produces mutually induced emf. If the second coil is closed current flows in it and so electrical energy is transferred from the first coil to the second coil without change in frequency.

3. List the types of Transformer based on Construction.

- Core type transformer, Shell type transformer

4. Mention the difference between core and shell type transformer. (Apr/May 2015)

In core type the winding surround the core considerably and in shell type the core surround the windings i.e windings is placed in central limb of the core.

5. Define Transformation Ratio and classify the Transformer based on Transformation ratio.

Transformation ratio is defined as the ratio of number of turns in the secondary winding to number of turns in primary winding.$K=N_2/N_1=E_2/E_1$
Types :Step up transformer & Step down transformer

6. List the various losses in a Transformer and state the Condition for Maximum efficiency.

Losses: i. Core loss ii. Copper loss

Condition for maximum efficiency:Iron loss = copper loss

7. What is the function of transformer oil in transformer?

1.It provides good insulation, Cooling

8. State why the transformer core is made of magnetic materials.

The transformer core is made of magnetic materials to provide a continuous magnetic path with the minimum air gap.

9. State the methods to reduce hysteresis and eddy-current losses in a transformer:

To reduce hysteresis loss, core is made up of CRGO (Cold rolled Grain oriented)Eddy current loss is minimized by laminating the core.

10. Draw the phasor diagram of a transformer in no load .(Nov/Dec 2014)

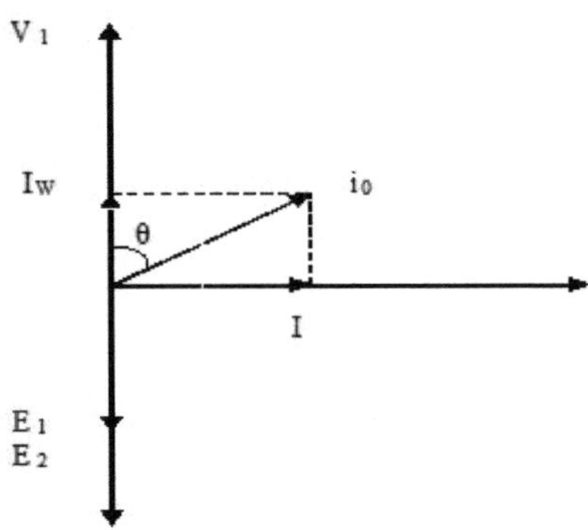

Phasor diagram of a transformer in no load

11 .Where does Iron loss occur in a transformer?

It occurs in transformer core and yoke

12. Why transformers are rated in KVA?

Copper Loss of transformer depends on current & its iron loss on voltage. Hence total losses depend on Volt-Ampere but not on power factor. That is why the rating of transformers is in KVA and not in KW.

13. Write the emf equation of a transformer.

E=4.44 fm f N (volts), where fm = maximum value of flux (Wb), f = frequency (Hz), N = number of turns

14. What are the applications of step-up and step-down transformers?

Step-up transformer: It is used in transmission side

Step-down transformer: It is used in distribution side.

15. Define regulation and efficiency of the transformer.(Nov/Dec 2014)

Regulation: The change is secondary terminal voltage from no load condition to full load condition expressed as a percentage of no load or full load voltage is termed as voltage regulation

Efficiency: The efficiency is defined as the ratio of output power in watts to the input power in watts

16. Give the principle behind the autotransformer.(Nov/Dec 2015)

Auto transformer is a transformer with one winding only part of this being common to both primary and secondary. In this transformer the primary and secondary are not electrically isolated from each other in the case of 2- winding transformer. Because of one winding, it uses less copper and hence is cheaper.

17.What are the Demerits of an auto transformer and state few applications?

- No Electrical isolation & Not suitable for higher power ratings.
- Used in laboratories, variable voltage regulators, variable voltage rectifiers etc.,

18. List the advantages of auto transformer?

- Only one winding required. Required voltage can be tapped off at the required turns.
- The main advantage is that the design saves on copper
- More economical compare to two winding transformer

19. Define all day efficiency.

Distribution transformers are energized throughout the day. Their secondaries are at no load most of the time in a day except during the hours of lighting period. Core loss occurs throughout the day. Copper loss occurs only when they are loaded and hence is less important. To judge their performance, all-day efficiency or operational efficiency is calculated. The all-day efficiency is defined by

$h_{all\ day}$ = Output in KWh/Input in KWh (for 24 hours)

20. What is the function of conservator in transformer?

The conservator's function is to take up contraction and expansion of oil without allowing it to come in contact with outside air.

21. What is the function of breather in transformer?

The breathing air is passed through the breather which extracts the moisture content

from the air. The breather has the drying agent silica gel.

22. What is a step down transformer? (Apr/May 2013)

If the no. of turns in secondary is lesser than no. of turns in the primary winding of the transformer, then it is called as step down transformer.

23. Draw the complete equivalent circuit diagram of a ideal transformer. (Apr/May 2013,Nov/Dec 2015)

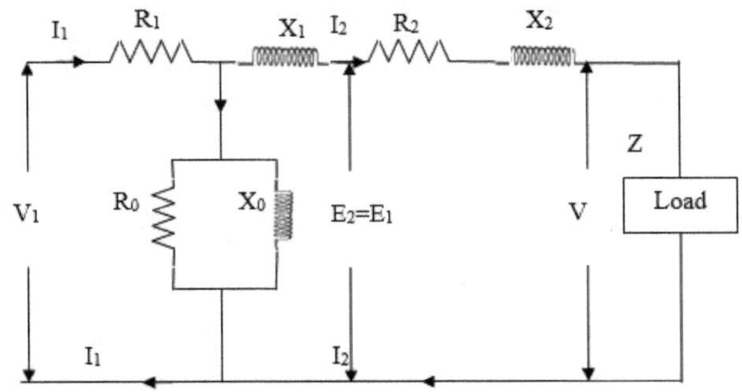

Equivalent circuit diagram of a ideal transformer

24.What is an ideal transformer and how does it differ from a practical transformer? (Apr/May 2015)

An ideal transformer is an imaginary transformer which does not have any losses and has 100% efficiency.

A practical transformer is one which do have some ohmic loss in the winding and the core and copper loss with efficiency less than ideal transformer.

25. What are the connections of 3-phase transformer?

Star-Star, Star-Delta, Delta-Star, Delta-Delta

PART - B

1. Explain the principle of operation of a transformer. Derive its EMF equation.
2. Explain the constructional details and working of core type and shell type transformers with neat sketches
3. Draw the phasor diagram of transformer when it is operating under load and explain.

4. Explain in detail step by step procedure to draw the equivalent circuit of transformer by conducting suitable O.C and S.C test.(May 2018, May 2019)
5. Describe the method of calculating the regulation and efficiency of a single phase transformer by OC and SC tests.
6. With a neat phasor diagram, explain about the single phase Transformer under load & no load condition. (Refer question number 3)
7. What is an ideal transformer and why the efficiency of a transformer is so high?
8. Derive an expression for saving of copper when an auto transformer is used.
9. State the various losses in a Transformer .Define efficiency of a Transformer and hence deduce the Condition for Maximum efficiency.
10. A 200kVA, 3300/240 V single phase transformer has 80 turns on the secondary winding. Assuming ideal transformer, calculate primary and secondary currents on full load, the maximum value of flux and the number of primary turns. (May 2018)
11. What is meant by auto transformer? Explain the principle of operation of auto transformer with neat sketch. (May 2018, May 2019)
12. Explain the operation of three phase core and shell type transformer with suitable sketch. (May 2019)

UNIT – II DC MACHINES
PART – A

1. **Define electric generator. What is a prime mover?**

The electric generator is machine that converts mechanical energy into electrical energy. It operates on the principle of dynamically induced emf. The basic source of mechanical power which drives the armature of the generator is called prime mover.

2.State the basic components required for generator action to exist:

A generating action requires following basic components to exist, (i) the conductor or a coil (ii) the flux (iii) relative motion between conductor and flux

3. **Write the emf equation for a dc generator and torque equation for a dc motor.(May 2018)**

The emf equation of a dc generator is given by, $E= (\Phi PNZ)/60A$.The torque equation of a DC motor is given by, $T= (0.159\Phi ZIaP)/A$ N-m, where P - No of poles; Φ – Flux per pole; N- Speed; Z - No. of armature conductors; A- No. of parallel paths; Ia – Armature current

4. **State the principle of working of D.C. motor.**

An electric motor is a machine which converts electrical energy into mechanical energy. Its action is based on principle that when a current carrying conductor is placed in a magnetic field it experiences a mechanical force whose direction is given by Fleming's left hand rule.

5. **Define magnetic reluctance.**

The opposition offered by the magnetic circuit to the establishment of magnetic flux in it is called Magnetic Reluctance. It is defined as the ratio of the mmf (F) to the flux (Φ). $S=L/\mu A$ (or) $S=F/\Phi$ and its unit is AT/Wb.

6. **State Fleming's Left Hand Rule.**

Fleming's Left Hand rule states that if the thumb, forefinger and middle finger are stretched in such a way that they are right angles to each other mutually, the forefinger points towards the direction f the magnetic field, middle finger towards the direction of flow of current then thumb will point the direction of force of the conductor.

7. **List the parts of dc machine.**

The parts of a dc machine are 1)Yoke 2)Poles 3)Pole shoes 4)Inter poles 5)Armature Core 6)Commutator 7)Brushes 8)Armature winding 9)Field winding

8. **What is the function of commutator in a D.C motor and generator?(May 2018)**

DC Motor: To convert the A.C voltage in the armature to D.C voltage, the commutator is used and it performs the function of rectification.

DC Generator: The commutator is to facilitate the collection of current from the armature conductors. It converts the alternating current induced in the armature conductors into unidirectional current to the external load circuit.

9. **State the various types of D.C. machines based on excitation.**

- Separately excited machine.
- Self excited machine (a)Shunt wound (b) Series wound (c) Compound wound.

10. **What are the functions of interpoles?**

The functions of interpole windings are (i) To neutralize armature reaction effect (ii) To supply the reversing emf and improve commutation (iii) To eliminate the sparking at the time of commutation (iv) Automatic neutralization of reactance voltage at all loads .

11.What is the function of brushes? Why brushes are made up of soft material?

The function of brushes is to collect current from commutator and make it available to the stationary external circuit. It connects the stationary external circuit to the rotating commutator. Brushes are stationary and resting on the surface of the commutator just making a contact with it. Thus as commutator rotates there is friction between brushes and commutator. To avoid wear and tear of commutator which is costly, the brushes are made up of soft material like carbon.

12.What is self-excited generator? How it gets excited?

When the field winding is supplied from the armature of the generator itself it is said to be self-excited. Initially without any current through field winding, the field poles possess some magnetic flux residing in them. This is called **residual flux** and the property is called residual magnetism. Thus when the generator is started, due to such residual flux, it develops a small emf which then drives a small current through the field winding. This tends to increase the flux produced. This in turn increases the induced emf thus field current and flux. The process is cumulative and continues till the generator develops rated voltage across its armature. This is Voltage building process in self excited generators.

13.Why the external characteristics of a DC shunt generator is more drooping than that of a separately excited generator?

In separately excited DC generator, E_a remains constant and I_aR_a is small. The external characteristics therefore droop slightly. A small voltage drop is added by reduction in E_a caused by cross magnetizing due to magnetic saturation. In shunt generator, as the terminal voltage drops due to I_aR_a, If reduces which causes further drop with reduction in E_a. The generator shifts to lower operating point in OCC. So the voltage droop is much sharper in shunt generator for a given I_f.

14.What is armature reaction?

The effect of magnetic field set up by the armature current on the distribution of the main field flux is called armature reaction. As a result of this the magnetic flux lines in the air gap gets distorted and the net magnitude of net magnetic flux get reduced.

15.State the necessity of starter in a dc motor.

The current drawn by the motor armature is given by the relation, $I_a = (V- E_b)/R_a$. When the motor is at rest, there is no back emf developed in the armature. If now full supply voltage is applied across the stationary armature, it will draw a very large current because armature resistance is relatively small. This excessive current will blow out the fuses and prior to that it will damage the commutator and brushes.

16.Draw various characteristics of D.C shunt generator.

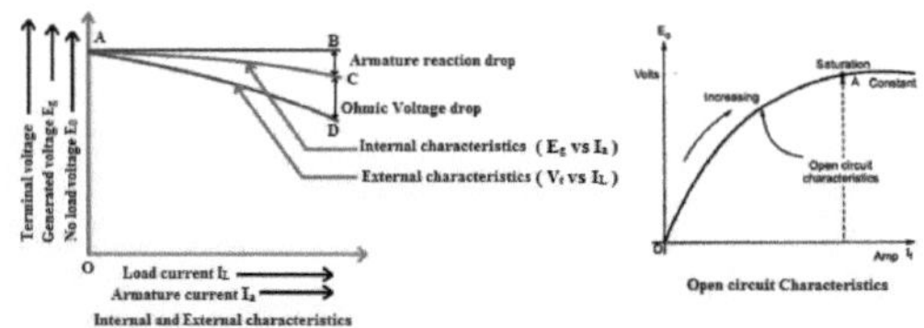

Characteristics of D.C shunt generator

17.Draw the circuit model of dc shunt motor.

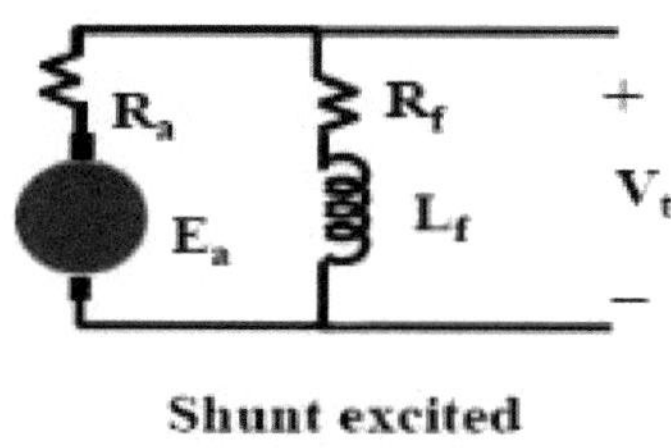

circuit model of dc shunt motor

18.Draw the speed torque characteristics for shunt, series and compound motors.

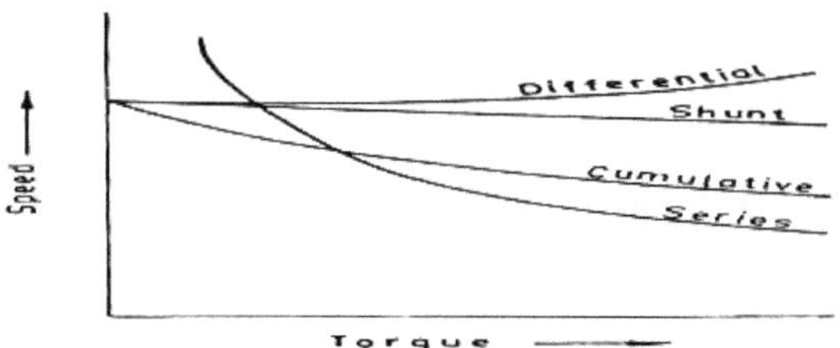

speed torque characteristics

19.What are the types of starters for DC machines?

3 point starter, 2 point starter, 4 point starter

20.Why should not dc series motor be started without load?

The speed of a dc series motor is given by the formula, $E = \phi ZNP/60A$;$N=60AE/\varphi ZP$ and $N=1/\phi$ and $\phi \;\alpha\; I_f = I_a$ (for series motor). If the motor is started without load, the armature current I_a will be very small and the speed becomes dangerously high, which damages the motor. Hence, the DC series motor should never be started without some initial load.

21.Specify the techniques used to control the speed of DC shunt motor for below and above the rated speed.

By varying the field current as well as armature voltage, the speed of a DC Motor can be controlled. The speed of a D.C motor can be controlled beyond the rated speed by field control method, because the flux per pole can be decreased to any value by decreasing the field current. (Field current can be decreased by inserting a field regulator)

22.List the different methods of speed control employed for dc series motor.

(i) Field diverter method (ii) Regrouping of field coils (iii) Tapped field control (iv) Armature resistance control (v) Armature voltage control for single motor (vi) Series parallel control for multiple identical motors

23.State the various applications of DC motor.

DC shunt motor: blower, fans machine tools, milling and drilling machines, centrifugal and reciprocating pumps and lathe machines

DC series motor: Cranes, hoists, trolleys, conveyor and electric locomotives

Cumulative compound DC motors: Punches, shear, heavy planers, rolling mills

Differential compound DC motors: They are not suitable for any practical applications

24.State the applications of various types of generators.

Shunt generator : commonly used in battery charging and ordinary lighting purpose

Series generator: Commonly used as boosters on DC feeders as a constant current generator for welding generator, arc lamps.

Cumulative compound generator: They are used for domestic lighting purposes and to transmit energy over long distance

Differential compound generator: They are very rare and used for special applications like electric arc welding.

25.Calculate the emf generated by a 4- pole , wave-wound armature having 45 slots with 18 conductors per slot when driven at 1200 rpm . the flux per pole is 0.016Wb

Given P=4, A=2 (in wave winding A=2), Z=45 X 18 =810 conductors, Φ =0.016 wb, and N=1200 rpm E= Φ PNZ/60A =(0.016x 4x 1200x810)/(60x2) =518.4 V

26.Why is the starting current very high in a dc motor?

A rotating d.c. motor generates a back-emf which opposes the supply voltage and reduces the current drawn by the motor. When the motor is stationary, it cannot generate this back emf and, so, the only opposition to current is the resistance as the machine starts to run, the resulting back emf, acts to reduce the current. The starting current is high because when the motor is not rotating no back-emf is generated, leaving the starting current to be determined by the armature resistance should be low.

27.List the types of DC generator. (May 2019)

i. Shunt generator
ii. Series generator
iii. Cumulative compound generator
iv. Differential compound generator

28.What do you mean by Universal motor? (May 2019)

The universal motor is a type of electric motor that can operate on either AC or DC power and uses an electromagnet as its stator to create its magnetic field. It is a commutated series-wound motor where the stator's field coils are connected in series with the rotor windings through a commutator.

PART – B

1. Discuss the construction and working principle of a D.C Generator with neat diagram. Derive the EMF equation of a D.C Generator. (May 2018, May 2019)
2. Explain in detail the characteristics of different types of DC generators with suitable diagrams.
3. Explain the armature reaction with neat sketch.
4. Explain the operating principle and construction of a D.C Motor. What is meant by back emf? What is its significance? (May 2018)
5. Derive the torque equation of Dc motor.
6. Explain in detail the characteristics of different types of D.C Motor with suitable diagram
7. Explain in detail about the 3 point starter.
8. Explain in detail about various methods to control the speed of DC shunt motor and DC series motor. (May 2018, May 2019)
9. Discuss the construction and working principle of Universal motor.

UNIT III – AC ROTATING MACHINES

PART A

1. **State the principle of 3 phase IM.**

While starting, rotor conductors are stationary and they cut the revolving magnetic field and so an emf is induced in them by electromagnetic induction. This induced emf produces a current if the circuit is closed. This current opposes the cause by Lenz's law and hence the rotor starts revolving in the same direction as that of the magnetic field.

2. Why an induction motor is called a 'rotating transformer'?

The rotor receives electric power in exactly the same way as the secondary of a two-winding transformer receiving its power from the primary. That is why an induction motor can be called as a rotating transformer i.e. one in which primary winding is stationary but the secondary is tree to rotate.

3. Why an induction motor will never run at its synchronous speed?

If the rotor runs at synchronous speed, then there would be no relative speed between the stator and the rotor; hence no rotor EMF, no rotor current and so no rotor torque to maintain rotation. That is why the rotor runs at a speed, which is always less than synchronous speed.

1. **Why are the slots on the cage rotor of induction motor usually skewed?**

- It helps to make the motor run quietly by reducing the magnetic hum
- It helps in reducing the locking tendency of the rotor i.e., the tendency of the rotor teeth to remain under the stator teeth due to direct magnetic attraction between the two.

5. **What is slip and slip speed in an Induction motor?**

The difference between the synchronous speed N_s and the actual speed of the rotor is called as the slip. Though it may be expressed in so many revolutions/second, yet it is usual to express it as a percentage of the synchronous speed. It also describes that the rotor slips back from synchronism.

It is denoted by's'. Slip s $=\{N_s\text{-}N/N_s\}*100$; Slip speed $=N_s\text{-}N$

6. **What are the advantages of slip-ring IM over cage IM?**

(i) Rotor circuit is accessible for external connection.

(ii) By adding external resistance to the rotor circuit the starting current is reduced with the added advantage of improving starting torque.

(iii) Additional speed control methods can be employed with the accessibility in the rotor circuit.

7. **why a 1phase induction motor is not self-starting?**

When **1phase** supply is given to the 1 phase stator winding, it produces a magnetic field that pulsates in strength in a sinusoidal manner. The field polarity reverses after each half cycle but the field does not rotate. Consequently, the alternating flux cannot produce rotation in a stationary squirrel-cage rotor. So a 1phase induction motor is not self-starting.

8. **How a 1phase induction motor can be made to self-start?**

To make a 1phase induction motor self-starting, a revolving stator magnetic field should be produced. This may be achieved by converting a 1 phase supply into 2 phase supply through the use of an additional (starting) winding. When the motor attains sufficient speed, the starting winding may be removed depending on the type of the motor.

9. **List the different types of 1phase induction motor based on the methods of making them self-starting.**

1. Split – phase motors, 2) Capacitor motors, 2.Capacitor-start motors, 2.2)Capacitor-start capacitor-run motors, 3)Shaded – pole motors.

10. **What is the slip of a 50Hz, 1**phase **, 4-pole induction motor running at 1440 rpm?**

Given, f = 50Hz,P = 4, N = 1440 Rpm, N_s = 120f/P = 120 x 50/4 = 1500 Rpm , Slip,s = (N_s-N)/N_s = (1500-1440)/1500 = 0.04, % s = 0.04 x 100 = 4%

11. **State the types of 3-phase induction motor based on construction.**

i. Squirrel cage Induction Motor, (ii) Phase Wound or slip ring Induction Motor

12. **What is the need for starters in 3-phase induction motors?**

To limit the high starting current by supplying reduced voltage to the motor at the time of starting. Such a reduced voltage is applied only for a short period and once rotor gets accelerated, full normal rated voltage can be applied.

13. **State the different types of starters used in induction motor.**

1. Stator resistance starter 2. Autotransformer starter 3. Star-Delta starter 4. Rotor resistance starter
5. Direct on line starter

14. **For domestic and commercial purposes which motor is best suited and why?**

Squirrel cage motor is used because it has moderate starting torque and constant speed characteristic hence commonly used in domestic pump sets.

15. **What is the frequency of the induced emf of an induction motor?**

$f_r = s * f$ where f_r - frequency of rotor induced emf ; S - slip & f - frequency of the supply voltage.

16. **Mention the characteristic features of synchronous motor.**

Synchronous motor is called so because the speed of the rotor of this motor is same as the rotating magnetic field. It is basically a fixed speed motor because it has only one speed, which is synchronous speed and therefore no intermediate speed is there or in other words it's in synchronism with the supply frequency.

17. **Name the various methods of starting a Synchronous Motor .**

i. Using pony motors ii.Using damper winding iii.As a slip ring Induction motor
iv. Using a small dc machine coupled to it.

18. **Define: Stepper motor and step angle?**

Stepper motor is a motor which rotates step by step and not continuous rotation. When the stator is excited using a DC supply the rotor poles align with the stator poles in opposition such that reluctance is less. A stepping motor rotates through a fixed angle for every pulse. The rated value of this angle is called the step angle and expressed in degrees.

19. **Mention the different types of stepper motor?**

- Variable Reluctance stepper motor (Single stack, Multi stack),
- Permanent magnet stepper motor,
- Hybrid stepper motor,
- Outer rotor stepper motor.

20. **Define: Holding torque and Detent torque of stepper motor?**

Holding torque is defined as the maximum static torque that can be applied to the shaft of an excited motor without causing continuous rotation.

It is defined as the maximum static torque that can be applied to the shaft of an unexcited motor without causing continuous rotation.

21. Write briefly about the construction and types of a Brushless DC machines.

1)Brushless PM machines are constructed with the electric winding on the stator and PMs on the rotor. There are several conventional PM machine configurations and other more novel concepts conceived in recent years to improve performance.2)The configuration of a PM machine and the relationship of the rotor to the stator determine the geometry and the shape of the rotating magnetic field. PM machines in which the magnetic flux travels in the radial direction are classified as radial-flux machines. 3)They are cylindrical in shape, and the rotor is usually located inside the stator but can also be placed outside the stator. PM machines in which the magnetic flux travels in the axial direction are classified as axial-gap machines. They can have multiple disk or pancake-shaped rotors and stators. The stator-rotor-stator configuration is typical.

22. What are the differences between mechanical and electronic commutator?

MECHANICAL COMMUTATOR	ELECTRONIC COMMUTATOR
Commutator arrangement is located in the rotor.	Commutator arrangement is located in the stator.
Shaft position sensing is inherent in the arrangement	It requires a separate rotor position sensor.
Sparking takes place. It requires regular maintenance.	There is no sparking. It requires less maintenance.
Sliding contacts between commutator and brushes.	No sliding contacts.

Comparison between mechanical and electronic commutator

23. State the advantages and disadvantages of three phase induction motor.(May 2018)

ADVANTAGES:

1. The working of the motor is independent of the environmental condition. This is because the induction motor is Robust and mechanically strong.
2. A Squirrel cage induction motor does not contain Brushes, Slip rings and Commentators. Due to this reason, the cost of the motor is quite low. However, Slip Rings are used in Wound type induction motor to add external resistance to the rotor winding.
3. Due to the absence of Brushes, there are no sparks in the motor. It can also be operated in hazardous conditions.
4. Unlike synchronous motors, a 3 phase induction motor has a high starting torque, good speed regulation and reasonable overload capacity.

DISADVANTAGES:

1. Speed control of an induction motor is very difficult to attain. This is because a 3 phase induction motor is a constant speed motor and for the entire loading range, the change in speed of the motor is very low.
2. Induction motors have high input surge currents, which are referred to as Magnetising Inrush currents. This causes a reduction in voltage at the time of starting the motor.
3. Due to poor starting torque, the motor cannot be used for applications

which require high starting torque.

24. Draw the basic circuit of capacitor start capacitor run motor.

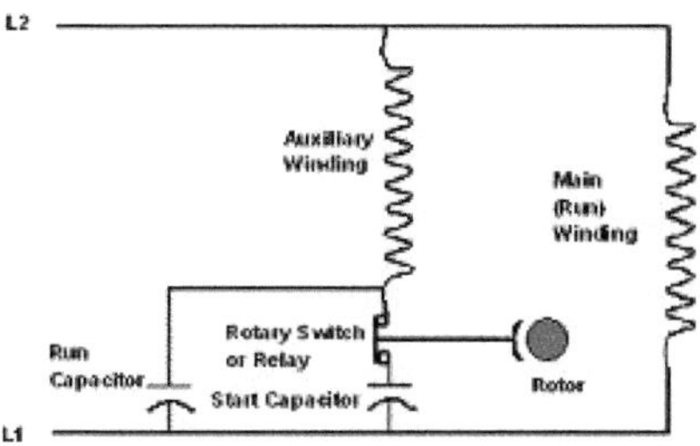

Basic circuit of capacitor start capacitor run motor

25. Compare salient pole alternator with non-salient pole alternator. (May 2019)

SALIENT POLE	CYLINDRICAL POLE
Salient pole rotors have large diameter and shorter axial length.	They are smaller in diameter but having longer axial length.
They are generally used in lower speed electrical machines, say 100 RPM to 1500 RPM.	Cylindrical rotors are used in high speed electrical machines, usually 1500 RPM to 3000 RPM.
As the rotor speed is lower, more number of poles are required to attain the required frequency	2 to 4 poles are used
Salient pole rotors generally need damper windings to prevent rotor oscillations during operation.	Damper windings are not needed in non-salient pole rotors.

Comparison of salient pole with non-salient pole alternator

26. List any two applications of stepper motor. (May 2019)

As the stepper motor are digitally controlled using an input pulse, they are suitable for use with computer controlled systems. They are used in numeric control of machine tools. Used in tape drives, floppy disc drives, printers and electric watches. The stepper motor is also used in X-Y plotter and robotics.

PART B

1. With the help of neat diagrams explain the construction and working of 3-phase induction motor and also obtain the equivalent circuit of 3-phase Induction motor. (May 2018, May 2019)
2. Explain the different starting methods of 3 phase induction motor with suitable diagrams and working principle.
3. (i) Explain the method of starting of synchronous motor.
4. Explain the methods of speed control of Induction motor.
5. Derive the expression for the starting torque developed by a 3-phase Induction motor and hence deduce the condition for maximum starting torque.
6. Give the constructional details of rotor of both salient pole and cylindrical rotor synchronous machines.
7. Explain the double field revolving theory of single phase induction motor.
8. Explain the working principle of synchronous motor and compare synchronous motor with induction motor. Discuss the torque equation of synchronous motor. (May 2019)
9. Discuss the construction and principle of operation of a Permanent magnet DC motor.
10. Explain the construction and principle of operation of Variable Reluctance Stepping motor.
11. Explain the construction and operation of hybrid Stepping motor.
12. Explain the modes of operation of the stepper motor. (May 2018)
13. Elucidate the working principle of permanent magnet stepper motor. (May 2019)

UNIT IV - MEASUREMENT AND INSTRUMENTATION

PART A

1. **What is meant by an instrument?**

Instrument is used as a physical means of determining quantities or variables. The instrument serves as an extension of human faculties and enables the man to determine the value of unknown quantity or variable which his unaided human faculties cannot measure. So an instrument in simple case consists of a single

2. **Enlist the applications of the measurement systems.**

(i) Monitoring of processes and operations: They simply indicate the value of condition of parameter under study and their reading do not serve any control functions. (ex.) ammeter, voltmeter, water & electrical energy meters in homes.

(ii) Control of processes and operations: A very useful application of instrument is in automatic control systems. In this method, both measurement and control are included.

(iii) Experimental Engineering Analysis: For solution of engineering problems, theoretical and experimental methods are available.

3. **What is measuring instrument and mention its types? (May 2018)**

The measurement of given quantity is the result of comparison between the quantity to be measured and a definite standard. The instruments which are used for such measurements are called Measuring Instruments. They are classified as (i) Indicating Instruments (ii) Recording Instruments (iii) Integrating Instruments.

4.What is the electrical current effect used to produce deflecting torque in a PMMC instrument?

When a current(I) carrying conductor of size l and d and N turns, cuts a magnetic field of flux density B and if the field is radial then the deflecting torque

T_d = NbldI = GI

5. Compare internal resistance of an ammeter and a voltmeter. Give reason.

The internal resistance of an ammeter is very low and the internal resistance of a voltmeter is very high.

6. What causes errors in moving iron instruments?

Temperature coefficient of spring, self heating of coils in voltmeters, Stray magnetic fields, changes of reactance of working coils, changes of magnitudes of eddy currents cause errors in moving iron instruments.

7. State two merits of PMMC ammeter.

The scale is uniformly divided. The power consumption is very low as 25 μW to 200 μW. The torque weight ratio is high which gives a high accuracy. The errors due to stray magnetic fields are very small. A single instrument may be used for many different voltage and current ranges.

8. State two sources of error in moving iron instrument.

Hysterisis Error, Temperature error, Stray magnetic fields, Frequency & eddy current errors

9. Define current sensitivity of a galvanometer.

The current sensitivity of a galvanometer is defined as the deflection produced by unit current. Current sensitivity = $S_i = \theta_F / I = Gi / K$ rad / A or G / 500K mm /µA.

10. List the various methods of providing control torque.

Gravity control, Spring control

11. What is the need for control torque and state the methods to provide it in Analog indicating instruments?

Control torque is needed to produce a torque equal and opposite to deflecting torque at the final steady position of pointer in order to make the deflection of the pointer definite. Controlling torque is achieved in analog instruments by two methods. They are (i) Gravity control (ii) spring control.

12. State the errors in PMMC instruments.

Weakening of permanent magnets due to aging and temperature effects. Weakening of springs due to aging and temperature effects. Change of resistance of moving coil with temperature.

13. What are the advantages and disadvantages of moving iron instrument?(Dec 2012)

Advantages:

- Used to measure both A.C and D.C quantites. . Accurate over a wider range of frequency and greater possibility of using shunts with ammeters. Suitable for economical production. Uniform scale.

Disadvantages:

- Temperature coefficient of spring, self heating of coils in voltmeters, Stray magnetic fields, changes of reactance of working coils, changes of magnitudes of eddy currents cause errors in moving iron instruments.

14.Is it posible to measure AC and DC using PMMC instrument. Justify.(May 2017)

PMMC instrument is **not** suitable for measurement of AC. Because the torque reverses if the cuttenr reverses. If the instrument is connected to AC, the pointer cannot follow the rapid reversals and the deflection corresponds to mean torque is zero. Hence these instrements cannot be used for AC.

11. What is phantom loading? (Dec 2015, May 2017)

When the current rating of a meter under test is high a test with actual loading arrangements will cause considerable waste of power. To avoid this phantom loading or fictitious loading is done. In phantom loading pressure coil is supplied with normal voltage and current coil circuit with separate low voltage supply to circulate rated current because the current circuit has low impedance. The total power consumed in this method is small.

12. If an induction type energy meter runs fast, how can it be slowed down .

Adjusting the position of braking magnet and making it move away from the centre of the disc can slow the energy meter down.

13. How to make adjustments in energy meters to reduce the error? (Nov 2013)

Preliminary light load adjustment, Full load unity factor adjustment,Lag adjustment (low power factor adjustment), Light load adjustment, Creep adjustment

13. List the errors in electro dynamometer type wattmeter.

Errors due to pressure coil inductance, Error due to pressure coil capacitance. Temperature errors.

Error due to mutual inductance Effects, Errors caused because of connections Eddy current errors, Stray magnetic field errors, Errors caused by vibration of moving system

14. What is the need for lag adjustment devices is single phase energy meter?

The energy meter will read true value of energy only when the phase angle between supply voltage and pressure coil flux is 90 deg. This requires that the pressure coil winding should be highly inductive and has a low resistance, but even with this phase of flux and voltage few degrees less than 90. So lag adjustments are necessary to bring this shunt magnet flux in exact quadrature with supply voltage.

15. List the errors in single phase energy meter.

- Errors caused by driving system:
- In correct magnitude of fluxes, Incorrect phase angles, Lack symmetry in magnetic circuit
- Errors caused by braking system:
- Changes in strength of brake magnet, Changes in disc resistance

- Self-braking effect of series magnet flux, Abnormal friction of moving parts.

16. What is "creep" in energy meter? (May 2014, Dec 2015)

In some energy meters a slow but continuous rotation is obtained even when there is no current flowing through the current coil and only pressure coil is energized. This is called creeping.

17. What are two classes of dynamometer wattcmeters?

Suspended-coil, torsion instruments. The moving or voltage coil is suspended from a torsion head by a metallic suspension, which serves as a lead to the coil. Pivoted-coil, direct-indicating instruments.

18. What is the expression for reactive power in 3-phase circuits?

Reactive power Q= 3VIsinφ, Phase angle φ=$\tan^{-1}$ Q/P, P= active power.

19. Which of the coils of a wattmeter has a high resistance and which is thicker?

Pressure coil of wattmeter has high non-inductive resistance to limit the current to small value which proportional to the voltage applied. Current coil of wattmeter is thicker to carry considerable current.

20. How is the error due to pressure coil inductance reduced/ eliminated?

Errors caused by pressure coil inductance compensated by means of a capacitor connected in parallel with a portion of multiplier (series resistance). Connecting this capacitance across multiplier reduces the circuit impedance purely depends on pressure coil resistance alone.

21. What are the special features incorporated in low power factor wattmeter?

The pressure coil circuit is designed to have low value of resistance to increase the current and operating torque.Compensation for pressure coil currentCompensation for inductance of pressure coil Small control torque

22.Why is a delay line used in the vertical section of the oscilloscope?

The electronic circuit causes a certain amount of time delay in transmission of signal voltages to deflection plates. To allow the operator to observe the leading edge of signal waveform, the signal drive for the vertical CRT plates must be delayed by at least the same amount of time.

23.How is the electron beam focused to a fine spot on the face of the cathode ray tube?

Electron beam from the cathode pass through the concave electrostatic lens aligned towards the axis of the CRT and after passing through the second concave lens focused at the phosphor screen. Focal length of the lens is adjusted by varying the potential difference between the two cylinders.

24.List the disadvantages of storage cathode ray tube.

Finite amount of time – storage tube preserves waveform power to the storage tube present as long as the image is to be stored. Trace of storage tube is not fine as a normal CRT. Writing rate of storage tube is less than conventional CRT which limits the speed of storage oscilloscope. Expensive and needs additional power supply.

25. Define transformation ratio of a potential transformer.

Transformation ratio (R) = primary winding voltage / secondary winding voltage

26. Define turns ratio of an potential transformer.

Turns ratio = number of turns of primary winding / number of turns of secondary winding

27. Define ratio error. (May 2013)

The primary current I_p is not exactly equal to the secondary current multiplied by turns ratio, i.e. $K_T I_s$. This difference is due to the primary current is contributed by the core excitation current. The **error in current transformer** introduced due to this difference is called current error of CT or some times **ratio error in current transformer**.

28. How does a P.T. differ from a power transformer. (Nov 2013)

(i) The Potential transformer use larger core and conductor sizes compared to conventaional power transformer.

(ii) Economy of material is not an important consideration at the time of design of PT. The accuracy is an important consideration.

(iii) The coxial primary and secondary windings are used in PT to reduce the leakage reactance. The primary winding is a single coil in potential transformers.

29. State the reason while current transformer must never be operated on open circuit? (Nov 2013)

If the secondary of CT is left open, then current through secondary becomes zero hence the ampere turns produced by secondary which generally oppose primary ampere turns becomes zero. As there is no counter m.m.f., unuposed primary m.m.f (ampere turns) produce high fluxin the core.. This produce excessive core losses, heating the core beyond limits. Similarly heay e.m.f.s will be induced on the primary and secondary side. This may damage the insulation of the winding. This is danger from the operator point of view also.

30. what is an instrument transformer? Give its various applications. (Dec 2016)

Instrument transformers are high accuracy class electrical devices used to isolate or transform voltage or current levels. The primary winding of the transformer is connected to the high voltage or high current circuit, and the meter or relay is connected to the secondary circuit.

The Instrument transformers are widely used in protection circuits of power systems for the operation of over-current, under-voltage, earth fault and various other relays.

31. Define turns ratio in a current transformer?

Turns ratio = number of turns of secondary winding / number of turns of primary winding

32. Define nominal ratio of an instrument transformer?

Nominal ratio = rated primary winding current / rated secondary winding current

33. Compare current transformer and potential transformer?

The voltage transformer may be considered as parallel transformer with its secondary winding open circuit. Current transformer is a series transformer operates with its secondary short circuit conditions.The primary winding current in a C.T is independent of secondary winding circuit conditions while primary winding of P.T depends on the secondary circuit.In P.T full line voltage appears across its terminals whereas in C.T small voltage appears.

PART-B

1. Explain the functional elements of an instrumentation system.
2. Explain the operating principle of PMMC type ammeter with a neat diagram. What special features are incorporated in its construction in order to reduce the errors? (**Dec 2015, Dec 2016, May 2017)**
3. Explain the principle, Construction of (i) Attraction type, Repulsion type moving iron instruments. Discuss their merits and demerits. **(May 2014, Dec 2012, Dec 2015)**
4. Explain in detail about 3 Phase wattmeter with neat diagrams. **(Dec 2014)**
5. Discuss the construction details and working principle of an induction type wattmeter. What are the advantages and disadvantages?
6. What is the working principle of a two element induction type energy meter. Explain, derive the expression for its deflecting torque.

7. Explain the operating principle of current transformer with a neat diagram. Mention the various causes of error and state the methods of reducing the errors (May 2018)
8. Explain the operating principle of potential transformer with a neat diagram. Mention the various causes of error and state the methods of reducing the errors.
9. Describe the functions of Digital storage oscilloscope with neat diagram.
10. With the help of the functional block diagram, explain the working of Data Acquistion System.

UNIT V BASICS OF POWER SYSTEMS

PART – A

1. **What are the three types of power used in AC circuits?**

(i) Real or Active or True power P=EI cosθ ii) Reactive power Q=EI sinθ iii) Apparent power S=EI

2. **Define Real power.**

The actual power consumed in an AC circuits is called real power and P=EI cos θ

3. **Define Reactive power.**

The power consumed by the pure reactance (X_L or X_C) in an AC circuit is called reactive power. The unit is VAR and Q=EI sinθ

4. **Define apparent power and Power factor. (May 2019)**

The Apparent power (in VA) is the product of the rms values of voltage and current.(**S** = $\mathbf{V_{rms}I_{rms.}}$)The Power factor is the cosine of the phase difference between voltage and current. It is also the cosine of the load impedance. **Power factor = cos φ** .The pf is lagging if the current lags voltage (inductive load) and is leading when the current leads voltage (capacitive load).

5. **What is meant by Complex power?**

Complex power (in VA) is the product of the rms voltage phasor and the complex conjugate of the rms current phasor. As a complex quantity, its real part is real power (P) and its imaginary part is reactive power (Q). and $S = P + jQ$

6. **What are the advantages of 3 phase circuits over single phase circuits?**

- Generation, transmission and distribution of 3 phase power is cheaper, more efficient and Uniform torque production occurs.
- Parallel Operation is easy
- Power delivered is constant
- For a given amount of power transmitted through a system, the three phase system requires conductors with a smaller cross-sectional area. This means a saving of copper and thus the original installation costs are less.

7. **State the relationship between line voltage& phase voltage and line current & phase current of a 3 phase delta and star connected system.**

For delta connected $V_{ph} = V_L$; $I_{ph} = I_L / \sqrt{3}$; For star connected $V_{ph} = V_L / \sqrt{3}$; $I_{ph} = I_L$

8. **Define Symmetrical System.**

It is possible in poly-phase system that magnitudes of different alternating voltage are different. But a three phase system in which the three voltages are of same magnitude and frequency and displaced from each other by 120° phase angle is defined as **symmetrical system.**

9. **Give some method available for measuring three-phase power.**

(i) Single wattmeter method. (ii) Two-wattmeter method. (iii) Three-wattmeter method.

10. **Explain the concept of balanced load.**

The load is said to be balanced when magnitudes of all impedances Z_{ph1}, Z_{ph2} and Z_{ph3} are equal and the phase angles of all of them are equal and of same nature either all inductive or all capacitive or all resistive.

11. **Define Phasor and Phase angle.**

A sinusoidal wave form or alternating electrical quantity can be represented in terms of a Phasor. A Phasor is a vector with definite magnitude and direction. From the Phasor the sinusoidal wave form can be reconstructed. Phase angle is the angular measurement that specifies the position of the alternating quantity relative to a reference.

12. **Distinguish between unbalanced source and unbalanced load.**

Unbalanced Source:

In unbalanced sources it will have negative sequence & zero sequence components whereas in a balanced source it has only positive sequence component.

Unbalanced Load:

If the individual load impedances are not identical then in general neither the line currents nor the line voltages at the load will have equal magnitudes. The phase sequence will affect both the magnitude and phase angle of current & voltage in the circuit.

13. **Which type of connection of 3Φ system is preferred at the point of utilization? Why?**

Three phase, 4 wire systems are used in utilization system so that either single phase or three phase load can be connected.

14. **While measuring power in a circuit by two wattmeter method, under what condition the two wattmeter reading will be equal and why?**

When the power factor is unity or when the load is purely resistive, then the two wattmeter reading will be equal.

15. **A star connected balanced load draw a current of 35A per phase when connected to a 440 V supply. Determine the apparent power.**

Apparent power=$\sqrt{3}V_LI_L$ = =$\sqrt{3}$ *440*35=**267 kVA**

16. **Write the equation for the phasor difference between the potentials of the delta connected networks.**

$V_{RY} = V_L\angle 0^0$ V; $V_{YB} = V_L\angle -120^0$ V; $V_{BR} = V_L\angle -240^0$ V

17. **Three coils, each having a resistance of 20Ω and an inductive reactance of 15Ω are connected in star to a 400V, 3 phase and 50 Hz supply. Calculate (a) line current, (b) power factor and (c) power supplied.**

Line current, $I_L = V_{ph}/ Z_{ph}$= 230.94 / 25 = 23 A
Power Factor, cos $\phi = R_{ph}/ Z_{ph}$= 20/25 = 0.8 lagging
Power Supplied, P = $\sqrt{3}\ V_L I_L \cos\phi$ = 51178W

18. **A 3 phase 400 V is given to balanced star connected load of impedance 8+6j Ω. Calculate line current.**

$I_L=I_{ph}$
$V_L = V_{ph} / \sqrt{3}$;= 400/$\sqrt{3}$ = 230.9 V
I= V_L/Z=230.9/(8+6j) = 23 -39°A

19. **When a 3 Phase Supply System is Called Balanced Supply System?**

If a three phase system has nominal voltage, frequency and phase shift of 120 degree with each other in all the phases, then the supply system is said to be balanced.

20. **What are the components of a power system?**

The components of power systems are Generators, Step up and Step down transformers, Loads and Transmission lines.

21. **What is meant by primary and secondary transmission?**

Transmission of electric power at 110 kV, 132 kV, 400 kV and 765 kV by three phase 3 wire overhead system is known as primary transmission.

Transmission of electric power at 33 kV by three phase 3 wire overhead system is known as secondary transmission.

22. **What is meant by primary and secondary distributions?**

The secondary transmission lines terminates at the substations where voltage is reduced from 33 kV to 11 kV lines which run along the road sides of the city forms the primary distribution. A primary distribution line terminates at the distributing substations where voltage is reduced from 11 kV to 400V. Thus three phase 4 wire system which connect the distributing substation and the consumer point forms the secondary distribution.

23. **What are the transmission level voltages we have in India?**

Primary transmission level voltage is 132 kV, 220 kV, 440 kV, 750 kV and secondary transmission level voltage is 33 kV or 66 kV.

24.Write down the formulae for converting Star to Delta.

"Star" "Delta"

$R_{ab}=(R_aR_b+R_bR_c+R_cR_a)/R_c$;

$R_{bc}=(R_aR_b+R_bR_c+R_cR_a)/R_a$;

$R_{ca}=(R_aR_b+R_bR_c+R_cR_a)/R_b$.

Formulae for converting Star to Delta

25.Write down the formulae for converting Delta to Star.

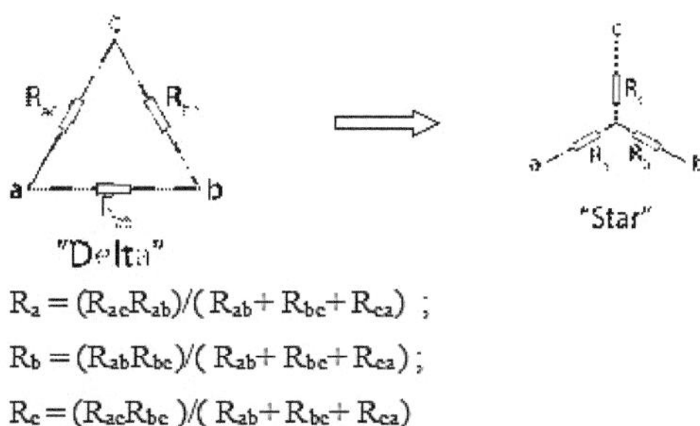

Formulae for converting Delta to Star

26. What are the advantages of underground system?(May 2018)

- (i) Suitable for congested urban areas where overhead lines may be difficult or impossible to install.
- (ii) Low maintenance.
- (iii) Small voltage drops.
- (iv) Fewer faults.
- (v) Not susceptible to shaking and shorting due to vibrations, wind, accidents, etc.
- (vi) Not easy to steal, make illegal connections or sabotage.

27. Write any two advantages of three phase power system. (May 2019)

- (i) The amount of conductor material required is less for three phase system.
- (ii) Voltage regulation of a three phase system is better.

PART – B

1. Explain structure of power system to deliver electric power to consumer place.
2. List the safety precuations of electrical power system.
3. Discuss the various levels of voltage in electric system.
4. Define Earthing.Describe the methods of earthing in brief.
5. Explain the various protective devices in detail.
6. Briefly explain about the switch fuse unit.
7. Elaborate in detail about Circuit braker and its types.
8. Explain Miniature circuit breaker and moulded case circuit breaker.
9. Describe the two methods of earth leakage circuit breaker.
10. Illustrate with an example of first aid(Electrical shock).

Table Of Contents

CHAPTER 1 -Transformer

CHAPTER 2 -DC Machines

Contents

UNIT I TRANSFORMER

Introduction - Ideal and Practical Transformer – Phasor diagram–- Per Unit System – Equivalent circuit- Testing- Efficiency and Voltage Regulation– Three Phase Transformers –Applications-Auto Transformers, Advantages- Harmonics.

UNIT II DC MACHINES

Introduction – Constructional Features– Motor and Generator mode - EMF and Torque equation –Circuit Model – Methods of Excitation-Characteristics – Starting and Speed Control – Universal Motor- Stepper Motors – Brushless DC Motors- Applications

UNIT III AC ROTATING MACHINES

Principle of operation of three-phase induction motors – Construction –Types – Equivalent circuit, Speed Control - Single phase Induction motors -Construction– Types–starting methods. Alternator: Working principle–Equation of induced EMF – Voltage regulation, Synchronous motors- working principle-starting methods – Torque equation.

UNIT IV MEASUREMENTS AND INSTRUMENTATION

Functional elements of an instrument, Standards and calibration, Operating Principle , types -Moving Coil and Moving Iron meters, Measurement of three phase power, Energy Meter,Instrument Transformers-CT and PT,DSO- Block diagram- Data acquisition.

UNIT V BASICS OF POWER SYSTEMS

Power system structure -Generation , Transmission and distribution , Various voltage levels,Earthing – methods of earthing, protective devices-switch fuse unit- Miniature circuit breaker moulded case circuit breaker-earth leakage circuit breaker, safety precautions and First Aid.

Printed by Libri Plureos GmbH in Hamburg,
Germany